COLLECTED ESSAYS
IN LITERARY CRITICISM

COLLECTED ESSAYS
in Literary Criticism

by
HERBERT READ

e

FABER AND FABER LTD
24 Russell Square
London

First published in mcmxxxviii
by Faber and Faber Limited
24 Russell Square London W.C.1
Second edition mcmli
Reprinted mcmliv
Printed in Great Britain by
Bradford & Dickens, London, W.C.1.

ACKNOWLEDGEMENTS

Acknowledgements are due to the following publishers for permission to include essays which first appeared under their imprint: The Cambridge University Press (*The Sense of Glory*, 1929); Messrs. Sheed & Ward (*Form in Modern Poetry*, 1932); and Messrs. William Heinemann, Ltd. (*In Defence of Shelley*, 1936). The remainder of the essays now collected are either from *Reason and Romanticism* (Faber & Gwyer, 1926) or have not hitherto appeared in book form.

PREFACE TO THE SECOND EDITION

In this edition several misprints have been corrected, but otherwise the volume remains substantially the same as when first published in 1938, except for the restoration to the essay on Henry James of a final paragraph from the original text.
January 1950   H. R.

CONTENTS

9

CONTENTS

INTRODUCTION

During the last quarter of a century we have witnessed the death of the 'polite' essay. A hundred years ago, in the hands of Macaulay, it was the very voice of authority, solemn and orotund. A generation later Arnold and Bagehot gave the form its last refinement; with Pater it was already in decline, expressive and subtle, but overwrought and literary.

Since Pater's time there have been good essayists, but gradually the form has been sacrificed to the increasing tempo of the Press. The quarterly and monthly magazines, the only effective patrons of this kind of journalism, have given way to the weekly reviews and daily newspapers; and though two or three of the old magazines still survive, they are moribund in the sense that they no longer appeal to a vital public. The exceptions, in my own time, have been the *Times Literary Supplement*, which until recently published every week a leading article of essay length, and the *Criterion*. It was in these two journals that most of the essays now reprinted first appeared.

The essay length is from 3,500 to 5,000 words. Less than 3,500 becomes an article or sketch—and to meet the exigencies of the daily and weekly it is generally much less—1,000 to 1,500 words only. The upper limit of the essay is no doubt also determined by journalistic considerations: anything more than 5,000 words is disproportionate to the fixed dimensions and miscellaneous character of a periodical, and is probably as much as the ordinary reader is prepared to absorb in a provisional format. Speaking from the writer's point of view, I would say that this upper limit also represents as much as any one with a sense of the form would want to write on a given subject—as much, that is to say, unless considerably more. Five thousand words give one room to turn round, to examine the various aspects of the subject, to summon the relevant evidence and to draw the necessary conclusions. It is a general view that the essay gives—not a biography nor a critical analysis, not a history nor a treatise. It is personal in its approach, but not intimate; objective rather than discursive. On any subject of permanent interest it should give the point of view of an age or generation; it should revise accepted opinions in the light of new knowledge.

Its function cannot be taken over by the 'feature' article or sketch. If the essay is to disappear from our literary practice, a very definite instrument of culture will disappear with it. The scholar will remain, for he has leisure or opportunity to study a subject at the sources; and there will be crowds round the literary snack-bars. But the figure in between, the amateur of letters, the man of cultured tastes, whose predominance gives a nation its degree of civilization—this type will lose its sustenance and disappear.

I have already admitted that by Pater's time the essay was decadent. I do not altogether share the current depreciation of Pater: his style was not always effete, and he had a fine sensibility. But for reasons which it would not be appropriate to discuss in a general introduction, his work marks the end of a certain attitude in English criticism—an attitude which he himself described as 'the perfect manner'—that 'certain shade of unconcern, the perfect manner of the eighteenth century, which may be thought to mark complete culture in the handling of abstract questions'. That manner gone, the field was open for industrious pedagogues and entertaining journalists to divide between them. They staked their claims so effectively that when a considerable essayist with a modern outlook and a scientific equipment did appear, he failed to find a permanent place. I am referring to the late J. M. Robertson, whose essays, never sufficiently appreciated in his lifetime, are now completely neglected. Perhaps Robertson was too solid for a generation already bent on distraction; and perhaps he had too many interests to command the devotion of a faction. Further, his style has none of the graces which entice the casual reader.

In any case, I doubt whether the particular kind of scientific attitude represented by Robertson was compatible with a fundamental respect for the irrational values of art. I only mention him to suggest that, with all his shortcomings, he was an essayist in the old tradition with something new to say; and he failed to obtain a hearing.

The scientific temper of our age is not necessarily one with which the artist, and the critic as representing the artist, need compromise. Art and science have always been independent methods of discovering and presenting the truth. But once a department of science was established with the mind itself as its subject, a new situation was created. For the scientist could not for long explore this realm without coming into contact with, and having to accommodate, those products of the human mind which we call works of art. Psychology, that is to say, impinges directly on the province of the literary critic —raids it and despoils it and leaves it a sorry desolation of unconscious prejudices. *It has been my contention that in this situation the critic must retaliate, and pick from the science of psychology his brightest weapons.* I have been gradually drawn towards a psychological type of literary criticism because I have realized that psychology, more particularly the method of psycho-analysis, can offer explanations of many problems connected with the personality of the poet, the technique of poetry, and the appreciation of the poem. The full extent to which I have developed this type of criticism is not represented

INTRODUCTION

in this volume—I must refer readers to my studies of Wordsworth (Faber, 1949) and Shelley (Heinemann, 1936) for more adequate essays in this manner. But over the fifteen years in which the essays now collected were written, my tendency, step by step with my increasing knowledge of modern psychology, has been to give literary criticism a psychological direction.

I admit that there still remains a more indulgent activity which deserves the name of criticism. Much as I dislike the idea of 'taste' (for the good taste of one generation is the bad taste of the next, and in time even the bad taste of a period becomes the 'chic' of a later age) there is nevertheless a certain exchange of appreciative gestures which is part of the civilized behaviour of a society. Every occasion we have for expressing our admiration or detestation of a poet or a painter is not necessarily an occasion for an analysis. We can float on the surface of a subject and still be aware of its depths. I do not wish, therefore, to make the psychological method in criticism the only method; I only wish to establish its relevance, and to suggest that under its guidance most of our literary judgements must proceed to a court of revision.

August 1938   HERBERT READ

Part One

GENERAL THEORIES

1. THE NATURE OF POETRY

I

ORGANIC AND ABSTRACT FORM

If a literary critic happens to be also a poet (*un poète manqué* is the usual taunt) he is liable to suffer from dilemmas which do not trouble the philosophic calm of his more prosaic colleagues. He may elaborate his theory and practice of criticism with perfect objectivity, looking on literature as so much material to be measured, compared and evaluated. That is the method of scientific criticism, and unless we confuse criticism with emotional impressionism, it must remain the only possible ideal of criticism. But the critic who is also a poet is in a special difficulty. With a certain objectivity he has elaborated his system of scientific criticism; but at other moments in his life, in another mood, he has felt a creative impulse, and submitting to this impulse has written poetry which owes nothing to his critical theories. These poems, whether good or bad, are nevertheless events in his life, much more vivid than any rational notions he may have acquired from reading other people's poetry. When such a critic-poet attempts to probe down into such a fundamental question as the form and structure of poetry, he cannot escape the evidence of his own experience, but must in some way establish an agreement between his theory and his practice.

Save for such experiences in my own case, this essay might have been simpler than it is. I should have been able to adopt a definite attitude or join a traditional school. In a broad sense my theory of poetic form would have been either classical or romantic. If I had adopted a purely intellectual attitude, it would have been classical, but when I stand up squarely to the traditional terms of classical theory, and attempt to relate them to my experience, I find there is no application—my experience cuts across the classical-romantic division.

I find, in fact, that it is necessary to distinguish between two kinds of form, which I will call *organic* and *abstract*. The abstract is evolved from the organic; but it represents a fixation of the organic in a particular mode. Let me illustrate the point by an analogy drawn from the more objective plastic arts. When the nomadic hordes known as the Scythians invaded south Russia in the eighth century B.C., they brought with them an art, limited in range, consisting of various metal ornaments used in the decoration of harness, weapons, and apparel. Such ornaments usually took the shape of very vigorous and lively representations of animals—stags, reindeer, lions, tigers, and eagles. The designs were generally stylized; that is to say, the natural form of the animal was distorted in the interests of linear rhythm and dynamic effect. The form of such objects I should describe as organic; every departure from truth-to-nature is at the same time an intensification of natural vitality.

The Scythians settled in south Russia and their art developed in a normal way. We find that the animal motives which they had first used singly began, after an interval of two or three centuries, to be used in stereotyped combinations. They were confronted in pairs to form an antithetic design; they were arranged in rows and series, and in the most complicated type evolved by this simple people the animals are interlinked in a chain or spiral which makes a rhythmical pattern over the whole of the decorated surface—a symphony, as it has been called.

In the early Scythian animal style, the form is single, integral, and organic. In the later style, the form is divorced from the original impulse and made to serve as a unit in an arrangement which is not related to the original impulse, but is an abstract or intellectual arrangement of given units.

Let me now give a general definition of these two types of form:

Organic form: When a work of art has its own inherent laws, originating with its very invention and fusing in one vital unity both structure and content, then the resulting form may be described as *organic*.

Abstract form: When an organic form is stabilized and repeated as a pattern, and the intention of the artist is no longer related to the inherent dynamism of an inventive act, but seeks to adapt content to predetermined structure, then the resulting form may be described as *abstract*.

It is then natural to ask whether these opposed entities of style correspond to any accepted categories in criticism. They may, I think, be directly related to the concepts 'romantic' and 'classical', provided these concepts are accepted in their proper, that is to say, their *historical*, sense. I wish to avoid these confusing terms as much as possible, though I think no confusion is necessary if we bear in mind the two distinct meanings of each term. In one case we can distinguish the meanings verbally, for 'classical' may be reserved for the historical sense, whilst 'classicistic' serves for the derivative and sentimental sense; and perhaps we ought to be bold enough to use 'romanticistic' as well as 'romantic'.[1]

The correspondence of organic and abstract forms with romantic and classical periods in the history of the plastic art, is obvious enough. The transition from the organic type to the abstract always coincides with the transition from a period of stress and energy to a period of satiety and solidity; and that is the historical distinction between romantic and classical periods. It is also quite clear that the classical and romantic periods are related to each other in a 'life-cycle' which is the

[1] The terms in general have been given a very precise definition by Sir Herbert Grierson in his Leslie Stephen lecture on 'Classical and Romantic' (reprinted in *The Background of English Literature*, 1925), and I am conscious of his definitions in the use I make of the terms in these essays.

recurring cycle of the growth, maturity, and decay of culture. But it is most important to remember that the term 'romantic' especially is often restricted to an art based on sentiment, which may be typical of inferior classical as well as of inferior romantic periods. To be quite clear, when referring to this type of romanticism, we might always call it 'sentimental-romanticism'.

The form which I propose to investigate in the following essays corresponds to the *organic unit* of the animal style in Scythian art, and more generally to the form typical of the romantic phase in any cultural development. It is the form imposed on poetry by the laws of its own origination, without consideration for the given forms of traditional poetry. It is the most original and most vital principle of poetic creation; and the distinction of modern poetry is to have recovered this principle. But before we can see how organic form takes shape, we must first consider the nature of the poet's personality; for upon the nature of his personality depends the form of his poetry.

I. THE NATURE OF POETRY

2
THE PERSONALITY OF THE POET

Many writers, especially novelists, have written in accordance with some theory of the nature of personality, and an enquiry into such working theories would be of great interest. But that is an aspect of the subject which I should like to exclude from the present enquiry, which is to be concerned not so much with personality, as objectively conceived by the writer, as with the writer's own personality—the subjective nature of personality, the part it plays in the process of writing: what, briefly, we might call the creative function of the personality. This is, perhaps, a vague subject, but its very vagueness is the excuse I offer for dealing with it. If we can introduce a few definitions into this twilight, a good service to criticism will have been rendered. As it is at present, this word 'personality' is tossed about, a more or less meaningless counter, from critic to critic. There is scarcely a literary judgement made anywhere in recent times that does not resolve itself into a statement such as: 'The work of so and so is good because it is the perfect expression of his personality.' This is not an exaggeration. I take the first book that comes to my hand. It is Volume I of the Cambridge Shakespeare, with a general Introduction by Sir Arthur Quiller-Couch. There I find this passage—three birds for a single stone:

'. . . who can doubt that every true man, small or great, leaves some print of himself on his work, or indeed that he *must* if his work be literature, which is so personal a thing. As

Sir Walter Raleigh puts it: "No man can walk abroad save on his own shadow." Yes, but as another writer, Mr. Morton Luce, well comments: "An author may be—perhaps ought to be—something inferior to his work."'

That reminds me of another passage, from *The Sacred Wood* of Mr. T. S. Eliot:

'Poetry is not a turning loose of emotion, but an escape from emotion; it is not the expression of personality, but an escape from personality'

'But, of course,' adds Mr. Eliot, 'only those who have personality and emotions know what it means to want to escape from these things'; and earlier in the same essay he has explained his meaning in these words:

'The point of view which I am struggling to attack is perhaps related to the metaphysical theory of the substantial unity of the soul: for my meaning is, that the poet has, not a "personality" to express, but a particular medium, which is only a medium and not a personality, in which impressions and experiences combine in peculiar and unexpected ways. Impressions and experiences which are important for the man may take no place in the poetry, and those which become important in the poetry may play quite a negligible part in the man, the personality.'

I do not quote these passages as texts, to attack or commend, but merely as illustrations of the use of the word 'personality' in modern criticism, and of the evident concern which critics have for its significance or otherwise. It will, however, be realized that the point of view of Mr. Eliot is a very exceptional one, and in fact a protest against a universal reliance on a vague concept. Mr. Eliot might hold that the notion of personality is *inevitably* vague; at least he does not attempt to define it. I think, however, that the attempt will be worth while.

We cannot hope to arrive at a definition of personality without encroaching to some extent on the science of psychology. Some of my readers will be uneasy at the prospect.

Nevertheless, this is where I take my stand, even against my best friends in criticism, such as Mr. Eliot himself. I believe that criticism must concern itself, not only with the work of art in itself, but also with the process of writing, and with the writer's state of mind when inspired—that is to say, criticism must concern itself, not only with the finished work of art, but also with the workman, his mental activity and his tools. If that is not admitted, no really useful progress can be made in this essay. But assuming we are agreed on the sphere of criticism, then I cannot conceive how the critic can avoid a dependence on general psychology. It may be said that psychology is a very doubtful science, and that none of its conclusions is established; but that is to set up as a better psychologist than the psychologists themselves. If we depart a single pace from the consideration of the work of art in isolation from all personal questions we involve ourselves in psychological considerations. It might be possible, for example, to plunge into the quarrel of Romantics and Classics with nothing in our armoury but an objective measuring-rod. An infallible distinction might be found in the use of the letter 'p', in feminine rhymes and false quantities; it would be infallible, but it would be dull. We should separate the sheep and goats, but the really interesting question—why some people are goats, and others sheep—that question would be left unsolved.

That is why, as a critic, I am tempted to seek an alliance with psychology, but I should like to distinguish between a general *entente* and a treaty of obligations. As a literary critic— that is to say, as a scientist in my own field—I insist on maintaining my territorial rights when I enter into treaty with another science. I accept just as much as seems relevant to my purpose, and I reject anything that conflicts with the evidence of my own special sensibility. But actually, if the literary critic will approach psychology without prejudice, he will find certain important conclusions which are generally accepted by psychologists themselves, and which he can apply with great profit to his understanding of literature.

23

I will take as an example, because it is relevant to the enquiry I am making, the theory of the mind as developed by the psycho-analysts, particularly by Freud. I am aware that there are certain fundamental aspects of psycho-analysis which are hotly disputed by psychologists in general—particularly that part of the theory which supposes the existence of an unconscious mind, or unconscious region of the mind. Now it happens that this particular hypothesis is the one which the literary critic is likely to be most tempted to adopt. Let him use every caution, for as one psychologist has warned us: 'All usages of the term "unconscious" that imply that it is an entity, such as saying that ideas are *in the unconscious*: or that the unconscious is dynamic, show a thoughtless or uncritical attitude—or ignorance.'[1] Freud himself, as we shall see, is not guiltless in this respect. I think, however, before we begin to criticize Freud, or even to use any of his terms, we should make sure that we know the meaning of them. It so happens that in a recent essay[2] Freud himself has given a concise résumé of his theory. He writes:

'The division of mental life into what is conscious and what is unconscious is the fundamental premise on which psycho-analysis is based; and this division alone makes it possible for it to understand pathological mental processes, which are as common as they are important, and to co-ordinate them scientifically. Stated once more in a different way: psycho-analysis cannot accept the view that consciousness is the essence of mental life, but is obliged to regard consciousness as one property of mental life, which may co-exist along with its other properties or may be absent.'

Then Freud shows how we are compelled to adopt the concept of the 'unconscious':

'We have found—that is, we have been obliged to assume—that very powerful mental processes or ideas exist which can

[1] Henry Herbert Goddard, 'The Unconscious in Psycho-analysis', *Problems of Personality* (1925), p. 300.
[2] *The Ego and the Id* (Eng. tr. 1927)

24

produce in the mind all the effects that ordinary ideas do . . .
without themselves becoming conscious . . . this is the point at
which psycho-analytic theory steps in with the assertion that
such ideas cannot become conscious because a certain force is
opposed to them, that otherwise they could become conscious, and that then one would see how little they differ from
other elements, which are admittedly mental. The fact that in
the technique of psycho-analysis a means has been found by
which the opposing force can be removed and the ideas in
question made conscious renders this theory irrefutable. The
state in which the ideas existed before being made conscious
is called by us *repression*, and we assert that the force which
instituted the repression and maintains it is perceived as
resistance during the work of analysis. . . . We see, however,
that we have two kinds of unconscious—that which is latent
but capable of becoming conscious, and that which is repressed and not capable of becoming conscious in the ordinary
way. . . . That which is latent, and only unconscious in the
descriptive and not in the dynamic sense, we call *preconscious*;
the term unconscious we reserve for the dynamically uncon-
scious-repressed. . . .'

That is a long quotation, but it is essential to use these terms
—'conscious', 'preconscious', and 'unconscious'—and to use
them in an accepted sense. The words as used by Freud have
been subjected to criticism and he has not been afraid to revise
his terms and make them more precise.

Freud says, in the work from which I have been quoting,
that 'in every individual there is a coherent organization of
mental processes, which we call his *ego*'; and this may serve as
the *preliminary* definition of 'personality' of which I am in
search. This ego is identical with the conscious flow of our
thoughts, the impressions we receive, the sensations we experience. Also, from this ego, this *coherent organization* of
mental processes, according to Freud, proceed the repressions
'by means of which an attempt is made to cut off certain
trends in the mind not merely from consciousness, but also

25

from their other forms of manifestation and activity'. Freud, following another Austrian writer, Georg Groddeck, further claims that the conduct of the ego throughout life is essentially passive—we are 'lived', as it were, by unknown and uncontrollable forces. But presumably these forces are inherent, differentiated in each individual—being, in fact, that reserve of instincts and passions which normally we repress, but which are never securely under the control of our conscious reason. To this reserve Freud gives the name 'Id', for it is the impersonal aspect of the 'Ego'.

Near to the word 'personality' we have another word, often used interchangeably with it, sometimes contrasted with it— I mean the word 'character'. This concept, too, we can bring into relation with the general scheme of Freudian psychology. Character can be explained as a disposition in the individual due to the repression of certain impulses which would otherwise be present in the personality; it is therefore something more restricted than personality. Character, which always has such a positive aspect, is really the result of certain fixities or negations imposed on the flow of consciousness. A flood only gains character and direction when it is confined between banks.

Before trying to show how the mind of the poet is related to these several concepts, let me draw confirmation of the rightness of Freud's general analysis of the mind from an unexpected quarter, a work first published nearly fifty years ago and neglected until recently revived by Dame Ethel Smyth. *The Prison*, by H. B. Brewster, is a philosophic dialogue of great force and originality, and there I found this definition of the personality:

'We live in a web of associated memories; our general map —the chart thanks to which we know more or less clearly where to put what, recognize analogies, form classes, make order out of chaos and accumulate experience—is a network of memories. And one of ourselves, the loudest voiced one, the one we usually think of when we say *I*, corresponds to the spot on that map where the most frequent and familiar memories cross each other, as the railroads of a country at its capital.'

It will be perceived how nearly this definition approaches Freud's conception of the ego as 'a coherent organization of mental processes'. Much more in Brewster's dialogue might be related to Freud's psychology; for example, that state of mind which Brewster opposes to the personality is nothing but Freud's unconscious 'id'.

It would be easy to give many further illustrations from literature which would give support to our preliminary definition of personality, but as they are so often bound up with, and even confused with, the notion of 'character', we must first make a clear distinction between the two. The word 'character' derives from the Greek word meaning an engraved sign, a distinguishing mark; and in common usage it always implies a man moulded to a pattern, firm, consistent, dependable. Again, the use of the word for that literary form known as 'the character' and practised by Theophrastus, Vauvenargues, and others, gives the same meaning: a consistent type. Descriptive psychologists adopt this same conception; the definition of Münsterberg may be quoted as typical. Character, he says, 'is the power to keep the selected motive dominant throughout life'. The difficulty about such a definition is that some 'power'—force, will or energy—is implied, for which there is no adequate theory of causation. The psycho-analysts have supplied this, and again I think their hypothesis is the most suggestive one for our purposes. They regard inhibition as the basis of character, and a definition which we may accept as representative is that of Dr. Roback, which reads: '[Character is the result of] an enduring psycho-physical disposition to inhibit instinctive impulses in accordance with a regulative principle.'[1] Now there are various words in that very condensed definition which need explanation. Inhibition I have already referred to, but if we do not care to accept it in its psycho-analytical sense, I think it will do for our definition

[1] 'Character and Inhibition.' *Problems of Personality*, p. 118.

27

if we merely regard the 'disposition to inhibit' as the 'will to hold in check', in the ordinary moralistic sense. Again, the phrase 'instinctive impulses' need not be given any but its normal meaning—there are many instincts besides the sex instinct, and if any one instinct is more in question than another, I think it is probably the gregarious instinct. There is a passage in that penetrating analysis of the character, Meredith's *The Egoist*, which describes this aspect of the problem very well:

'Within the shadow of his presence,' Meredith writes of Sir Willoughby Patterne, 'he compressed opinion as a strong frost binds the springs of earth, but beyond it his shivering sensitiveness ran about in dread of a stripping in a wintry atmosphere. This was the ground of his hatred of the world; it was an appalling fear on behalf of his naked eidolon, the tender infant Self swaddled in his name before the world, for which he felt as the most highly civilized of men alone can feel, and which it was impossible for him to stretch out hands to protect. There the poor little lovable creature ran for any mouth to blow on; and frost-nipped and bruised, it cried to him, and he was of no avail! Must we not detest a world that so treats us? We loathe it the more, by our measure of our contempt for them, when we have made the people within the shadow-circle of our person slavish.'

This does not mean that the man who avoids the herd will thereby form his character; you do not inhibit an instinct by avoiding its activity. But the man who maintains a certain integrity in the midst of the herd, that man is by way of forming his character. Dr. Roback quotes very appositely Goethe's couplet:

Es bildet ein Talent sich in der Stille:
Sich ein Charakter in dem Strom der Welt.

'A talent is formed in solitude; a character in the stream of the world'[1]—a sentiment which I would ask the reader to

[1] Stendhal has said the same thing: '*On peut tout acquérir dans la solitude, hormis de caractère.*' *De l'Amour*, Fragments Divers, 1.

remember because I am presently going to suggest that this difference between the conditions necessary for the formation of a character and for the formation of what Goethe calls a talent and what I am here calling a personality, corresponds precisely with the difference between rhetorical and lyrical literature, which is the difference often loosely implied in the terms 'classical' and 'romantic' literature.

But first I must draw attention to the final clause in Dr. Roback's definition of character: it is 'an enduring disposition to inhibit instinctive impulses *in accordance with a regulative principle*'. That, of course, implies that there is an element of self-determination in character. It is obvious that characters vary enormously in value, and I think a little consideration will show that the differences in value are due to differences in intelligence. A man without any intelligence, a lunatic, is a man most decidedly without any character. A man with a perverse intelligence, like Don Quixote, is a deformed character, a caricature of the real thing. Another negative aspect to remember is, that character once formed is not affected by experience. It is possible for groups of men to endure, over lengthy periods, the same experiences (I am thinking particularly of the experiences of war) and to emerge at the end of it with their characters not in the least changed. Character is in fact armour against experience; it is not in itself deflected by experience. From whatever direction we approach it, we get the notion of fixity; and once a man's character is determined, it is hardly possible to speak of his moral or spiritual development. A character is 'set', 'hard-boiled' as the slang phrase vividly expresses it. Not even the emotions will dissolve it, or move it. The emotions indeed are irrelevant to character; they are waves which break themselves in vain against its base. History is full of examples of men of character who have exercised their justness and firmness in spite of the emotional claims of friendship and love.

Character, in short, is an impersonal ideal which the individual selects and to which he sacrifices all other claims, especially those of the sentiments or emotions. It follows that character must be placed in opposition to personality, which is the general-common-denominator of our sentiments and emotions. That is, indeed, the opposition I wish to emphasize; and when I have said further that all poetry, in which I include all lyrical impulses whatsoever, is the product of the personality, and therefore inhibited in a character, I have stated the main theme of my essay.

One problem absorbs me above all others: it is what I will call *the intermittency of genius.* Why, more often than not, does a poet blossom out in his adolescence and early manhood, and then wither to pedantry and dullness? Why does inspiration work fitfully and often at intervals of many years? Why, to put these questions in concrete terms, did Milton cease writing poetry for twenty-five years? Why did a poet like Gray write only one poem of supreme excellence? Why, for a brief decade did the great poetic genius of Wordsworth pour out its richness, and then lapse into comparative poverty? One could ask a hundred questions of this kind, but the reader is not to imagine that I am going to provide a universal key to answer them all. I think, however, that this problem of the relations of personality to character does provide the right setting for such questions, and if psychology can solve *its* problem, then with the aid of psychology we shall be on the way to solving our own literary problem.

It would be too simple a solution to say that, character and personality being so opposed, inspiration will flow so long as the personality does not harden into character. In psychology you have always to reckon with the phenomenon of compensation. If you suppress one instinct, you revive another; we are infinitely complex machines, so that a check on one action is apt to release the spring of another action. The man of character may have repressed the conscious functioning of certain instincts; he cannot, however, prevent them from forcing their way underground into the preconscious and unconscious states described by Freud. The physical potentiality of the instincts remains in the body, though their surface workings may be suppressed. What is suppressed in consciousness may be found active in the imagination, which might be identified with the preconscious of Freud's phraseology. Dr. Jung confirms this supposition, remarking that 'the unconscious feeling of the intellectual is peculiarly fantastic, often in grotesque contrast to an exaggerated, rationalistic intellectualism of the conscious. In contrast to the purposefulness and controlled character of conscious thinking, the feeling is impulsive, uncontrolled, moody, irrational, primitive, archaic indeed, like the feeling of a savage.'[1] Along these lines, I think, we might explain the art of certain intellectual types of the present day—I mean, in literature, the writings of the 'Surréalistes' in France, of Franz Kafka in Germany, and even the later writings of Mr. James Joyce; and in painting, the art of men like Paul Klee and Max Ernst. Let me interpose here this axiom of criticism: by explaining the nature of a work of art, we do not explain it away. Art always rises superior to its origins. It is an entity of direct appeal; we do not, in the process of appreciation (no process but an immediate insight) unfold the process of creation.

To return to my main argument: this phantasy proceeding from the unconscious as a balance or compensation for instincts repressed in the interests of character, may be identified with *fancy*; and this I think fits in well, not only with the modern types of art and literature already mentioned, but generally with the distinction between fancy and imagination in the literature of the past. For the sake of a tidy correspondence, it ought to be possible to relate *imagination* to the preconscious, and this I think can be done without much difficulty. But I must avoid, if only for lack of space, the endless controversy which revolves round these two words; I have, besides, on another occasion discussed the relationship which exists between the intellect and fancy.[2]

[1] 'Psychological Types.' *Problems of Personality*, p. 300.
[2] *English Prose Style*, chap. ix.

But now we must enlarge our description of *personality*. As a preliminary I have suggested that the term might be identified with Freud's 'Ego'—a coherent organization of mental processes. But the coherence of this organization is not to be confused with the fixed organization of a character—any more than the coherence of a work of art is to be confused with the concision of a machine. The nature of this coherence is very well defined in an essay on personality by Mr. Ramon Fernandez.[1] He has been discussing Nietzsche's conception of personality which he finds wanting in just this element of coherence.

'To be coherent', he explains, 'does not mean that one *feels oneself* the same, nor *that one acts* in the same way in all circumstances, but rather that one is ready to meet every circumstance when once a certain inward perspective has been established; it does not mean that one never changes, but that the changes of the world always find you ready to select your own point of view . . . the more complicated the personality grows, the more unstable it becomes, and the more it submits to the influence of the mind. . . . The ideal personality would be that of a man who showed himself ever capable of adapting his being to the movements of his thought, and whose thought would be ever in accord with the universal; who, in such conditions, considering himself with stern impartiality, would accept gladly that idea which for the moment may take the lead; because thought which ceaselessly renews itself will make him—in Emerson's phrase, "live always in a new dawn", but at the same time it will prevent him from falling into incoherence, being guaranteed by its own laws.'

Such a conception of personality is admittedly based on the most exact, the most complete and fearless revelation of a personality that we possess: Montaigne's Essays. I perhaps need quote[2] only one of a hundred passages in which this notion is put forth. It is a sufficiently famous one:

[1] *De la personnalité* (1928), pp. 86–7.
[2] From the translation by E. J. Trechmann (Oxford, 1927), p. 266.

32

'What I do I do thoroughly, as a matter of habit, and make one step of it; and I seldom take any step that steals away and hides from my reason, and that is not very nearly guided by all my faculties in agreement, without division or inner revolt. My judgement takes all the blame or all the praise for it; and the blame it once takes it takes always, for almost from birth it has been one: the same inclination, the same direction, the same strength. And in the matter of general opinions, I have since my childhood occupied the position I had to hold.'

It will be seen that in both authors we have the idea of a free disposition which is that of the sensations and memory—the sensual being—and that this being is given coherence, is defined or outlined, by a judgement which is innate. The ego is a synthesis of the sensations, is generated by conscious experience, by that inward perspective which Montaigne exercised so freely for our delectation. The judgement is not imposed on the sensations from without, as if by an external agency—that is the process of repression which results in character; judgement emerges from the history of our sensations, is elected by them, and the coherence of personality is indeed the coherence of a natural process; not the coherence of an arbitrary discipline.

Mr. Fernandez's book, from which I have just quoted, has much more to offer us that is suggestive; its only fault, in my opinion, is that it tends to confuse the coherence of the personality with the fixity of the character; at least, it does not clearly mark off the functions of character. But speaking of the restricted, the too limited notion of personality in Corneille, he gives us a perfect description of character—he describes it as 'the tragic conformity of a man to his definition'—Freud would say 'to his "ego-ideal"'. The personality knows no such definitions, no such ideal; it is an active process of thought, a balance of relations maintained between our various feelings and sentiments. From this process, this play of thought, comes a certain act of belief, the *illative* act described by Newman. The nature of belief in general is not a subject to embark on now.[1] I would merely suggest that the reality of the personality—its operative efficiency—is dependent on a belief in the existence of the self, a belief that may have little support in objective evidence, but is made possible by that insight into the future, that belief in the continuity of experience, which is the will to live. This is obviously a state of mind very different from that involved in character: the whole difference between blind compulsion to an external and arbitrary ideal, and an organic coherence intuitively based on the actual world of sensation.

I should like for my last illustration to pass from Mr. Fernandez to a friend of his whose work he has criticized so intelligently: I mean Marcel Proust. Proust's great work rivals Montaigne's in the deliberate light it throws on this problem of personality.

'Frequent discussions with Marcel Proust,' writes Mr. Fernandez (p. 23), 'who would adopt instantaneously no matter what point of view, have revealed to me that man dehumanizes himself by excess of affectivity at least as much as by excess of rationality. . . . To wish to introduce unity into the life of sensation and affectivity, by separating out one's sentiments and giving them a structure without ever leaving the level of concrete life, was not that precisely to put oneself in quest of a personality?'

Proust was very much occupied by this problem of personality and gave most attention to the very aspect of the problem that I now wish to consider here—I mean the extent to which the personality depends on the memory, and particularly on the memory of sensations. There is a famous excursus, coming almost exactly in the middle of Proust's long epic, which is a key to the author's whole philosophy of art and life. He has just related how, in a moment of complete physical collapse, there comes to him, by an instinctive act of recollection, the living image of his grandmother; and it is

[1] It was the subject of a very adequate enquiry by the Reverend M. C. D'Arcy, S.J.—*The Nature of Belief* (London, 1931).

only at this moment, more than a year after her burial, that he becomes conscious that she is dead. This causes Proust to reflect that 'at whatever moment we estimate it, the total value of our spiritual nature is more or less fictitious, notwithstanding the long inventory of its treasures, for now one, now another of these is unrealizable, whether we are considering actual treasures or those of the imagination'—or those actually of the memory. Then Proust goes on to make this very significant, and for his work, quite essential analysis of the personality:

'For with the cloudiness of memory are closely linked the heart's intermissions. It is, no doubt, the existence of our body, which we may compare to a jar containing our spiritual nature, that leads us to suppose that all our inward wealth, our past joys, all our sorrows, are perpetually in our possession. Perhaps it is equally inexact to suppose that they escape or return. In any case, if they remain within us, it is, for most of the time, in an unknown region where they are of no service to us, and where even the most ordinary are crowded out by memories of a different kind, which preclude any simultaneous occurrence of them in our consciousness. But if the setting of sensations in which they are preserved be recaptured, they acquire in turn the same power of expelling everything that is incompatible with them, of installing alone in us the self that originally lived them.'[1]

Mr. Fernandez is very critical of this passage and therefore of Proust's method in general. He does not deny its acuteness, nor its significance—for Proust. But far from being the key to Proust's genius, he regards it as a confession of Proust's weakness. Mr. Fernandez's criticism at this point would be much clearer if it were combined with a distinction between personality and character; as it is, the inadequacy of Proust's analysis is impugned against such notions as the integrity of our sentiments, our ideals, our spiritual progress.

[1] *Cities of the Plain*, by Marcel Proust, translated by C. K. Scott Moncrieff. Vol. i, p. 219.

'If Proust is to be believed,' Mr. Fernandez writes, 'not only can man not guarantee his sentiments, and consequently his acts, and consequently man must be an eternal failure, but also he must renounce the consolation of feeling that he progresses despite this discontinuity and this intermittent blindness. . . . It is the problem of spirituality, of the value of the ideal, of the future and of human progress, that is set by the Proustian analysis of the intermissions of the heart. . . . If the intermissions of the heart and their corollaries represent the depths of human nature, the supreme experience of our ego, then the spiritual life must be ranged in its entirety in the category of the imagination, and the intelligence is the highest point of human development to which we may pretend . . . the victory of the intelligence would mark the defeat of the spirit.'

But is so much implied in Proust's analysis? It is, I think true that, as Proust says elsewhere, the respect for moral obligations, faithfulness to friends, the achievement of a task, the observance of a discipline, have a surer foundation in blind habits than in the momentary and ardent flights of our sensibility. But is this not equivalent to saying that character as we have defined it is formed by the inhibition of the instinctive life—that, put inversely, the full and free life of the personality must be sacrificed in the interests of any fixed ideals, whether of morality or the imagination? But does this mean that no alternative progress is possible for the personality? That is the momentous question to which we are finally driven, and which I will now try to answer.

It may have been noticed how closely Proust's analysis agrees with Freud's. It is the phenomena of the mind in its conscious, unconscious, and even preconscious phases of repression and censorship, that Proust is describing in words not far removed from the scientific vocabulary of psycho-analysis. But I doubt very much that Proust had any exact knowledge of psycho-analysis; at many points we must regard his work as a confirmation, or an anticipation, of the observations of

Freud. Proust speaks of the heart, and Freud of the mind; but these are interchangeable concepts.

I will not carry the parallel any further. But I do wish to point out how closely Proust's description of the intermissions of the heart can apply to that other parallel phenomenon—the intermissions of genius, or inspiration, to which I have already referred. We all have our moments of inspiration, and perhaps they differ, as between an ordinary mortal and a genius, only in the degree of their intensity. Poets have not often described their creative experiences, but there is one account, quoted by Mr. Percy Lubbock in his Introduction to the *Letters of Henry James*, that is quite unique in the beauty and fullness of its revelation. Henry James began one night to feel his way towards a novel which he had in mind, and among the working notes for this novel were found some pencilled lines from which I should like to quote the essential passage:

'Infinitely interesting—and yet somehow with a beautiful poignancy in it that makes it strange and rather exquisitely formidable, as with an unspeakable deep agitation, the whole artistic question that comes up for me in the train of this idea ... of the donnée for a situation that I began here the other day to fumble out. I mean I come back, I come back yet again and again, to my only seeing it in the dramatic way—as I can only see everything and anything now; the way that filled my mind and floated and uplifted me when a fortnight ago I gave my few indications to X. Momentary side-winds—things of no real authority—break in every now and then to put their inferior little questions to me; but I came back, I come back, as I say, I all throbbingly and yearningly and passionately, oh mon bon, come back to this way that is clearly the only one in which I can do anything now, and that will open out to me more and more, and that has overwhelming reasons pleading all beautifully in its breast. What really happens is that the closer I get to the problem of the application of it in any particular case the more I get *into* that application, so that the more doubts and torments fall away from me, the more I

37

know where I am, the more everything spreads and shines
and draws me on and I'm justified of my logic and my passion. . . . Causons, causons, mon bon—oh, celestial, soothing,
sanctifying process, with all the high sane forces of the sacred
time fighting, through it, on my side! Let me fumble it gently
and patiently out—with fever and fidget laid to rest—as in the
old enchanted months! It only looms, it only shines and shim-
mers, *too* beautiful and too interesting; it only hangs there too
rich and too full and with too much to give and to pay; it only
presents itself too admirably and too vividly, too straight and
square and vivid, as a little organic and effective Action. . . .'

Referring to this confession, Mr. Lubbock says: 'It is as
though for once, at an hour of midnight silence and solitude
he opened the innermost chamber of his mind and stood face
to face with his genius.' I think, in the consistent phraseology
I have tried to adopt, we might say that in such a mood of
creative activity, the author stands face to face with his personality. He stands fully conscious of the wavering confines of
his conscious mind, an expanding and contracting, a fluctuating horizon where the light of awareness meets the darkness of
oblivion; and in keeping aware of that area of light and at the
same time watching the horizon for a suggestion of more
light, the poet induces that new light into his consciousness; as
when, at twilight, no stars are visible to a casual glance, but
shine out in answer to a concentrated stare. Such lights come,
of course, from the latent memory of verbal images in what
Freud calls the preconscious state of the mind; or from the still
obscurer state of the unconscious, in which are hidden, not
only the neural traces of repressed sensations, but also those
inherited patterns which determine our instincts. But it is not
inspiration alone—not the sudden ingress of light—which
makes the poet; that is only the intermission which, if isolated,
leads to an easy despair. The essential faculty is an awareness of
one's own personality, and the capacity to cultivate its inherent activities 'without division or inner revolt', as accurately
described by Montaigne. Montaigne was not a poet, though

38

he might have been an inspired novelist. But that is beside the point; what distinguishes one kind of artist from another is not their states of mind, their mental machinery, but a difference in the distribution of sensational development—the difference, that is to say, between a poet and painter is a difference between verbal-aural and plastic-visual sensibility; a difference of material, not of method. And that, it seems, is another way of saying with Mr. Eliot that 'the poet has, not a "personality" to express, but a particular medium, which is only a medium . . . in which impressions and experiences combine in peculiar and unexpected ways'.

It looks, therefore, as though the one thing an artist must avoid is the fixity of character. This conclusion is forced on us from still another point of view. A man of character is generally distinguishable as a man of action. Or as Keats wrote in a letter to his friend Bailey (22nd November 1817):

'Men of Genius are great as certain ethereal Chemicals operating on the Mass of neutral intellect—but they have not any individuality, any determined Character—I would call the top and head of those who have a proper self Men of Power.'[1]

If we say that there is a fundamental opposition between the artist and the man of action, the statement is acceptable enough. At least, it would fit typical artists like (to mention only poets) Shakespeare and Blake. It would explain the sudden withering of Wordsworth's genius: he acquired a character. But what of Milton and Goethe? Well, of Milton we can say that he was a poet of one kind in his youth, that he then became a man of action and was silent for twenty-five years, and then became a poet once more, but of a different kind. Of Goethe I cannot speak with any confidence, but I suspect that a complete analysis might reveal a real poet and a real personality, but a somewhat fictitious character. Finally—to repeat a suggestion I have already made—may we not perhaps explain the dreary quarrel of romantic and classic as an opposition between two kinds of art, springing respectively from

[1] *Letters* (Oxford, 1930), p.72.

character and from personality? It is an explanation that would work out very well in practice. We have only to think of Dryden and of Dr. Johnson, and to compare them with Shakespeare and Keats.

The only objection which I can foresee to this theory of personality in literature is the one raised in a general way by Mr. Fernandez: it does not account for the moral and intellectual development in a poet like Shakespeare. Between *Romeo and Juliet* and *Measure for Measure*, between *Hamlet* and *The Tempest*, there is a vast difference which we can only call, in Nietzsche's phrase, a transvaluation of all values. But the poet and his poetry remain the same. The medium, the material—all pedantry apart—is one. But then must we conclude, because a man of character is an admirable spectacle, in his fixity of demeanour and directness of action, a type to be envied and imitated, that therefore this other type of man, this mobile personality of which poets are made, can show no compensating virtues? Must we not rather conclude that the virtues of personality inhere in its very mobility?[1] For though thought by its own nature is capable of logical development, it can be informed by the whole personality, and therefore made real, only when that personality is free to adapt itself to the movements of thought. Thought and personality go hand in hand, and their goal, whether confessed or not, is that state of vision or inspiration which all great spirits have attained.

[1] Its 'negative capability', as Keats called it in a letter to his brothers (28th December 1817):

'I had not a dispute, but a disquisition, with Dilke upon various subjects; several things dovetailed in my mind, and at once it struck me what quality went to form a man of achievement, especially in literature, and which Shakespeare possessed so enormously—I mean *Negative Capability*, that is, when a man is capable of being in uncertainties, mysteries, doubts, without any irritable reaching after fact and reason. Coleridge, for instance, would let go by a fine isolated verisimilitude caught from the Penetralium of mystery, from being incapable of remaining content with half-knowledge.'
—*Letters* (Oxford, 1930), p. 77.

I. THE NATURE OF POETRY

3
POETIC DICTION

In one of his lectures on Shakespeare, Coleridge defined the principle of modern poetry in these words:

'No work of true genius dares want its appropriate form, neither indeed is there any danger of this. As it must not, so genius can not, be lawless: for it is even this that constitutes its genius—*the power of acting creatively under laws of its own origination.*'

Because people have no clear definition of poetry, and because a very different kind of activity has too often usurped the title of poetry, this principle has for long periods been obscured. It thus comes about that every poet who strives for this principle—from Wordsworth to Hopkins or Mr. Eliot—has to wear the trappings of a rebel, and what is the assertion of a law of discipline is treated as a declaration of independence.

No further progress can be made in this essay without a direct statement on the nature of poetry. This cannot have the exact proportions of a logical definition. Poetry is properly speaking a transcendental quality—a sudden transformation which words assume under a particular influence—and we can no more define this quality than we can define a state of grace. We can only make a number of distinctions, of which the main is the broad but elemental one between poetry and prose. I use the word 'elemental' deliberately, because I believe the difference between poetry and prose to be, not one of sur-

41

face qualities, not of form in any sense, not even of *mode* of expression, but absolutely of essence. It is not a case of the mind, in need of expression, choosing between two ways—one poetry, the other prose. There is no choice for the particular state of mind in which poetry originates. It must either seek poetic expression, or it must simply not be expressed; for an altogether lower tension, involving a different kind of mentality, must be substituted before the activity of prose expression can intervene.

I do not wish to imply by these words any particular theory of aesthetics. The difference in tension really corresponds to a difference in the historical evolution of language. Poetry is a more primitive mode of expression than prose, and that is why the language of primitive peoples often seems poetic to us. And we have now, thanks to the labours of Lévy-Bruhl, abandoned the idea that what is primitive is necessarily inferior. In the circumstances in which they operate, the mind and language of the savage are more effective than the mind and language of the civilized man. But the world of one is not the world of the other, nor is the world of poetry the world of prose. The point of view I am expressing has probably been worked out in most detail and force by Vico (*Scienza Nuova*, Book II, chaps. ii and iii); the following summary by his disciple Croce makes this clear:

'Poetry is produced not by the mere caprice of pleasure, but by natural necessity. It is so far from being superfluous and capable of elimination, that without it thought cannot arise: it is the primary activity of the human mind. Man, before he has arrived at the stage of forming universals, forms imaginary ideas. Before he reflects with a clear mind, he apprehends with faculties confused and disturbed: before he can articulate, he sings: before speaking in prose, he speaks in verse: before using technical terms, he uses metaphors, and the metaphorical use of words is as natural to him as that which we call "natural".'[1]

[1] *The Philosophy of Giambattista Vico.* By Benedetto Croce. Trans. by R. G. Collingwood (London, 1913), p. 48.

I have, in the preceding section of this essay, put forward a theory of the poet's personality which has some justification in modern psychology and is supported by the experience of various imaginative writers. The theory of poetic form which follows has been worked out on the basis of my own practice, and on the basis of my own vivid experience of the presence of poetic values in other poets. I want to keep the discussion as far as possible to a practical level. But I have found considerable support for my theories not only in Vico, but in more recent philosophy. There is some support in Croce, for the theory I advance necessarily assumes an intuitive quality in all art; but there is more in the works of another Italian, Leone Vivante, whose two books, *Intelligence in Expression* and *Notes on the Originality of Thought*, are unduly neglected; but perhaps both Croce and Vivante owe a good deal to Vico and De Sanctis. The relevance of some of Signor Vivante's observations may be judged from the following paragraphs:

'In the poetic period not only the attribute, but every word, every moment of thought, gathers up, renews the whole. The subject is recalled in its concept in every word of the proposition, that is, it progressively takes fresh value, fills up of itself and governs every new moment. Thus reality at every point is drawn up from the unknown. The new expressive moment in its particular significance forms itself in the meaning of the whole, which in the new moment is not inferred but renewed: and myriads of *nexus*—resemblances, accords, unities, *ex principio*—form themselves. On the other hand, constructive thought loses the *nexus* or necessities of principle proper to thought in its integral originality: if we except the *nexus* belonging to formal logic, to a conception schematically material and spatial—a position of mere existences and of spatial and quantitative relations and ideal abstract identities. In other words, in constructive thought *nexus of inherence* are comparatively prevalent, in poetic thought *nexus of essence*.'[1]

[1] *Notes on the Originality of Thought*, pp. 164–5. Translated by Professor Brodrick-Bullock (London, 1927).

'In prose the period is more subject to rules, whether in the collocation of words, in the structure of the phrase, or in the use of words; i.e. it is subject to conventional usage. Uncommon words can hardly be introduced; it seems wayward and arbitrary to use them, and in general we cannot depart from common usage—while in poetry a like "transgression", a like inversion or the uncommon use of a word passes, as such, unobserved. And this is due to the boldness which words have in poetry—because their meaning is entirely present, their every reason or value is present and active in them, in every moment of expression; and because, on the other hand, the very material, as it were, calls forth activity to form itself according to all its intrinsic values and forms and, being one with activity, is itself concept.'[1]

All art originates in an act of intuition, or vision. But such *intuition* or vision must be identified with *knowledge*, being fully present only when consciously objectified. This act of vision or intuition is, physically, a state of concentration or tension in the mind. The *process* of poetry consists firstly in maintaining this vision in its integrity, and secondly in expressing this vision in words. Words are generally (that is to say, in prose) the *analysis* of a mental state. But in the process of poetic composition words rise into the conscious mind as isolated objective 'things' with a definite equivalence in the poet's state of mental intensity. They are arranged or composed in a sequence or rhythm which is sustained until the mental state of tension in the poet is exhausted or released by this objective equivalence.

To this description of the process of poetry there is one qualification to make. If we take it at its bare worth, it might be held to justify those theories of 'pure poetry' which have had much vogue lately. These theories imply that the intuition or vision of the poet is expressed simply by a *musical* equivalence in the words. This I think may be possible in

[1] *Intelligence in Expression*, p. 3. Translated by Professor Brodrick-Bullock (London, 1925).

isolated words and phrases, particularly those of a high-sounding 'proper' meaning ('In Xanadu did Kubla Kahn . . .'), but poetry in general disproves the theory of pure poetry. Words, their sound and even their very appearance, are, of course, everything to the poet: the sense of words is the sense of poetry. But words have associations carrying the mind beyond sound to visual image and abstract idea. And the poet, even as he becomes conscious of words in the act of composition, feels them tincturing his consciousness not only with sound, but also with colour and light and power—in short, with meaning. Poetry depends, not only on the sound of words, but even more on their mental reverberations.

So much by way of a theoretical preamble. Historically, I believe that this theory of poetry is illustrated by the main tradition of English poetry which begins with Chaucer and reaches its final culmination in Shakespeare. It is contradicted by most French poetry before Baudelaire, by the so-called classical phase of English poetry culminating in Alexander Pope, and by the late Poet Laureate. It was re-established in England by Wordsworth and Coleridge, developed in some degree by Browning and Gerard Manley Hopkins, and in our own day by poets like Wilfred Owen, Ezra Pound, and T. S. Eliot.

The distinction is not merely that between 'classical' and 'romantic'. This division cuts across in a different direction. The real distinction is between the poetic process as I have defined it, and a process adequately described by Dryden as *wit-writing*. In the Introductory Letter to *Annus Mirabilis* Dryden wrote:

'The Composition of all poems is or ought to be of wit; and wit in the Poet, or *Wit-writing*, (if you will give me leave to use a School distinction), is no other than the faculty of imagination in the Writer; which, like a nimble Spaniel, beats over and ranges through the field of Memory, till it springs the Quarry it hunted after; or, without metaphor, which searches over all the Memory for the Species or Ideas of those things which it designs to represent. *Wit written* is that which is well defin'd, the happy result of Thought, or product of Imagination.'

And further:

'The first happiness of the Poet's Imagination is properly Invention, or finding of the thought; the second is Fancy, or the variation, deriving or moulding of that thought as the Judgment represents it proper to the subject; the third is Elocution, or the Art of clothing and adorning that thought so found and varied, in apt, significant and sounding words. The quickness of the Imagination is seen in the Invention, the fertility in the Fancy, and the accuracy in the Expression.'

This is an excellent description of the practice of Dryden and of others of his school, and that the practice results in a verbal art of a high order, no one would deny. But such art is not poetry; it is no more than elocution, or, as we should now say, eloquence.

To give but one illustration:

> *Will all great Neptune's ocean wash this stain*
> *Clean from my hand; no, this my hand will rather*
> *The multitudinous seas incarnadine*
> *Making the green one red.*

—Which is poetry. But the following lines are wit-writing, or eloquence:

> *Lo! thy dread empire, Chaos! is restor'd;*
> *Light dies before thy uncreating word;*
> *Thy hand, great Anarch! lets the curtain fall,*
> *And universal darkness buries all.*

I think Wordsworth was the first poet to be fully conscious of the difference between poetry and wit-writing, and his various Prefaces contain admirable definitions of the nature of poetry. These definitions are of great psychological exactitude, but since they are consistent with the general theory of poetry already enounced (and indeed, the main inspiration of it), and

46

since I have dealt with them in detail in a book on Wordsworth,[1] I will not review them now. It is sufficient to emphasize the historical fact, that Wordsworth emancipated himself
and the whole tradition of English poetry from the prevailing
tyranny of wit-writing. which had lasted for about a century
and a half.

Wordsworth's restorations (one cannot speak of innovations, for there is nothing new in Wordsworth that is not to
be found in the Ballads, or in Shakespeare and Milton), were
confined to the sphere of what he called poetic diction. He
saw, and saw rightly, that the defect of wit-writing was fundamental, and therefore to be sought in the very act of composition. He concluded that it was a *verbal* defect—and this verbal
defect he identified with artificiality. All his efforts were concentrated on this end: the return to naturalism and simplicity
of diction. But he was only partially right. Artificiality was
only one of the symptoms of the disease. The real defect involved the state of the poet's mind in its completeness, and
was reflected, not only in diction, but also throughout the
whole poetic process—in modes of feeling, in diction, rhythm
and metre. Wordsworth's mode of feeling was fully involved:
to be exact, we should say that it was a divergence in his emotional reactions to experience (arising out of his experiences in
France in 1792) that was the primary cause of his dissatisfaction with the poetry of the eighteenth century (to which he
had hitherto been devoted). To his changed emotional outlook, the wit-writing of Dryden and Pope would naturally
appear as so much 'gaudiness and inane phraseology'. But if
he had looked deeper, he would have found that more than
phraseology was involved. It will now be seen that what
precisely was involved was the whole theory of personality
and character which I have been outlining in this essay.

Nevertheless, the course of poetry in the nineteenth century
was determined by Wordsworth. Not one poet—not Shelley
nor Keats, not Landor nor Tennyson, not even Swinburne—

[1] *Wordsworth* (London, 1931; new edn., 1949).

47

but was affected by the revolution in poetic diction originated by Wordsworth. They were affected, but did little to develop the situation as Wordsworth left it. Against the magnitude of Wordsworth's experiment, all the minor tinkerings of the nineteenth century are as nothing—until we come to Browning and Gerard Manley Hopkins. Browning had no particular theory of diction: he wanted his verse to be expressive, and expressive it was—of his personality. But what he did do was considerably to enlarge the scope of poetry by adding certain categories of content to it, such as those embodied in his dramatic monologues and his psychological studies generally. His influence is important because its tendency is to encourage an objective attitude in the poet. Matthew Arnold should perhaps not be passed over; he adds little to Wordsworth's achievement, but he did experiment in free verse, and the originality that is claimed for contemporary writers of free verse is excessive when 'The Strayed Reveller' is borne in mind. But that graceful experiment bore little fruit. Hopkins's experiments, however, were of far greater potential influence though they did not begin to be operative until thirty years after his death. I deal with the subject more fully in a later essay (pages 339–48).

Any complete history of the evolution of modern verse technique would have to find a place for other poets—for Whitman, who contributed nothing very intelligent to its technical development, but rather a blind emotional force; for W. B. Yeats, who is not so conventional as romantic enthusiasts imagine; for T. E. Hulme and Ezra Pound. It was with the school which Hulme started and Pound established that the revolution begun by Wordsworth was finally completed. Diction, rhythm, and metre were fully emancipated from formal artifice, and the poet was free to act creatively under laws of his own origination. It was not always understood that, having cast off the tyranny of obsolete laws, the poet was under the necessity of originating his own, and much of the free verse that has been practised since 1914 compromises the theory by its feebleness. Nevertheless, the theory is right, and all true poetry of to-day, as all true poetry of the past, conforms to it. For, properly understood, this theory is not the theory of a particular school; it is the theory of all essential English poetry.

At all great epochs of change and of crystallization it is the medium of verse that has hitherto embodied the first and the final accents of intelligence. The first formulation of the particular spirit of the Renaissance is found in the poetry of Jacopone; and it was only under the direct influence of Franciscan literature that the plastic arts took on, in Giovanni Pisano and Giotto, the elements of a new conception of life. The priority of poetry seems to hold good for all epochs of Western civilization down to and including the Romantic Movement of the last century. It holds good even of later and minor movements, such as that of the Symbolists in France and of the Pre-Raphaelites in England. But of the definitely new conceptions which promise to be distinctive of the twentieth century we find little sign in poetry. There is, that is to say, no adequate literary equivalent in England for the impressive organization and intellectual content of the modern movement in painting. There may be psychological reasons for this unusual precedence of the visual arts, and to speculations of this kind it is tempting to devote some space. But for the present we must consider the practical possibility of inherent defects in traditional poetic form. Why that form did not succumb to the forces that changed design in the plastic arts is still another question. It is largely a question of a lack of intelligence at certain crises in the history of poetry since Baudelaire.

Such a crisis is always marked by a discussion of the technique of verse, and no such discussion has been so general and on the whole so profound as the one that marked the emergence of the classical English style in the Elizabethan period. And in this discussion there were no documents so practical and so decisive as Thomas Campion's *Observations in the Art of English Poesie* (1602) and Samuel Daniel's *A Defence of Ryme*

D   49

(1603).[1] Sidney's more famous *Apologie for Poetrie,* published in 1595, had been written about 1581, before the dawn. It has a more general and pervasive charm than these two militant pamphlets, because it is written from a more absolute stand-point. At the same time it lacks the empirical interest of the later works, which were composed at the highest and intensest moment in the history of the English tongue. Here we touch the pulse of a crisis, feel the life flowing, and see intelligence determining the result. The cause in question was more than the ostensible one—the use of rhyme. It was the cause of native and original vigour against academic and pedantic bonds. Surprisingly it is Campion, inveighing against 'the childish titillation of riming', who furthers the academic cause. In the setting out of his case he makes certain just obser-vations on the abuse of rhyme, as 'that it inforceth a man often-times to abjure his matter, and extend a short conceit beyond all bounds of arte', and his experiments in unrhymed verse are lively and were not without their influence on the de-velopment of blank verse. He brought even Daniel to an admittance that 'a tragedie would indeede best comporte with a blank verse, and dispence with Ryme', and to an advocacy of certain precautionary measures against 'this over-glutting the eare with that alwayes certaine, and ful incounter of Ryme'. But Campion could advance no very positive reasons for the abjuration of all rhyme beyond the fact that the custom of the Greeks and Latins was against it. His graceful pamphlet was easy prey to Daniel, who is full of lusty good sense and the right humour of originality. He goes straight to the point, and con-tends that the genius of our language has its own peculiar laws:

'Every language hath her proper number or measure fitted to use and delight, which, Custome intertaining by the allow-ance of the Eare, doth indenize, and make naturall. All verse is but a frame of wordes confinde within certaine measure; differing from the ordinarie speach, and introduced, the better to expresse mens conceipts, both for delight and memorie.

[1] The Bodley Head Quartos, No. XIV (London, 1925).

Which frame of wordes consisting of *Rithmus* or *Metrum,*
Number or Measure, are disposed into divers fashions, according to the humour of the Composer and the set of the time;
And these *Rhythmi* as *Aristotle* saith are familiar amongst all
Nations, and *è naturali & sponte fusa compositione*: And they fall
as naturally already in our language as ever Art can make
them; being such as the Eare of it selfe doth marshall in their
proper roomes, and they of themselves will not willingly be
put out of their ranke; and that in such a verse as best com-
portes with the Nature of our language.'

There are two observations in this passage which are of
present moment, for they possibly indicate considerations
which we have since forgotten. One relates to what we might
call the inherent rhythm of our language, determined by custom and evident to the ear, and the other to the disposition of
number or measure according to *the set of the time*. It is possible
that by 'the set of the time' Daniel meant no more than the
dictates of fashion; but even this phrase may have a useful
sense implying the instinctive harmony of expression and
actuality. And here we come to the crux of the modern
situation; for have we any assurance that the modern poetry
has arrived at this intimate sympathy with the pace or rhythm
of contemporary life which is the condition of all vigorous
art? But there are two questions here which must not be confused: the nature of poetic rhythm, and its relation to what
we must call the rhythm of life. 'Every versifier', Daniel
observes in another place, 'that well observes his worke, findes
in our language . . . what numbers best fitte the Nature of her
Idiome, and the proper places destined to such accents, as she
will not let in, to any other roomes then into those for which
they were borne.' 'A dunce like myself', said Swinburne,
'measures verse by ear, not by finger.' This latter remark is
quoted by Professor Sonnenschein, whose treatise[1] on rhythm

1 *What is Rhythm?* An essay by E. A. Sonnenschein. Accompanied by an
appendix on Experimental Syllable-Measurement, in which Stephen Jones
and Eileen Macleod have co-operated. (Oxford, 1925.)

has the merit of 'fitting the facts' in a remarkably inclusive way. One thing in the eternal discussion of rhythm is certain, that verse, both historically and creatively, takes its form as a rhythmical sequence independent of any analysis into feet and measures. First the poet and then the metrist. Professor Sonnenschein keeps this truth well in mind, and his definition of rhythm is based on it. 'Rhythm', he says, 'is that property of a sequence of events in time which produces on the mind of the observer the impression of proportion between the durations of the several events or groups of events of which the sequence is composed.' Among the merits of this definition is the fact that it speaks of *durations*; 'for *time*, in the sense of the duration of events, is the fundamental feature of rhythm'. It also speaks of *events* in time, and implies the possibility of measuring them. There exists an instrument called the kymograph, which by its operations promises to put at rest all the age-long controversies of the metrists. For the kymograph, like the camera, cannot lie.

Briefly, the kymograph can measure exactly the duration of every syllable in speech; it can therefore reveal the exact quantity of spoken verse. For example, a simple line of Tennyson's, when measured, shows the following ratios of duration:

The long light shakes across the lakes
12 : 31 : 27 : 45 : 7 : 34 : 9 : 55

When this scientific measurement is applied on a large scale to the main body of 'refined English verse', the results show beyond doubt that 'quantity is nothing less than a *structural element* in the best kind of English verse, side by side with accent'. Syllables are only relatively long or short, and even then may vary with the context; or they may be of equal value in a foot (isosyllabic), or protracted, or even, where the rhythm demands it, merely imaginary. Professor Sonnenschein is, of course, mainly concerned with the analysis of traditional verse forms, and no one interested in this aspect of the subject can

afford to neglect his book. He does not, however, make any
attempt to apply his definitions and discoveries to the extension of the possibilities of poetry. He does not seem to realize,
for example, that his definition of rhythm is not merely applicable to refined extracts from Tennyson and Keats, but that it
is equally applicable to 'The Strayed Reveller' and 'The
Waste Land'. In fact, Professor Sonnenschein's definition,
without more ado, substitutes the element of proportion in
rhythm for the element of regularity; and this is precisely
what the best *vers libriste* poets, in France, England, and America
have been contending for. One cannot deny proportion to a
rhythm like this, which is contemporary free verse:[1]

> *sunlight was over*
> *our mouths fears hearts lungs arms hopes feet hands*
> *under us the unspeaking Mediterranean bluer*
> *than we had imagined*
> *a few cries drifting through*
> *high air*
> *a sail a fishing boat somebody an invisible spectator*
> *maybe certain nobodies laughing faintly*
> *playing moving far below us*
> *perhaps one villa caught like pieces*
> *of a kite in the trees here*
> *and here reflecting*
> *sunlight.*

Nor to this passage, from 'The Strayed Reveller';

> *Is it then evening*
> *So soon? I see, the night-dews,*
> *Cluster'd in thick beads, dim*
> *The agate brooch-stones*
> *On thy white shoulder;*
> *The cool night-wind, too,*
> *Blows through the portico,*

[1] From a poem by E. E. Cummings, in '1924', No. 2, August 1924.

Stirs thy hair, Goddess,
Waves thy white robe!

Nor can one, for that matter, concede regularity to a rhythm like this:

> *Pray, do not mock me,*
> *I am a very foolish, fond old man,*
> *Fourscore and upward, not an hour more nor less;*
> *And, to deal plainly,*
> *I fear I am not in my perfect mind.*
> *Methinks I should know you and know this man;*
> *Yet I am doubtful: for I am mainly ignorant*
> *What place this is, and all the skill I have*
> *Remembers not these garments; nor I know not*
> *Where I did lodge last night.*

and lines like these, which demand such an elaborate quantitative analysis, are in effect totally free from any but the most superficial regularity:

> *Open, ye everlasting Gates, they sung,*
> *Open, ye Heav'ns, your living dores; let in*
> *The great Creator from his work returnd*
> *Magnificent, his Six days work, a World;*
> *Open, and henceforth oft; for God will deigne*
> *To visit oft the dwellings of just Men*
> *Delighted, and with frequent intercourse*
> *Thither will send his winged Messengers*
> *On errands of supernal Grace. So sung*
> *The glorious Train ascending: He through Heav'n,*
> *That open'd wide her blazing Portals, led*
> *To Gods Eternal house direct the way.*

If, then, we are to substitute for the concepts of measure (that is, for regular, accented feet) a concept of rhythm dependent on nothing but its own innate rightness as tested by the ear, we must inquire more closely into the nature and origins of such rhythms. How are they come by? The conventional metrist will say that at any rate in the case of Shakespeare and Milton, and even in the case of Arnold, they are variations on the basis of a regular measure. But this is casuistry, for all rhythm, even the rhythm of prose and of speech, is only perceptible by contrast to a hypothetical norm of regularity—a uniform temporal beat or simple iambic sequence. Certainly all free verse of rhythmical structure is related to such a norm or basis. But actually no rhythms are consciously constructed by a system of normal measurements: they are rather spontaneous sense perceptions. And any comparative study of rhythms reveals the fact that they are relative. They vary from age to age and from language to language. Chinese and Polynesian rhythms are perceptible to us, but they are foreign to our habits. English rhythms have a good deal in common with Germanic rhythms, but both are quite different from French or Spanish rhythms. Even within the limits of our own language, if we observe carefully purely local dictions, we find surprisingly different rhythms. A man from Newcastle and a man from Hull speak in entirely different *tempi*. But we must beware of a loose connotation of the word 'rhythm', which is better kept for aesthetic effects. We can, however, resort to the word 'idiom', so aptly used by Daniel. A living language analyses into idioms: idioms are the live organisms of speech—words are molecules and letters atoms. Now this organic unit, this idiom, is instinct with rhythm; it has irrefrangible intonation, and poetic rhythm is but the extension and the aggregation of these primary rhythms. Even measured, regularly accented verse is successful only in so far as it makes use of or accommodates itself to these idioms. Free verse, which includes the slightest as well as the widest divergence from regular pattern, is but the free use of these idioms.

Idioms arise out of the contacts of daily life. They are the response of the human organism to the elements around it. They reflect the speed of life, the pressure of life, its very

GENERAL THEORIES

essence. Idioms are the vocal chimings-in of man in the rhythm
of life, and have their parallels in the beating of drums and
the dancing of limbs. All the arts are built up from these primary elements, and their reality, their actuality, depends on
this strict relation. To build up poetry with dead idioms is
like living a life of dead habits and obsolete manners. But such
is precisely the sickness of nearly all modern poetry: it rings
false in the actual turmoil of the day.

We can only seize the real rhythm instinctively. It *has* been
found—in the modern ballet, in American rag-time music,
and in a minute quantity of modern poetry. But when we
have found the rhythm we are only at the beginning of art.
We have found no more than the instruments of art.

'It is not the observing of *Trochaicques* nor their *Iambicques*
[writes Daniel in one place] that wil make our writings ought
the wiser: All their Poesie, all their Philosophie is nothing,
unless we bring the discerning light of conceipt with us to
apply it to use. It is not bookes, but onley that great booke of
the world, and the all-overspreading grace of heaven that
makes men truly judiciall.'

That warning against pedantry applies equally to the makers
of new rhythms, for no amount of originality will benefit us
if it lack 'the discerning light'. Technique we may learn from
observations, but this final necessity is a gift of a more individual nature, depending not so much upon the influences of
environment as upon an inborn capacity. Or, to speak more
exactly, it depends upon a convergence of these two factors—
upon the right mind co-operating with the finest sensibility,
and then freely expressing itself.

I. THE NATURE OF POETRY

4
THE STRUCTURE OF THE POEM

It might be objected that whilst the theory of poetry which I am putting forward in these pages may be accepted as a theory of poetic essence, it will not account for poetry in being, which involves, besides essence, embodiment and structure. The question is: how can the poet pass from the metaphor and the lyric poem which is in reality no more than an extended metaphor, to those larger epic conceptions by which we measure the greatness of poets? To discuss the length of poetry might seem at first sight a very trivial approach to a serious subject. But actually it involves those first principles of the poetic faculty which we have been discussing. Most poets aspire to write long poems, and we might almost say that the distinction between a major and a minor poet is the capacity to write a long poem successfully. I cannot think of any poet whom one would venture to call 'major', whose work consists entirely of short pieces; though naturally there are many minor poets, with an exquisite talent for short pieces, who have many long, dreary, and unreadable poems to their discredit.

How long is a long poem? is the simple question that might first be asked. The *Divine Comedy* and *Paradise Lost* are poems of the first order, and they are extremely long. The characteristic poems of Chaucer, Shakespeare, Dryden, Pope, Wordsworth, Shelley, and Robert Browning are of comparable length. But is *The Ancient Mariner* a long poem? And the *Ode:*

Intimations of Immortality or *Lamia*? Is Donne's *Progress of the Soul*, or Mr. Eliot's *Waste Land*? Obviously there is no general rule, and in the absence of a linear measure, we are driven to seek a qualitative one. Between the short poem and the long poem there is a difference, but it is not so much a difference of length as of essence.

The difference really turns on the question of lyricism. We often call the short poem a *lyric*, which meant originally a poem short enough to be set to music and sung for a moment's pleasure. From the poet's point of view, we might define the lyric as a poem which embodies a single or simple emotional attitude, a poem which expresses directly an uninterrupted mood or inspiration. A long poem, it would follow as a corollary, is one which unites by artifice several or many such emotional moods; though here the artifice might imply a single dominating *idea* which in itself might be an emotional unity—a question which I discuss in detail in the next essay.

In this short paragraph we have used several terms which are far more significant than a casual reading would reveal. I want especially to stress the words *emotion* and *idea*, in their particular contexts. It might be found that they are the very words which, dominating the nature of a poem, lead to the essential distinction we wish to make between a long poem and a lyric. But before broaching that essential distinction there are certain descriptive features to be disposed of. For example, of the long poems already mentioned, some are properly described as epic, others as philosophic, some are odes and some are direct narratives. *The Canterbury Tales* are long because they could not very well be shorter: the poet has a series of stories to tell in verse, and he uses his verse with economy and despatch to achieve the end. Such length in a poem is at once necessary and arbitrary; it is a necessity of the content, but so far as the poetic quality of the poem is concerned, the length is arbitrary; I mean, it is not the poetry that makes for the length, but the story.

Most epic poetry is of this nature, though 'epic' is not an exact term. The *Iliad* is an epic in one sense; *Paradise Lost* in quite another sense. The *Iliad*, like the *Canterbury Tales*, is lengthy by reason of its story; and so, I think, is all true epic poetry. But Milton, in his poem, had more in mind than the story; the story of the Fall is merely the kernel, or theme, round which he elaborates, firstly, a dramatic myth, and secondly, a philosophical thesis. Here the epic, we might say, is dominated by an idea; though in the construction of a dramatic myth another faculty is involved, which I will discuss presently.

I confess I have never understood what precisely an ode is. It is difficult to find anything in common between Cowley's *Ode, Of Wit* and Dryden's *Ode on St. Cecilia's Day* and, say, Wordsworth's *Ode: Intimations of Immortality*. An ode, in practice, implies a certain architectonic mastery of rhythmic variations; a structure which, I suppose, has its analogies in music, but which, from a strictly poetic point of view, does not differ from the long poem in general; just as, from the point of view of eating, a wedding cake terraced like a tabernacle does not differ from plain plum cake. The ode, that is to say, is not essentially long or short; it might conceivably be a lyric, as I believe Wordsworth's *Ode* to be.

It will be said that the philosophic poem, such as *De Rerum Natura*, the *Divine Comedy*, and, to take a modern example, *The Testament of Beauty*, does not need to be discussed at this point because it is obviously not lyrical in nature, and is invariably long. But what are we to say of a poem like *The Phœnix and the Turtle*, not a long poem by any means, but decidedly a philosophical one: indeed, a poem in which all the force and beauty of this kind of poetry is distilled in purest essence? There are many poems of Donne's, too, which superficially are lyrical in form, but philosophical in content. If only negatively, the philosophic poem shows that the difference between the long poem and the short poem is not to be found in the nature of its content.

Let us consider a final possibility: that there is no poetic difference between the long poem and the short poem: that there is a certain art of poetry, which arises we do not quite know how, from the music of vowels and consonants, the sound and associations of words, the surprise of images and metaphors; in the now consecrated phrase, that there is 'pure poetry', and that the rest is prose, or padding. According to this theory, most poems would tend to be short, if only for the sufficient reason that it is impossible for any poet to sustain his inspiration for long; and actually, when the advocate of 'pure' poetry is pressed for examples, he can only quote you a few short lyrics, perhaps *Kubla Khan*, and for the rest, nothing but disinterred lines and couplets. I have already pointed out the general limitations of this theory: it is actually a species of solipsism. It confuses the thing and its attributes. It ignores what the world has agreed to call poetry in favour of an *a priori* definition of poetry. For what the advocate of 'pure' poetry is defining is not poetry, but only a species of poetry, namely, 'pure' poetry. Let us admit, even, that word-music, image and metaphor are the bloodstream of poetry, without which it cannot for a moment exist. Yet beyond these are structure and conception—structure which is the embodiment of words in a pattern or form; and conception, which is the projection of the poet's thought into a process from which, or during the course of which, words are generated.

That is to say, there can be no words with their accompanying music, no images with their visual immediacy, no metaphors with their more-than-verbal meaning, unless there is either an intuition of form, which I take to be an emotion about fitness, size, appropriateness, tension, tautness, and so on (as in the sonnet); or, not alternatively so much as in addition, a progressive invention which will carry the poet on from word to word, line to line, stanza to stanza, book to book, until the invention is exhausted.

Form and conception are present in the lyric, but they are

60

unobtrusive; the duration of the poetry is so short, the emotion so immediate (and relatively simple) that we do not perceive (it is the poet's business to conceal) the time-structure. Form and conception are fused in the act of creation. When form dominates the conception (that is to say, when the conception is limited enough to be seen as a single unit—to be held from the beginning to the end in one mental tension), then the poem can be defined properly as 'short'. On the other hand, when the conception is so complex that the mind must take it in in disjointed series, finally ordering these series in a comprehensive unity, then the poem is properly defined as 'long'.

In a successful sonnet, for example, or in *Kubla Khan*, the music of the first words has not died in the mind when the last words sound; nor is the configuration of the poem—its rhythm and closed form—for a moment lost. Its total effect is not only in the sound, but also in the shape. But in the long poem, the music is an accompaniment which is never lost, which is not co-extensive with the form. It is the difference between the still beauty of a lake, looked at as a whole, and the beauty of the stream which we follow from its source to the sea, never seeing it at one time as a whole, but always aware of its continuity, its sameness in variation, its music in progression.

Having made this distinction and leaving the short poem on one side, we can perhaps ask a very relevant question: Is the long poem worth while? It is a banal question, but necessary, because the long poem is very often attempted. It would be too rash to assume that it was extensively read; in fact, we know that in general the reading public is bored with the long poem. But is it the fault of the length of the poem, of the long poem in itself; or are the long poems given to us in some sense unsuccessful? And in any case, if no one reads them, why do poets go on writing them?

There is a passage in one of Keats's letters which answers this last question. Writing to his friend Bailey in 1817, he says:

'I have heard Hunt say and I may be asked: why endeavour after a long poem? To which I should answer: Do not the Lovers of Poetry like to have a little Region to wander in where they may pick and choose, and in which the images are so numerous that many are forgotten and found new in a second Reading—which may be food for a week's stroll in the summer? Do not they like this better than what they can read through before Mrs. Williams comes down stairs? a Morning work at most. Besides a long Poem is a test of Invention which I take to be the Polar Star of Poetry, as Fancy is the Sails, and Imagination the Rudder. Did our great Poets ever write short Pieces? I mean in the shape of Tales— This same invention seems indeed of late years to have been forgotten as a Poetical excellence.'[1]

Invention, fancy, imagination—here are terms which we have already used in another context perhaps with another meaning. What I think Keats means, if I may venture to transpose his ideas into words which seem more consistent with the present argument, is that the long poem is a test of inspiration —though inspiration, which may on occasion mean motivation, is far from being a satisfactory word. That is to say, Keats thought that if the inspiration of the poet could hold out without flagging until it has embodied many moods and feelings *throughout the course of a narrative,* then the reader, in his turn, would find in the poem, not merely a single and momentary impression of loveliness, but a vast assembly of verses and images through which he may wander and find, now one sympathetic response, now another, according to his mood or feeling. In one case (the lyric) the poet immediately subdues the reader, and achieves his desired effect; in the other (the long poem) he drops his jewels in a chosen path, and allows the reader to pick up any that may catch his eyes.

From the poet's point of view, the long poem means, according to the view expressed by Keats, charging the narrative with a certain density or opacity. This is achieved by a

[1] *Letters,* I, pp. 55-6.

liberal use of epithets, similes, and metaphors, which, though poetic in themselves, may have the effect of impeding the narrative. Take almost any passage from *Hyperion*:

> *In pale and silver silence they remain'd*
> *Till suddenly a splendour, like the morn,*
> *Pervaded all the beetling gloomy steeps,*
> *All the sad spaces of oblivion,*
> *And every gulf, and every chasm old*
> *And every height, and every sullen depth*
> *Voiceless, or hoarse with loud tormented streams*
> *And all the everlasting cataracts,*
> *And all the headlong torrents far and near,*
> *Mantled before in darkness and huge shade,*
> *Now saw the light and made it terrible.*
> *It was Hyperion:—a granite peak*
> *His bright feet touch'd, and there he staid to view*
> *The misery his brilliance had betray'd*
> *To the most hateful seeing of itself.*
> *Golden his hair of short Numidian curl,*
> *Regal his shape majestic, a vast shade*
> *In midst of his own brightness, like the bulk*
> *Of Memnon's image at the set of sun*
> *To one who travels from the dusking East:*
> *Sighs, too, as mournful as that Memnon's harp,*
> *He utter'd, while his hands, contemplative,*
> *He press'd together, and in silence stood.*

As a static poem it is very beautiful; as a piece of narrative it is halting, and the interest, surfeited with conceits, is apt to lag for the action. If from the passage you omit lines 4–11, 19–20, you do not injure either the descriptive force or the narrative action.

It is perhaps hardly fair to compare Keats and Chaucer, for there is a clash between idealistic and realistic values. But let us take a passage from Spenser's *Faerie Queene*:

There in a gloomy hollow glen she found
A little cottage, built of stickes and reedes
In homely wize, and wald with sods around,
In which a witch did dwell, in loathly weedes,
And wilfull want, all carelesse of her needes;
So choosing solitarie to abide,
Far from all neighbours, that her deuilish deedes
And hellish arts from people she might hide,
And hurt far off vnknowne, whom euer she enuide.

The Damzell there arriuing entred in;
Where sitting on the flore the Hag she found,
Busie (as seem'd) about some wicked gin:
Who soone as she beheld that suddein stound,
Lightly vpstarted from the dustie ground,
And with fell looke and hollow deadly gaze
Stared on her awhile, as one astound,
Ne had one word to speake, for great amaze,
But shewd by outward signes, that dread her sence did daze.

At last turning her feare to foolish wrath,
She askt, what deuill had her thither brought,
And who she was, and what vnwonted path
Had guided her, vnwelcomed, vnsought?
To which the Damzell full of doubtfull thought,
Her mildly answer'd; Beldame be not wroth
With silly Virgin by aduenture brought
Vnto your dwelling, ignorant and loth,
That craue but rowme to rest, while tempest ouerblo'th.

With that adowne out of her Christall eyne
Few trickling teares she softly forth let fall,
That like two Orient pearles, did purely shyne
Vpon her snowy cheeke; and therewithall
She sighed soft, that none so bestiall,
Nor saluage hart, but ruth of her sad plight

64

Would make to melt: or pitteously appall;
And that vile Hag, all were her whole delight
In mischiefe, was much moued at so pitteous sight.

Here nothing can be omitted without detracting from the descriptive force of the whole passage. There is only one simile in the four stanzas—'like two Orient pearls'—and this is too short, too vivid and too just to do anything but enhance the movement of the narrative. This does not mean that the passage from Spenser is better *poetically* than the passage from Keats; it merely means that Spenser's is the better *narrative* poetry; but if the object of the poem is to narrate, I think we might say that it is a better poem.

My point is, that Keats was mistaken in his approach to the long poem, and that both *Endymion* and *Hyperion* are failures as narrative poems just because Keats was trying to do something which cannot legitimately be done. He was misusing a definite form of poetry. His poems may be compared with motor-cars moving slowly in procession at a Carnival of Flowers, which must be stripped of their lovely decorations before they can resume their proper speed.

It must not be imagined, however, that all the virtue of a narrative poem lies in its efficiency in forwarding the action. Prose is sufficient for that purpose. Poetry always, in every kind, resides in the word and its associations. In narrative poetry the words must convey the action with speed and economy, but then they must be fine emotive words; words such as we find, indeed, in the passage I have quoted from Spenser.

A narrative poem, then, may properly be called a long poem, but only in virtue of the content. The story is told, is perhaps invented; the poetry springs into being as the story unfolds. The story is the inspiration (and in this case also the motivation) of the poetry. The length of the poem is not motivated by the force of the poetic inspiration; but the poet will be poetically inspired by the narrative to the extent that he visualizes the events of the narrative, and is moved by the visualization. He will be moved so long as, in the famous phrase, he keeps his eye on the objects, on the visualized events.

But that does not achieve Keats's purpose in writing a long poem, which is to have 'a little Region to wander in'. Invention, which he calls the Polar Star of Poetry—surely this is not merely the capacity to tell a story? Is it possible that there are other modes of poetry, which satisfy Keats's purpose, but which are neither lyrical nor narrative? What of that other kind of poem whose characteristic it is to be dominated by an idea?—

> An Orphic song indeed,
> A song divine of high and passionate truths
> To their own music chaunted.

That was Coleridge's conception of the long poem, the ideal he quoted to Wordsworth[1] to explain his disappointment with the *Excursion*. He tells us what he had expected:

'. . . the colours, music, imaginative life, and passion of *poetry*; but the matter and arrangement of *philosophy*; not doubting from the advantages of the subject that the totality of a system was not only capable of being harmonized with, but even calculated to aid, the unity (beginning, middle, and end) of a poem. Thus, whatever the length of the work might be, still it was a *determinate* length; of the subjects announced, each would have its own appointed place, and excluding repetitions, each would relieve and rise in interest above the other.'

'The totality of a system'—the phrase somehow does not call up poetic associations. The famous poem of Lucretius is perhaps the only one that is at once systematic in the sense desired by Coleridge, and also poetic. Coleridge discusses Lucretius, and in this very context he utters his famous judgement that Lucretius was most poetic when he was least philosophical, and most philosophic when least poetical. I have been inclined, as the following essay shows, to accept this dictum of Coleridge's as expressing a very probable truth,

[1] Letter of 30th May 1815.

but it has been claimed, by one whose capacity to appreciate Latin poetry is far greater than mine,[1] that Coleridge's dictum needs considerable qualification: in fact, it is based on the narrow lyrical notion of poetry which we are now examining. For in major poetry, as Matthew Arnold was so eager to point out, expression occupies a subordinate rank.[2] He quotes Goethe's opinion, that what distinguishes the artist from the mere amateur is Architectonicé in the highest sense: that power of execution which creates, forms, and constitutes; not the profoundness of single thoughts, not the richness of imagery, not the abundance of illustration. The modern poet, says Arnold, has three things to learn from the classical writers of the ancient world:

'He will learn from them how unspeakably superior is the effect of the one moral impression left by a great action treated as a whole, to the effect produced by the most striking single thought or by the happiest image. As he penetrates into the spirit of the great classical works, as he becomes gradually aware of their intense significance, their noble simplicity, and their calm pathos, he will be convinced that it is this effect, unity, and profoundness of moral impression, at which the ancient Poets aimed; that it is this which constitutes the grandeur of their works, and which makes them immortal.'

Arnold, it will be remembered, applied this test to Keats; dismissing *Endymion* as 'so utterly incoherent, as not strictly to merit the name of a poem at all', he fixed his attention on *Isabella, or the Pot of Basil*. Admitting that 'this one short poem contains, perhaps, a greater number of happy single expressions which one could quote than all the extant tragedies of Sophocles,' he yet asks:

'But the action, the story? The action in itself is an excellent one; but so feebly conceived by the Poet, so loosely constructed, that the effect produced by it, in or for itself, is absolutely null.'

[1] Hugh Sykes Davies in *The Criterion*, September 1931.
[2] Preface to the 1852 edition of his Poems.

Arnold, I think, effectively discounts Coleridge. We may doubt whether the totality of a system, or any purely philosophic theme, can be made the subject of a poem (necessarily a long poem) unless it is translated into action or imagery. It is the quality of the emotion that is really involved. By far the easiest method of securing the necessary emotional tension throughout the length of a 'long' poem is to embody its theme in a dramatic myth, which is the way of Milton in *Paradise Lost*. The only other method is to secure a consistent and continuous vitality of expression by the operation, in every line of the poem, of a dominant emotion. This is the way of Lucretius in *De Rerum Natura*. Poetry of any length is visual or it is tedious; it may be visual by virtue of its action, or by virtue of its imagery. It can never, whilst still remaining poetry, be merely informative or conceptual.

It is for this reason that I think it is dangerous to admit, as Mr. Lascelles Abercrombie does in *The Idea of Great Poetry*, that the far richer and greater effects of the long poem can be achieved 'by means of a unity far less direct', and 'a form less immediately impressive and, therefore, no doubt, less lovely' than the means employed in a successful sonnet. There are really no degrees of poetry; at least, there is no easy transition from poetry to prose. The two forms of expression are distinct in kind; we must speak in either one mode or the other. It is not enough even to be 'visual'; prose can be 'visual'. Poetry must be visual in a swift, intuitive way. It must also, by its daring, adventure into a world of sense and sound beyond the reach of the mundane instruments of prose. That is its faculty of Invention, about which Keats speaks. Invention and Imagery—Poetry is an essence distilled by these emotional activities. But it is not an essence which we can dilute with the water of prose, to make it go a long way. There are many varieties of poetic expression, just as there are many voices that sing; but none of them forgoes its proper harmony.

I. THE NATURE OF POETRY

5
THE NATURE OF METAPHYSICAL POETRY

The word *lyric* has lost most of its original meaning; it now conveys, if it conveys anything at all, a certain quality in writing which we may for the moment be content to call 'emotional'. A lyric poem has in addition certain formal characteristics, such as brevity, simplicity, and directness, and this has led to the notion which we have just examined, that a good poem cannot be long, or that a long poem can only be good 'in parts'. It is fairly obvious that those poems the world agrees to call lyrical are exclusively concerned with the record of sensibility—of direct sensibility, as in 'The Solitary Reaper', or of those vaguer reactions of direct sensibility that are 'the bliss of solitude'. Some lyric poets are sensible of the beauty of the actual phenomenon, others are sensible of the ideal associations of phenomena. But they agree, and it is essential to bear this in mind, in deriving their emotions from a direct awareness of the world—of its women, its flowers, its atmospheres, and its subtleties.

The occasionality of such emotional awareness has resulted in the practice, and then in the theory, of an emotional unity in the poem. An emotion is fleeting and must be seized in its uniqueness; all elements that do not contribute to its expression must be rigorously excluded: clarity, succinctness, simplicity—these are the virtues of the lyric, and, in modern minds, of all poetry. All the elaborate rules, and even all the revolts against any rules, exemplified in modern poetry, have their origin in the peculiar needs of the lyric.

The occasionality of the lyric does not, however, deprive it of a more general utility; a lyric is simply a perception, and all thought is based primarily on perceptions. From the accumulation of selected perceptions, expressed as lyrics, it is obvious that a general view of life may be constructed, and this general view may possess great ethical and aesthetic value. But it will remain a view, a *Weltanschauung*; it cannot become metaphysical until it is converted into concepts. But, in the mind of the modern theorist, to convert perceptions (i.e. emotional perceptions) into concepts is to destroy their poetic quality. In reality, however, such a result is by no means inevitable.

Let us examine more carefully the use of the word *emotion* in this connection. I gather from the critics who have established the lyrical standard of poetry that they use the word in its general psychological sense. Even in psychology any exact scientific use of the word is difficult, as McDougall has shown;[1] and while our critics do not normally expect poetry to embody or inspire primary emotions like anger or fear, the emotions they do demand of poetry differ in degree rather than in kind from these. The tenderness expressed and induced by a lyric may even be so influential as to cause a 'lump in the throat', even as fear is accompanied by certain visceral disturbances; and physiology may yet identify and classify the various glandular excretions and their appropriate lyrical responses. Nor am I disposed to deny that the state of attention or contemplation induced by metaphysical poetry may not also have its basis in some material agitation of the human cortex or glandular system. But the business of the literary critic is to identify the mental rather than the physiological significance of the material in his hands, and in this sense a more useful distinction can be made in the content of the emotions; though immediately we desert the field of a material science we are driven to the use of inexact terms. But terms are inexact only because they mean different things to differ-

[1] *Social Psychology*, chap. iii.

ent people: to those who are willing to understand, they can convey an exact meaning; and, when I contrast the abstract and the concrete contents of emotions, I do not thereby imply that an abstract content is something vague and indefinable. To the scientific poet, as to the scientific philosopher, abstract conceptions have their exactitudes. With this understanding, I may distinguish the concrete character of the content of the lyric, which in its purest state is concerned with the direct awareness of phenomenal environment, from the abstract character of what I am going to call metaphysical poetry.

Metaphysical poetry is abstract because, like metaphysics, it deals with concepts. But, as poetry, it is no less 'emotional' than lyrical poetry—though, since the emotion is differently manifested, it is a question whether that state of vivid contemplation inspired by metaphysical poetry had not better be described by another word. For my present purpose I do not think so, for it is necessary at all costs to maintain a nexus between lyrical poetry and metaphysical poetry in the word *poetry*; and since I despise all distinctions based on the technique or *décor* of poetry, I prefer to justify this nexus in the word *emotion*, which denotes a common foundation in physical fact. Later I shall illustrate the actual character of metaphysical poetry. For the present I will define it as the emotional apprehension of thought—or, to use words suggested by Dante, as thought transmuted into the imagery of dreams: 'e il pensamento in sogno transmutai.'

But first it is necessary to indicate certain misconceptions, the most serious of which is to imagine that metaphysical poetry is didactic, *and nothing but didactic,* in the deadest sense of the word. It is assumed that metaphysical poetry is the writing of metaphysics or science in the manner of verse, and that while as such it may be a wonderful display of technical virtuosity, it is not poetry in the strict (that is, the lyrical) sense of the word; and some frankly didactic poem, such as *The Botanic Garden* of Erasmus Darwin, is given as an illustration. Lucretius and Dante are slighted by implication. Now it is very difficult to dissociate the idea of didacticism from the idea of metaphysical poetry, but it is essential to any understanding of the subject that this should be done. *The Botanic Garden* is didactic and is not poetry; the *Commedia* is didactic and is poetic. Can we completely disengage the two ideas and say, for instance, that the didacticism of the *Commedia* has nothing at all in common with its poetry? The question is clearer when it is made more general: when it is said, for example, that the *art* of the Middle Ages was didactic.[1] In this case we do not mean that didacticism was of the essence of art; we only mean that the artists of the Middle Ages, urged perhaps by their own religious consciousness, and certainly by the consciousness of their religious environment, inevitably expressed themselves in religious subjects. The result was didactic, but was the process? Surely the process was simply one of *feeling*—of feeling for the significance of the subject in hand—and rarely one of purpose. The purpose perhaps only existed in the minds of the ecclesiastical syndicate that ordered the general design of a cathedral: the artists executed their orders with quite a different intention. In the same way the design of a poem may be didactic, and the fact that design and execution are alike the work of one mind does not alter the fact that aesthetically they may be distinct. Design is generally a question of reasoning—perhaps from given premises—whereas expression is a question of instinct or emotion. But the design may obviously have logical beauty, and it might be held that such beauty is the only aesthetic quality that a metaphysical poem can have. In this connection it is valuable to note Dante's attitude as expressed in the dedicatory epistle to *Can Grande* (Epistola X of Mr. Paget Toynbee's edition of the Letters of Dante). In § 9 he describes the form or manner of treatment

[1] Cf. Émile Mâle, *L'Art religieux du XIIIᵉ Siècle en France* (Paris, 1910, p. 1): 'Le moyen âge a conçu l'art comme un enseignement. Tout ce qu'il était utile à l'homme de connaître, l'histoire du monde depuis sa création, les dogmas de la religion, les exemples des saints, la hiérarchie des vertus, la variété des sciences, des arts, et des métiers, lui était enseigné par les vitraux de l'église ou par les statues du porche.'

of the *Commedia* as 'poëticus, fictivus, descriptivus, digressivus, transumptivus; et cum hoc definitivus, divisivus, probativus, improbativus, et exemplorum positivus'.[1] The conjunction of these several epithets shows either that Dante did not regard the 'poetic' as incompatible with the definitive, the analytical, the probative, etc., or that otherwise he used the word *poëticus* in the sense we should use the word *lyric*, and did not see any reason why his poem should be wholly, or even mainly, lyrical. In § 15 of this epistle he states the aim of the whole and of the part as being 'to remove those living in this life from a state of misery, and to bring them to a state of happiness'; and he goes on to say (§ 16) that 'the branch of philosophy to which the work is subject, in the whole as in the part, is that of morals or ethics; inasmuch as the whole as well as the part was conceived, not for speculation but with a practical object'. This emphasis on the doctrinal purpose of his poem, *totius et partis*, seems to prove very clearly, as the peculiar use of the word *poeticus* had indicated, that Dante did not regard his philosophy as inconsistent with his poetry, and this fact should be given its due weight, especially since there is a tendency nowadays to regard the intellectual structure of the *Commedia* as irrelevant to its poetry. But nevertheless Dante nowhere presumes that his poem is poetical *because* it is philosophical, and the conclusion of the matter is, that while metaphysical poetry always exists in association with a mind that is didactic, insomuch as its life is a life of thought, yet it derives its poetic quality from another source, which is emotional. As an illustration we might represent thought and emotion as two separately revolving pulleys: one, emotion, has a revolution a thousand times greater than the other; but by the operation of a lever the two pulleys are connected, and immediately thought is accelerated to the speed or intensity of emotion.

In the case of Lucretius there is throughout a vigour and a resonance which are very attractive; in fact, the more his

[1] My quotations and translations are in each case taken from Mr. Toynbee's edition (Oxford, 1920).

great poem is read the more it seems to cohere and become a unity, a part of one's mental life. And it is tempting to abandon all other pretensions and claim that this coherence of design and thought and unifying vitality is the sign and proof of the possibilities of metaphysical poetry. A sufficient case could be made out on this basis, but here I prefer to follow a more exact distinction, finding the nature of metaphysical poetry in the intensity rather than in the vigour of expression. For when the vitality of Lucretius's poem is analysed it is found to proceed from one of two causes: it is due either to the frequent interpolation of lyrical phrases, or, when these are absent, to a rather masterful rhetoric, a rather too facile manipulation of elemental metaphors. But he remains a very great poet, the most *interesting*, perhaps, of all the Latin poets. His lyric moods are very pure:

> *nam saepe in colli tondentes pabula laeta*
> *lanigerae reptant pecudes quo quamque vocantes*
> *invitant herbae gemmantes rore recenti,*
> *et satiati agni ludunt blandeque coruscant;*
> *omnia quae nobis longe confusa videntur*
> *et velut in viridi candor consistere colli.*[1]

The peculiar dichotomy of Lucretius's poem is seen when it is realized that lines so simply lyrical as these serve as a metaphor to explain the invisibility of atomic movement. Lyrics are embedded like jewels in the chain of an argument. The argument remains:

> *inque dies quanto circum magis aetheris aestus*
> *et radii solis cogebant undique terram*
> *verberibus crebris extrema ad limina in artum,*
> *in medio ut propulsa suo condensa coiret,*

[1] II, 317–22. Munro's text (1864), who translates thus: 'For often the woolly flocks as they crop the glad pastures on a hill, creep on whither the grass jewelled with fresh dew summons and invites each, and the lambs fed to the full gambol and playfully butt; all which objects appear to us from a distance to be blended together and to rest like a white spot on a green hill.'

tam magis expressus salsus de corpore sudor
augebat mare manando camposque natantis,
et tanto magis illa foras elapsa volabant
corpora multa vaporis et aeris altaque caeli
densebant procul a terris fulgentia templa.[1]

Science was never so effectively written, before or since Lucretius's day. But though it is impossible to seize all the subtlety of lines written in a language we never speak, all the same I think it is evident that this beauty is a beauty of force; it is an aural clarion and deceives, and even deafens, the mind, whereas it should pervade it convincingly.

As the lyric lies like an episode breaking into the intellectual flow of *De Rerum Natura*, so in the case of the English metaphysical 'school' we find an inverse process, giving rise to another possible misreading of the term 'metaphysical poetry'; a metaphysical metaphor or concept is included in a poem predominantly lyrical in mood. In reality very few of the metaphysical school were metaphysical in any sense, and the name only adds confusion to literary criticism. Their characteristics—'stranger than seven antiquaries' studies'—are well enough known; and their faults have been ably summarized and controverted by Johnson in his *Life of Cowley*. But the quality that was really distinctive in the experiments of Donne and some of his followers Johnson missed altogether; all that he could grudgingly allow to 'this race of authors' was a virtuous erudition: 'To write on their plan it was at least necessary to read and think.' In this way he did considerable injustice to Donne, as is shown by the quotations he uses, which never represent the Donne that appeals to a modern

[1] V, 483–91. Munro translates thus: 'And every day the more the heats of ether round and the rays of the sun on all sides compressed the earth into a close mass by oft-repeated blows on its outer edges, so that thus buffeted it was condensed and drawn together about its centre, ever the more did the salt sweat squeezed out of its body increase by its oozings the sea and floating fields, and ever the more did those many bodies of heat and air escape and fly abroad and condense far away from earth the high glittering quarters of heaven.'

mind. In Donne we do as a matter of fact find the first consciousness of felt thought, and his compasses and mandrakes are small matters in comparison to this. The new consciousness is so incidental that at first it seems accidental; but it continues to be incidental, not only in the metaphysical school, but in others that came after them, and we must ascribe its rarity to its difficulty. It begins to be present in lines like the following:

> Earths hollownesses, which the worlds lungs are,
> Have no more wind than the upper valt of aire.
> We can nor lost friends, nor sought foes recover,
> But meteorlike, save that we move not, hover.
> Onely the Calenture together drawes
> Deare friends, which meet dead in great fishes jawes.[1]

It may be asked: what metaphysics is there in a passage like this? The only answer is that only a metaphysician could have written it. Only a mind habituated to thought would visualize its thoughts in precisely that way. Donne's metaphors, even when they are most 'poetical', are still a part of his thought:

> All their proportion's lame, it sinkes, it swels.
> For of Meridians, and Parallels
> Man hath weav'd out a net, and this net throwne,
> Upon the Heavens, and now they are his owne.
> Loth to goe up the hill, or labour thus
> To go to heaven, we make heaven come to us.
> We spur, we reine the starres, and in their race
> They're diversely content t'obey our pace.
> But keepes the earth her round proportion still?
> Doth not a Tenarif, or higher Hill
> Rise so high like a Rocke, that one might thinke
> The floating Moone would shipwracke there, and sinke?[2]

[1] From *The Calne* (Oxford edition), 1912, p. 178.
[2] From *An Anatomie of the World, The First Anniversary* (Oxford edition), pp. 239–40.

Poorer poets bring lights into their rooms, but Donne, like all true metaphysical poets, strikes fire in the very process of his reasoning.

If we turn to a contemporary of Donne's—to George Chapman—we discover an even better augury of what the metaphysical poet might be. It would, in fact, be difficult to exaggerate the wealth of possibilities that came into existence with Chapman's individual poetry; but after Chapman came Milton, destroying this indigenous growth. Although a contemporary of Donne's, Chapman was not at the time often associated with Donne; he was not considered one of the metaphysical school—which shows, indeed, how prone contemporary opinion is to judge authors by their superficies: Donne by his conceits and Chapman by his 'full and heightened style'. When we get to the essence of these authors we find in Donne a mind poised at the exact turn of the course of philosophy—drawing his inspiration right back from scholastic sources, and yet at the same time eagerly surveying the new future promised by the science of Copernicus and Galileo. Chapman, on the other hand, is in a remarkable degree the forerunner of humanist philosophy—of Hume and Spinoza in particular. He is aware, above all things, of 'the consent and sacred harmony of life'. He brings ethics even into his title-page (e.g. *Caesar and Pompey*: A Roman Tragedy, declaring their Warres. Out of whose events is evicted this proposition: *Only a just man is a freeman*). And his theory of tragedy, as expressed in the dedication of *The Revenge of Bussy D'Ambois,* is more definitely didactic than Aristotle's even, and more uncompromising than Dante's theory of poetry: 'And for the authentical truth of either person or action, who (worth the respecting) will expect it in a poem, whose subject is not truth, but things like truth? Poor envious souls they are that cavil at truth's want in these natural fictions; material instruction, elegant and sententious excitation to virtue, and deflection from her contrary, being the soul, limbs, and limits of an authentical tragedy.' But who, in reading *The Revenge of*

Bussy D'Ambois, pauses for an instant conscious of the bore-
dom of its ethical purpose? It is, on the contrary, one of the
most sustained poetic dramas in English literature. But the
poetry is not 'easy';[1] it is musical, like lyrical poetry, but it
has an opacity, or 'charged' effect, characteristic of all good
metaphysical poetry; as though behind each word lurked
considerable processes of thought:

> *And know ye all . . .*
> *That in this one thing all the discipline*
> *Of manners and of manhood is contained;*
> *A man to join himself with th' Universe*
> *In his main sway, and make (in all things fit)*
> *One with that All, and go on, round as it;*
> *Not plucking from the whole his wretched part,*
> *And into straits, or into nought revert,*
> *Wishing the complete Universe might be*
> *Subject to such a rag of it as he;*
> *But to consider great Necessity,*
> *All things as well refract as voluntary*
> *Reduceth to the prime celestial cause,*
> *Which he that yields to with a man's applause,*
> *And cheek by cheek goes, crossing it no breath,*
> *But, like God's image, follows to the death,*
> *That man is truly wise. . . .*

The philosophical spirit in both Donne and Chapman was, I
think, derived directly from Dante and the early Italian poets,
rather than from more immediate forerunners in Spain and
France; and it is to these, and particularly to Dante and Cavalcanti, that we turn for the most obvious illustration of the
nature of metaphysical poetry. In reality there existed at that
time a perfectly conscious theory of metaphysical poetry. It
had come into existence with Guinicelli, who succeeded in

---

[1] It is important, in this connection, to remember the dedicatory epistle
to Ovid's *Banquet of Sense,* which embodies Chapman's very direct affirma-
tions on the subject of his metaphysical poetry.

escaping from the convention of direct lyricism, giving to his poetry a depth and beauty definitely related to a philosophical interest. 'Amore e cor gentile' is not only one of the most beautiful love poems ever written: it is also one of the most metaphysical. Love is no longer an affair of the heart, but is rather an affair of the brain. It is a symbolism in which the most abstract ideals of the intellect can be made personal and actual. And it was this symbolism that became the sustaining element in all Dante's work. In the *Convivio* (Trattato Secondo, cap. i) Dante distinguishes the four values or interpretations of literature—the literal, the allegoric, the moral, and the anagogic. The first three are normal values and present no novelty. In the fourth value we have the whole meaning of metaphysical poetry. Dante defines the *senso anagogico* as occurring 'quando spiritualmente si spone una scrittura, la quale, ancora nel senso litterale, eziando per le cose significate, significa delle superne cose dell'eternale gloria'.[1] In effect, this value depends on a form of personification which we have not developed to any extent in England (Donne's *Anatomy of the World* is the only example that occurs to me), and which consists of a bold interfusion of thought and actuality. The common idea of 'personification' in literature is peculiarly bloodless: there is not, in fact, any idea at all of actually associating thought with a living person: personification is merely a convenience that enables us to address a virtue or an abstraction in the third person singular. It was far otherwise with Dante and Guido Cavalcanti: they in perfect seriousness identified their love of philosophy with their love of women; and in singing of their love of women they made an allegory that expressed their love of philosophy. In that manner they made their writing *sovra senso*, or anagogic. Or, more exactly, all experience, whether intellectual or sensual or instinctive, was regarded as equally and contemporaneously the subject-matter of their poetry. The result was a desirable continuity

---

[1] 'When a writing is spiritually expounded, which even in the literal sense, by the very things it signifies, signifies higher matters of eternal glory.'

or coherence; imagination, contemplation, and sensibility becoming fused within the perfect limits of a human mind. 'The poet was inspired with an overmastering desire to link the present with the past and with the future, to blend all knowledge into one coherent system, and to bring the experiences of life into one harmonious whole. For this purpose allegory was an indispensable instrument. But the basis of the allegory was no mere fancy. His conception of allegory postulates the existence of facts, for allegory is the agency by which earthly passion is brought into relation with Philosophy and Theology, and becomes their servant and interpreter.'[1] In modern lyrical poetry this degree of coherence is never reached; we have instead a consciousness of the divorce of personality from the processes of thought. All the poet's senses and thoughts radiate from and return to one minute centre of self, and as a result he becomes disparate and insignificant in the process of nature, and a prey to *acedia* and despair. Thought, if indulged in at all, is not related to experience, though psychologically it may be a ratiocination balancing the abnormal exploits of the personality. But with Dante and Cavalcanti, and with Donne and Chapman, and even with Wordsworth, thought is the expression of experience—of all the experiences registered by the brain; and on the capacity of that brain for analysing its experiences, and even more on its capacity for selecting its experiences, will depend the value of the thought. If in addition that brain has the ability to reduce its thought to the emotional unit of the poem, we shall have the purest kind of metaphysical poetry as a result.

Dante achieved this result. The *Commedia* is the complete expression of a very complete mind—a mind that saw as much beauty in the *Summa* of St. Thomas Aquinas as in the episode of Paolo and Francesca, and did not find these beauties inconsistent. It is in every sense a metaphysical poem, complete and unified, and as a whole is a perfect demonstration

1 William Walrond Jackson, D.D., 'Introduction' to his translation of the *Convivio* (Oxford, 1909), p. 18.

of the sufficiency of metaphysical inspiration. That the ground-work of the poem is metaphysical would not be disputed, but it is possible to show that the metaphysics is itself poetic, in detail as well as in design—that there exists at one and the same time abstract thought and feeling for that thought, expressed in poetry. I am not going to claim that this unity is to be discovered at all frequently in the *Commedia*. It is a difficult achievement, and in Dante's case there was even a special difficulty in that one of his 'features' is the almost complete unoriginality of his thought: the world was not a problem to him, to be resolved by experimental effort, but the particularly neat scheme so amply provided by St. Thomas Aquinas. This vicariousness is not without its effect on the metaphysical quality of Dante's poetry, for the fusion of thought and emotion is surely more apt to be produced when thought has all the freshness of a personal discovery. But only *more* apt: that freshness is not exclusively the condition of emotion in thought is evident enough to all who enjoy an abstract argument. Besides, the exposition of a philosophy to which are attached no considerations of personal pride or vanity makes for the exclusion of all kinds of subjective impurities—makes, in fact, for that very objective clarity that is so distinctive of Dante's poem:

> *O abbondante grazia, ond'io presunsi*
> *Ficcar lo viso per la luce eterna*
> *Tanto, che la veduta vi consunsi!*

> *Nel suo profondo vidi che s'interna,*
> *Legato con amore in un volume,*
> *Ciò che per l'universo si squaderna;*

> *Sustanzia ed accidenti, e lor costume,*
> *Quasi conflati insieme per il modo,*
> *Che ciò ch'io dico è un semplice lume.*

GENERAL THEORIES

La forma universal di questo nodo
Credo ch'io vidi perchè più di largo,
Dicendo questo, mi sento ch'io godo.[1]

The history of Guido Cavalcanti's canzone beginning 'Donna mi priega' is the history of all metaphysical poetry. It is an analysis or definition of love, and was the most admired of Guido's poems in his own day. In the fourteenth century it inspired several elaborate commentaries, some of them by distinguished philosophers of the time. It passed into obscurity with the Renaissance; it probably had a brief revival of interest in the seventeenth and eighteenth centuries; but in the nineteenth we find it the object of almost impassioned scorn. D. G. Rossetti describes it as 'a poem beside the purpose of poetry, filled with metaphysical jargon, and perhaps the very worst of Guido's productions. Its having been written by a man whose life and works included so much that is impulsive and real is easily accounted for by scholastic pride in those early days of learning. I have not translated it, as being of little interest. . . .'[2] Even Gaspary cannot stomach it, and sarcastically remarks that the lady who had questioned Guido 'must have been very learned if she was satisfied with his reply. . . . Here we have the apparatus of the scholastic philosophy, the logical divisions and distinctions, the definitions, syllogisms, and terminology of the schools. Image and sentiment, the foundations of all poetry, are entirely lacking.'[3] This latter sentence is entirely untrue, and I am indeed content

[1] *Paradiso*, canto xxxiii, 82-93. Wicksteed translates as follows : 'O grace abounding, wherein I presumed to fix my look on the eternal light so long that I consumed my sight thereon! Within its depths I saw ingathered, bound by love in one volume, the scattered leaves of all the universe; substance and accidents and their relations, as thought together fused, after such fashion that what I tell of is one simple flame. The universal form of this complex I think that I beheld, because more largely, as I say this, I feel that I rejoice'.

[2] *The Early Italian Poets*, Introduction to Part II.

[3] *The History of Early Italian Literature*, by Adolph Gaspary, translated by Hermann Oelsner (1901), pp. 207-8.

to quote this famous poem as an example of true metaphysical poetry. The second stanza reads:

> *In quella parte, dove sta memora,*
> *Prende suo stato, si formato, come*
> *Diafan dal lume, d'una oscuritate,*
> *La qual da Marte viene, e fa dimora,*
> *Egli è creato, ed ha sensato nome:*
> *D'alma costume, e di cor volontate:*
> *Vien da veduta forma, che s'intende,*
> *Che prende nel possibile intelletto,*
> *Come in suggetto, loco e dimoranza.*
> *In quella parte mai non ha possanza,*
> *Perchè da qualitate non discende,*
> *Risplende in se perpetuale effetto:*
> *Non ha diletto, ma consideranza;*
> *Si che non puote la gir simiglianza.*[1]

One might leave the subject there, counting on the sufficiency of Calvalcanti and Dante, and of Donne and Chapman; but there are certain 'obvious' poets that one cannot neglect to mention if only to disclaim them—I mean particularly Milton, Shelley, and Browning. Wordsworth is dif-

---

[1] It is difficult to translate such concentrated poetry as this. Charles Lyell (*The Lyrical Poems of Dante Alighieri*, London, 1845) has made the following attempt (p. 134):

> *Within the soul's recess where memory dwells*
> *Love has its seat, there formed as brightness is*
> *By light, in thing transparent that was dark;*
> *Which darkness is from Mars, and permanent.*
> *Love is produced, and has its name from sense;*
> *A habit of the soul, a will of the heart;*
> *It springs from beauty seen and contemplated;*
> *Which takes, in the receptive intellect,*
> *A dwelling-place, as in a subject fit.*
> *There, matter it has none, nor has it weight;*
> *For purely spiritual is its quality.*
> *Love shines transplendent, long as beauty charms.*
> *In contemplation is its whole delight,*
> *Hence it can yield no likeness to itself.*

ferent. But Milton, in his later phase, perhaps did more to destroy the true tradition of metaphysical poetry than any other agent. His thought was a system apart from his poetic feeling, and in the violence wrought by his too forceful fashion he almost crushed the life out of an only too subtle advance of human consciousness. He did not think poetically, but merely expounded thought in verse: psychologically he was conscious all the time of a dualism—on the one side the thought to be expounded, on the other side the poetic mould into which his thought had to be smelted. The true metaphysical poet is conscious of no such dualism: his thought is in its very process poetical. This distinction so briefly expressed may seem a trifle upon which to dismiss so established a reputation as Milton's is in this particular sphere, and it must be admitted that the whole matter needs careful analysis and consideration; for the present I prefer not to endanger a good cause by enlisting a doubtful ally. Shelley, too, I prefer to leave unquoted: his case is a very complicated one, which I have dealt with at length in another book.[1] Shelley is certainly a metaphysical poet: he has his intellectual system and it is implicit in almost everything he wrote. But in the writing the thought became so transcendental, so far removed from the actuality of objective images, that the poetry is as it were released and floats away like a bubble from the pipe in which it was blown. As for Browning, he was neither mystical nor metaphysical, and I am not sure that it would not be legitimate to say that he was just wordy. It may be admitted, however, that he has very definite claims to be considered as a psychological poet; and if 'Bishop Blougram's Apology' is not so good of its kind as is Cavalcanti's canzone beginning 'L'ardente fiamma della fiera pesta' (it is not so sincere), yet 'Bishop Blougram' and parts of *The Ring and the Book* and certain of the *Parleyings* are good enough to establish the *genre* in its own rights. But the *genre* is definitely psychological, consisting of the analysis of motives and personalities, and

[1] *In Defence of Shelley* (London, 1936).

differing entirely from the metaphysical, which should confine itself to the statement of ideas. Leibniz has defined an intelligent author as one who includes the most of reality in the least possible compass,[1] and it would be difficult to improve on this definition. And in that case it is difficult to see how psychological poetry, which is descriptive, can compete with metaphysical poetry, which is synthetic. It is for this reason, if for no other, that Wordsworth tends to emerge out of the immediate welter of his epoch with something more of solidity than we can associate with the merely descriptive evocations of his contemporaries. In fact, we might go a long way to find a better example of metaphysical poetry than certain lines from the fragment of *The Recluse*:

> . . . *I must tread on shadowy ground, must sink*
> *Deep—and, aloft ascending, breathe in worlds*
> *To which the heaven of heavens is but a veil.*
> *All strength—all terror, single or in bands,*
> *That ever was put forth in personal form;*
> *Jehovah—with his thunder, and the choir*
> *Of shouting Angels, and the empyreal thrones—*
> *I pass them unalarmed. Not Chaos, not*
> *The darkest pit of lowest Erebus,*
> *Nor aught of blinder vacancy, scooped out*
> *By help of dreams, can breed such fear and awe*
> *As fall upon us when we look*
> *Into our Minds, into the Mind of Man,*
> *My haunt, and the main region of my song.*
>
>   *. . . if I oft*
> *Must turn elsewhere—to travel near the tribes*
> *And fellowships of man, and see ill sights*
> *Of madding passion, mutually inflamed,*
> *Must hear Humanity, in fields and groves*
> *Pipe solitary anguish; or must hang*

[1] *Discourse on Metaphysics*, § v.

Brooding over the fierce confederate storm
Of sorrow, barricadoed evermore
Within the walls of Cities; may these sounds
Have their authentic comment,—that even these
Hearing, I be not downcast or forlorn!

The first part of this quotation is a gesture, and it may be advanced that as such it comes dangerously near to being rhetorical. But rhetoric is only reprehensible when it is hollow, as it mostly is; when it is compact with thought, as this rhetoric of Wordsworth's is, it is powerful beyond any other mode of expression. Blake recoiled in horror from three of these lines: he saw in them a rebellion against the very basis of humanistic religion. And if to-day we can no longer share Blake's apprehension, we can instead appreciate the profundity, the intellectual significance, and the emotional power of these verses. The second part of the quotation does not lack something of such qualities also, but I use it rather with the special intention of illustrating how words like 'confederate' and 'authentic comment' can be lifted from their prosaic origins and made the very keywords of a poetic vigour.

With Wordsworth the metaphysical tradition in English poetry for the time being ends. The possibility of recovering this lost tradition remains to be considered.

I began by defining metaphysical poetry as the emotional apprehension of thought, and I am not sure that I can do better than leave the definition simply so, trusting that the quotations I have meanwhile made use of may quite sufficiently illustrate my meaning. It has been seen very noticeably, I hope, that a degree of economy is implied in the word 'apprehension'—that economy of thought, in fact, breeds its corresponding intensity, which is to be identified with the poetry itself. More anxiously I hope that it has been seen in exactly what sense the epithet 'emotional' has been used. Now that my illustrative matter is complete, as far as may reasonably be allowed, 'emotional apprehension' should appear as a fairly 'hard', even as a necessarily 'dry', process. It is important beyond everything, in this era of emotional or 'common-sense' philosophies, not to confuse this mental process in which emotion is the product of thought, with that other vaguer, easier process, which is the emotionalization of thought, or thought as the product of emotion. Metaphysical poetry is determined logically: its emotion is a joy that comes with the triumph of the reason, and is not a simple instinctive ecstasy. It is, finally, but the precise statement of such abstractions as the poet derives from his experience. In the scholastic sense, it is the poetry of universals.

In conclusion, it is perhaps worth while to refer to the characteristics of our own age, and in that way arrive at some more definite idea of the possibilities of metaphysical poetry to-day. This leads us on to very opinionative ground; we strike deeply into subconscious prejudices. But, generally, we can recognize the disintegration of religion and with this dis-integration the disappearance of some of the most powerful inducements to poetic inspiration. To what degree this dis-integration is permanent is another question, and not one to be discussed here. It is rather to be feared that the crowd, as an organized society, will find inferior outlets for its emotional forces. But we may claim a certain independence for the poet. If he is the product of his age, yet he is not generated by the pressure of a specific unanimism, but rather stands within his environment and absorbs the spectacle around him; and in this sense negation is as good a sounding-board for thought as any more positive state of society. And however pitiful our social life may be, yet there does exist an intelligent minority of considerable vigour and positive achievement: I refer par-ticularly to the modern physicists, whose work would seem to provide a whole system of thought and imagery ready for fertilization in the mind of the poet. For, if the assumptions of this essay are accepted, it will be seen that science and meta-physical poetry have but one ideal, which is the satisfaction of the reason. For science we accept without question the axiom

that logical method and the satisfaction of reason are the final
tests to be used in the attainment of a system of truth, but for
art such an ideal appears at first sight to be paradoxical and
detrimental—even as science, in another age, found the ideals
of religion inimical, and nearly fatal. Ideals, however, survive
only so long as they serve the interests, economic or emotional, of the multitudes among which they exist: they, as all
human attempts at fixation, are at the mercy of more brutal
forces. Very few ideals—perhaps only those immuring the
instincts of self-preservation—are so old as history; and such
an ideal as scientific method in poetry must be accepted subject to the contingency of all ideals. The scientific ideal does
at any rate carry us into the full stream of all that is valuable
in our age. Science has established a large number of 'phenomena', but these phenomena remain discrete. They lack
synthetic unity. Perhaps mathematical philosophy is working
in one direction to establish this unity; metaphysical poetry,
working in a different direction, can, without presumption,
aim at the same end.

I. THE NATURE OF POETRY

6

OBSCURITY IN POETRY

One of the greatest pleasures of a literary life, to which a reader may be driven by a too close familiarity with the poetry of his own language, and equally by an increasing awareness of the narrow range of creative expression in general, is the exploration of the poetry of another language. This pleasure seems to me to increase with the nearness of a language—its contemporaneity and its consanguinity. I know that the pleasure can be got from a dead language like Latin or Greek; even a schoolboy can be moved by the sonority of Lucretius or by the more liquid sequences of Virgil. The first reading of Dante in the original is a memorable stage in one's poetic education. Racine, in my own experience, is a more uncertain acquisition: I seem to enjoy the poetic quality of his alexandrines—the grace that rises superior to the monotony—but the apprehension is not so direct and instinctive as I require it to be; as I find it in more recent French poets such as Baudelaire, Laforgue, Rimbaud and most definitely in a poet who has always affected me strangely: Guillaume Apollinaire.

These intimations of poetic essence—for they deserve no stronger name—have never seemed to me to be certain enough to form the basis of a critical opinion, and I have always been chary of committing myself when any but the poetry of my native language was concerned. For poetry is such a function of language—almost an impersonal fruit of its slow growth—

that it seems contrary to nature that any one not born to a language should be capable of extracting its essence. I would even go further and suggest that no one whose blood is not coeval and congenital with the language he uses ever attains the last perfection of poetic expression. There is no great *English* poetry written by a Scotsman, a Welshman or an Irishman.

This brings me within distance of racial theories for which I have nothing but contempt. Though I believe that poetic values are the highest values of a culture, I do not connect them with political values; though I would never trust a Scotsman with our poetry, I am quite content to be governed by him; for the life of action and the life of the imagination have nothing in common, to our eternal distress.

It has seemed to me, still speaking from my own experience, that the discovery and appreciation of German poetry is a partial exception to these general observations. I feel sure, at least, that the pleasure I have derived from the gradual discovery of the poetry of a few German poets—Goethe, Hölderlin, George, and Rilke—is appreciably different in kind from the sensations accompanying my explorations in other languages. It cannot be altogether due to the fact that my German is self-taught; so, to a large extent (it is also a small extent), are all my languages. And it is useless to suggest that affinity of language can account for the peculiarity of the pleasure: if the gap between Scots and English cannot be bridged when the poetic essence is to be reached how can we leap from English to German?

In the circumstances I have looked for another explanation, and think I have found it in the quality of a particular kind of poetry: for it is only a few German poets that are concerned, and perhaps in them I find an enhancement of poetic qualities I value in English poetry. I cannot find my thrill in Schiller, nor even in Kleist. Even in Goethe the pleasure is intermittent; it is only a few of his lyrics that yield their essence or, to make the metaphor more exact, that give me the necessary shock.

In these lyrics—and I might equally well for this purpose take any representative lines from Dante or Racine or Baudelaire —I experience the poetry as a direct *impact*; a sensation of sound, and of sound allied to expressive epithet and metaphor. But in the case of George and Rilke the sensation is almost one of sight. Light seems to be involved: a visual perception. But not a visual perception of the image alone; rather an intuition of a presence: in Hobbes's phrase, a sudden glory.

Actually I believe the sensation has to do with the immediate obscurity of the verse, and is strictly parallel to the pleasure I derive from obscurity in English poetry. Rilke in one of his poems cries:

> Singe die Gärten, mein Herz, die du nicht kennst;
> wie in Glas eingegossene Gärten, klar, unerreichbar.

And that is the perfect analysis of the sensation: the vision of an unknown garden, embedded in glass, clear but unattainable. Vision without meaning, concrete, synthetic, but held in suspense, contemplated without question. But the vision must be won; it is not immediate; it breaks on the concentrated awareness of the reader like a summer dawn. It is the experience which all so-called obscure poetry tries to communicate; but with the rarest success. I am now suggesting that the experience may be obtained from foreign poetry even when that poetry, to a native, may not be particularly obscure. The language acts as an extra veil for the foreigner, and when the veil is penetrated, then he experiences the sudden shock of revelation.

Admittedly, however, this experience is only frequent when the poet in question has a certain tendency towards obscurity even in his own language. Most Germans find Rilke an obscure poet—if only the Rilke of the Duinese Elegies. There is, therefore, a positive value in obscurity which must be affirmed, in opposition to those who expect poetry to be as plain as a pikestaff—or some less obscure object.

Hopkins was fully aware of this quality in poetry, and in one of his letters[1] describes how it affected him:

'Granted that it [his poem, 'The Wreck of the Deutschland'] needs study and is obscure, for indeed I was not over desirous that the meaning of all should be quite clear, at least unmistakable, you might, without the effort that to make it all out would seem to have required, have nevertheless read it so that lines and stanzas should be left in the memory and superficial impressions deepened, and have liked some without exhausting all. I am sure I have read and enjoyed pages of poetry that way. Why, sometimes one enjoys and admires the very lines one cannot understand, as for instance, "If it were done when 'tis done", sqq., which is all obscure and disputed, though how fine it is everybody sees and nobody disputes. And so of many more passages in Shakespeare and others.'

The empirical argument might be used with good effect—much unquestioned poetry *is* obscure. That Shakespeare is an obscure poet is witnessed, not only by Hopkins, by also the immense libraries of elucidatory criticism which have been devoted to his text. The obscurity is not explained away even by the scholar's usual assumption that anything he cannot understand must be due to a printer's error. The poetry remains in the obscurity—is, in some way, the obscurity itself.[2] We therefore need some further explanation of the nature of obscurity in poetry.

The germ of a theory of obscurity may be found in the passage already quoted from Vico, to the effect that 'man, before he has arrived at the stage of forming universals, forms imaginary ideas. Before he reflects with a clear mind, he

[1] *Letters of Gerard Manley Hopkins to Robert Bridges* (Oxford University Press, 1935), p. 50.

[2] Obscurity should be distinguished from *ambiguity*, which quality has been brilliantly analysed by Mr. Empson in his *Seven Types of Ambiguity* (London, 1930). Ambiguity is essentially *grammatical*; obscurity is *imaginative*. As we shall see, it arises *before* the logical, and therefore grammatical, stage of expression.

apprehends with faculties confused and disturbed: before he can articulate, he sings: before speaking in prose, he speaks in verse: before using technical terms, he uses metaphors, and the metaphorical use of words is as natural to him as that which we call natural.' The first kind of wisdom in pagan times, Vico says, was *poetic* wisdom—a metaphysic, proceeding not from reasoning or abstraction, as modern philosophy does, but from sensibility and imagination. The metaphysic of such men was poetry, and poetry originated in the necessity of creating a metaphysic—an explanation of the universe. Necessity, we say, is the mother of invention, and invention is another word for imagination. Imagination is a substitute for knowledge—before knowledge was possible, imagination filled the unexplained vacuum created by the questioning existence of man. Naturally such poetry was divine—it invented gods to explain all that was beyond man's power of apprehension, and these gods were clothed in the colours of man's imagination. We may observe the same process in the unfolding minds of children: the poetry of Fairyland. Further, these first men who created gods were called poets, which etymologically means creators. And Vico points out that their creations embodied the three essentials of great poetry: sublimity, popularity, and the emotional power which renders poetry effective. The very character of poetry, Vico concludes, is precisely this: to render the impossible credible.

From this conception of a poetic *metaphysics*, Vico proceeds to the conception of a poetic *logic*. *Logos* in its original sense meant a fable or an oracle, and poetic logic is the elaboration of a myth. Out of this poetic logic, as a necessary result, came the metaphor, to this day the most common of all poetic tropes. It originated in mythology, which endowed inanimate things with human sentiments and passions. A metaphor is a shorthand fable. It is a fable summarized in a phrase, and it still retains all the irrationality of its origins. The simplest metaphors relate inanimate things to the human body, or to human actions: *mouth* for any opening, the *teeth* of a saw or a comb, a *tongue* of land, the *gorge* of a mountain, a *handful* for a small number, *heart* for the middle of anything, the *flesh* of a fruit; the wind *whistles*, and so on. Many other 'figures of speech' have a similar pre-logical origin, but so much is obvious. All I want to emphasize is the fact that Vico establishes the priority of poetic logic, or the logic of the imagination, and differentiates it in kind from the logic of prose, which is the logic of reasoning.

Vico's theory was first published in 1725 and though it is not often acknowledged, I fancy a consciousness of it was gradually diffused among critics during the eighteenth century and was the beginning of that movement in criticism sometimes associated with romanticism, but which it is preferable to call empirical criticism in opposition to that *a priori* criticism based on the pedantic tradition of classicism. We find a consciousness of it, I think, in Thomas Warton's commentary on Milton's shorter poems, first published in 1785, a landmark in the history of English criticism. Warton, for example, commenting incidentally upon the image of Satan in *Paradise Lost,* Book IV:

> *His stature reached the sky, and on his crest*
> *Sate HORROR plum'd—*

criticizes his pedantic predecessor, Dr. Newton, for regarding the passage as an extravagant metaphor in which 'Horror is personified and made the plume of his helmet'. 'Other and better explanations might be offered,' suggests Warton. 'But, I believe, we have no precise or determinate conception of what Milton means. And we detract from the sublimity of the passage in endeavouring to explain it, and to give a distinct signification. Here is a nameless terrible grace, resulting from a mixture of ideas, and a confusion of imagery.'[1]

That Coleridge was conscious of Vico's theories, or arrived unconsciously at similar ideas, as he seems to have had a habit of doing, might be easily demonstrated. But it would serve

[1] *Poems, etc.,* ed. T. Warton, (2nd edition, 1791), p. 505.

me better to quote Coleridge as a poet rather than as a critic.
A poem like 'The Ancient Mariner' is full of obscurities.
Indeed, we might say of Coleridge's poetry in general, that
its poetic worth is in inverse ratio to its logical sense, reaching
its greatest intensity in the incoherent imagery of 'Kubla
Khan.'

Henri Bergson, who may perhaps be regarded as the culmination of the anti-Cartesian movement of thought initiated
by Vico, gives a convincing description of the poetic activity
in his last book.[1] He is investigating the nature of mysticism,
and turns first to the musician for an analogy. What, he asks,
could be more constructive, more scientific than a symphony
of Beethoven's. But in addition to his work of arrangement
and rearrangement, his selection, which is carried out on the
intellectual plane, the composer projects himself to a point
beyond this scheme and there he seeks the final direction or
inspiration: and this point is an emotional complex which the
intelligence can help to resolve into musical terms, but which
in itself is more than music and more than intelligence. And
so with the inspired writer, be he poet or mystic. He projects
himself beyond the region of the concepts and words in which
the normal thought processes are expressed. He reaches beyond this plane to a point where the mind feels a pressing
need for creation. The existence of this need has only to be
plainly felt once in a lifetime, but it will always be there, a
unique emotion, an impulse or urge received from the very
base of things. To obey it incontinently, it is necessary to forge
words, to create ideas, but this means to abandon communication, and therefore writing. But the poet attempts to achieve
the impossible. He will seek the essential emotion, the form
which wants to create its matter, and with this he will confront
the ready-made ideas, already existing words, stereotyped
notions of reality. In the process he will feel the form becoming explicit in symbols of its own creation, fragments of its
own materialization. But how can these elements, each unique

[1] Les Deux Sources de la morale et de la religion (Paris, 1932), pp. 270 ff.

of its kind, be made to square with words already expressive of things? It becomes necessary to violate words, to do violence to such elements. Still success will never be assured: the poet is continually asking himself whether he is justified in going to extremes; every partial success depends on chance. But if he succeeds, he achieves a thought capable of taking on a new aspect for every new generation—he enriches humanity with a capital sum which is not spent at once, but goes on earning interest indefinitely.

To the evidence of the philosopher we may add that of a philosophical poet, Paul Valéry. A disciple of Mallarmé, a metaphysician and a scientist, he has given us the most penetrating criticism of the art of poetry that has been written in our time. In an article devoted to Mallarmé,[1] and even to this very question of obscurity which is raised so acutely by Mallarmé's poetry, Valéry begins by deploring the facility demanded by the reading public; for his part, he requires a power of resistance in a book, and a capacity in the reader to match the care and zeal of the writer with corresponding virtues of patience, leisure, and distinct and deliberate attention. He refutes the notion that complexity or obscurity is to be dismissed as romanticism. Romanticism is afraid of ideas, of the process of thought involved in this mode of creation, and relies for its effect on descriptive epithets, contrasts of detail, 'jewelled' words. But Mallarmé advances far beyond such a method; we feel in his verse the presence and the firm design of abstract thought.

But I must not follow Valéry in his particular views on Mallarmé's poetry; I am concerned with certain general ideas which he enunciates. He describes how this least primitive of poets nevertheless acquires the most powerful quality of primitive poetry: its magical formula, its quality of incantation, and he has a finely emotive paragraph claiming that the very efficacy of such poetry depends on the obscurity of the words used:

[1] *Nouvelle Revue Française,* May 1932.

'What is sung or articulated in the most solemn and the most critical moments of life; what we hear in a Liturgy; what is murmured or groaned in the extremity of passion; what calms a child or the afflicted; what attests the truth of an oath—these are words of a particular tone and expression which cannot be resolved into clear ideas, nor separated out, without making them absurd or silly. In all these cases, the accent and inflexion of the voice outweigh anything intelligible conveyed to us: it is our life rather than our mind which is addressed—I would say that such words incite us to *become* rather than excite us to *understand*.'

This, of course, is to resort to the magical apology for poetry, deplored by scientific critics like Mr. Empson. But M. Valéry does not stay there. He proceeds, in fact, to adopt Vico's theory, without any acknowledgement, and perhaps unconsciously. Poetry, he says, goes back to some stage of human development anterior to writing and criticism. 'I find', he adds, 'a very ancient man in every true poet; he still drinks at the source of language; he invents "verses"—just as the most gifted primitive man had to invent "words", or the ancestors of words.' Most people are deaf to the words they use: their words are expedients necessary for expression, and they use them in a purely practical spirit. 'But poetry remains pagan: for every soul it requires a body—there is no meaning, no idea which is not an issue of some remarkable figure of speech, made up of tones, intervals, and intensities. . . .

'. . . the *given* language acquired in childhood, being of a statistical and communal origin, is generally not well fitted to express shades of thought far from practical: such a language scarcely lends itself to ends more profound or more precise than those which determine the actions of everyday life. Therefore technical languages come into being—and among them literary language. In all languages sooner or later a *mandarin's language* appears, sometimes far removed from the customary language; but generally this literary language is derived from the other, from which it draws words, figures of speech, and phrases best fitted to express the effects which the literary artist aims at. Thus it happens that some writers make up a language of their own. . . . Mallarmé created a language almost entirely his own by a refined choice of words and by using exceptional turns of speech which he invented or adapted, always refusing the immediate solution suggested to him on every side. And this is no more than defending himself, precisely in the details and elementary functioning of mental life, *against automatism.*'

We see, therefore, that essentially obscurity lies not in the poet, but in ourselves. We are clear and logical at the cost of being superficial or inexact. The poet, more exactingly, seeks absolute precision of language and thought, and the exigencies of this precision demand that he should exceed the limits of customary expression, and therefore *invent*—invent sometimes words, more frequently new uses of words, most frequently phrases and figures of speech which reanimate words, and among these, above all, *metaphor*. Metaphor, in fact, for such a poet becomes the normal mode of expression, and I think we should always be prepared to judge a poet, to the exclusion of all other qualities, by the force and originality of his metaphors.

Originally, no doubt, as Vico suggests, the metaphor arose from the habit of ascribing the attributes of the human organism to inanimate objects. The name implies a transference of attributes, and the ordinary dictionary definition of a metaphor is 'the application of a name or descriptive term to an object to which it is not literally applicable (e.g. *a glaring error*).' Such a conception is very inadequate for the uses of poetry. We might define metaphor summarily as the discovery of an illuminating correspondence between two objects but that too is inadequate for the subtleties of the process. In fact, the modern poet has passed beyond the metaphor to a new figure of speech. This has been called the *image*—'The image', writes a modern French poet, Paul Reverdy, 'is a pure creation of the mind. It cannot emerge from a comparison but only from the bringing together of two more or less distant realities. . . . An image is not striking because it is brutal or fantastic—but because the association of ideas is remote and exact. . . . No image is produced by comparing (always inadequately) two disproportionate realities. A striking image, on the contrary, one new to the mind, is produced by bringing into relation without comparison two distant realities whose relations *the mind alone* has seized.'

Jacques Maritain, with particular reference to Reverdy's definition,[1] notes that the image thus conceived is the opposite of *metaphor*, which compares one known thing with another known thing the better to express the former by covering it with the latter. The image *discovers* one thing with the help of another, and by their resemblance makes the unknown known. But it is not a logical resemblance. As a modern philologist, Karl Vossler, says in another connection[2] (he is dissecting the image of the 'shining moon'—in Latin there was a connection between the two words *luceo* and *luna*, but no one knows whether a 'shining moon' or a 'moon-like shine' came first, whether the moon entered into the shining or the shining into the moon), 'linguistic comparisons of this kind are not logical acts of thought at all. They are the dream of a poet, in which things come together, not because they are being differentiated or because they are being identified, but because they are thought and felt together in an emotional unity.'

I halt on the threshold of philology, for finally it is to the philosophy of language that this enquiry leads us, to one of the most interesting and fundamental of all sciences. An affirmation of obscurity in poetry must force on us a reconsideration of the function of language. Obscurity in poetry cannot be regarded as merely a negative quality, a failure to attain a state of perfect clarity. It is a positive value, but more, it is a whole series of such values. Apart from the pure and unmean-

[1] *Art and Scholasticism* (London, 1930), p. 192.
[2] *The Spirit of Language in Civilization* (London, 1933).

ing sound-value of words, and apart from their irrational magic, their power of incantation—aspects of the question I have not thought worth more than a mention—there is a fundamental obscurity in the actual thought process involved —an obscurity due to the honesty and objectivity of the poet. He works outwards from an emotional unity. This unity may be clothed in what Vossler calls 'an inner language form'; but between this inner language form and the outer language form in which our everyday rational thoughts are expressed, there is no necessary correspondence. In order to remain faithful to the inner language form, the poet must invent words and create images, he must mishandle and stretch the meaning of words. The emotional unity of the poem is given; the correspondence in words must be created; and that is why the poet is called a creator.

It is a mistake, therefore, to ask a poet to explain his poems. That is to make the wrong approach to poetry, to knock at the wrong door. This emotional unity which is the *raison d'être* of every poem cannot be measured by the instruments of reason. Otherwise it would be simpler to express it in prose. The poem must be received directly, without questioning, and loved or hated. It has a necessary and eternal existence; it is impervious to reason, and if it has no discoverable meaning, it has immeasurable power. The poet has created in words an objective equivalence of his emotional experience: the words may not make sense, but they make the emotion— follow the contour of the thought—and reproduce, as nearly as possible, 'the mind's internal echo of the imperfect sound'. It was Rilke who said that 'the poet is farther away from men than from things'. That is perhaps why he seems so strange to us. But the things he approaches are eternal things, and because they endure in his words, his words grow familiar to men, until they are accepted without questioning, but always with fresh recognition.

I. THE NATURE OF POETRY

7
MYTH, DREAM, AND POEM

At first it would seem that nothing is so remote from the scientific mind of to-day as the myth. Scholars may still read Homer and Ovid as a literary exercise, and perhaps a few people can read their poems as simple and enthralling stories. But the myths of these ancient poets do not mean anything to the average man, and even the myths that are nearer to us and embodied in our own culture—the myths of Christ, of Hamlet, and of Faust—even these have lost their simple virtue. Unless we are peasants or mystics, we can only believe in the Christian legend by an effort of the will, *quia impossibile*; and as for Hamlet and Faust, they are the myths of the mythless, of men wandering through the world without faith in themselves or their destiny.

At the same time we may observe that the farther science penetrates into the mystery of life, the more it reverts to a mythological world. I refer more particularly to the science of the individual psyche, where all science culminates; for we know nothing unless we know ourselves. And the more we learn about ourselves by the objective methods of observation and analysis, the more we realize that our knowledge is already crystallized in the ancient myths. Nowhere do we meet these myths playing so vital a part as in the pages of Freud. Myths that were dead are now alive again, and it may be that in the course of time all the old gods and heroes, that for centuries peopled and pacified the minds of men, will return and resume their symbolic functions.

Oedipus lives again, and Electra; and Eros has been revived to indicate that our poor words, sex and love, no longer adequately represent the force and necessity of our most passionate instincts. We feel a need to personify feelings so intimate and acceptable. But death, which is so universally dreaded, for that reason remains an abstract conception; even Freud has not yet dared to personify that instinct which finally triumphs over Eros. 'The picture which life presents to us', he says, 'is the result of the working of Eros and the death-instinct together and against each other.' Eros, but not Thanatos; and indeed Thanatos, the god of death, has no familiar claim on our imagination. Man has been afraid to create a recognizable figure of death: he would have been too constant and too terrifying. Death, apart from a few fleshless and inhuman symbols (such as the skull) remains deeply buried in the unconscious.

Yet death is present in all the great myths, though at first we do not recognize him. Generally he is the loathly worm, the gorgon or dragon which must be slain by the hero, who is always Eros in disguise. Evade the dragon—that is the condition on which alone love can be consummated.

A little research would discover the symbols of life and death on every side of us—threaded through the fabric of our history and legend, our poetry and painting, our dreams and our speech. It is even possible that in many subtle ways these symbols dominate each individual life. It would only be possible to prove such an hypothesis, in any normal case, by a process of psycho-analysis. There are certain cases, however, which are not normal: in particular, there is the case of the poet.

The poet is distinct from the reporter (who is rather the scientist, in so far as the scientist makes use of words). That is to say, the poet is a man who creates his own myths. But we must ask, by what process does such a myth, the unique creation of an individual, come into being? We say that the poet is inspired, or possessed. He is no longer in his right mind, but is visited by voices that come, it seemed once from the sky, but we now say from deep within the self. A man's *right* mind—by that we mean his conscious mind. When he is not in his right mind, then he is in another mind—a mind which from the point of view of normal and practical life is certainly his *wrong* mind; but which from the point of view of the imaginative life, is the mythical mind. And this mythical mind is the mind we all know in our dreams, partially, incoherently; but the poet knows it with a penetrating and selective validity.

It is tempting to identify poetry and the dream; or shall we say, to avoid qualifications of a technical and linguistic nature, the imagination and the dream. Freud has found it necessary to distinguish between various stages or degrees of dream activity, and it is with the most superficial level, which we call day-dreaming, that he tends to identify the poetic imagination. At the same time he would be willing to admit that the myth, the dream which has become valid for a whole people, has a significance which reaches into the very depths of the unconscious. Jung, who has dealt much more fully with this aspect of the myth, has found it necessary to suppose the existence of a racial psyche from which the myth is precipitated into the individual mind of the poet: an hypothesis for which there is, of course, no objective evidence.

The myth and the poem differ in this: the myth persists by virtue of its *imagery*, and this imagery can be conveyed by means of the verbal symbols of any language. The essence of a myth is diffusable. But a poem persists by virtue of its *language*; its essence belongs to that language and cannot be translated. Very rarely a poem in one language may inspire a poem of comparable poetic value in another language; but generally it is only the imagery which is translated intact. Nevertheless, a poem is more than an essence of language; it is this essence allied to imagery. In later stages of human development it may be this essence allied to abstract thought, or discourse; but this is the rarest type of poetry and invariably a prelude to poetic decadence. Visual or verbal, all art is predominantly eidetic, emotionally aware of the plastic reality of its images.

In this art resembles the dream. We all remark on the vividness of our dreams. Confusion there may be, but no vagueness or mistiness. Each person or object has a separate and discrete existence, and the landscape of dreams is as carefully and distinctly composed as the landscape in a medieval painting. The dream, in fact, is a combination of acute sensational awareness with an unnatural order. The order or composition of what we call nature, which is our human and superficial vision of reality, is plethoric and arbitrary, and all art except the most crudely naturalistic is based on a selection and arrangement of a few elements. The dream, too, is selective; but whereas art tends to arrange the selected elements according to some intellectual or instinctive scheme (such as balance, symmetry, proportion, and harmony) the dream arranges its selected elements according to some symbolic intention, the significance of which can be explained only by a complete analysis *of the dreamer*.

There is not, however, any clear distinction between the dream and the work of art, for the more we examine the history of art, the more evident it becomes that the works of art which survive are those which most nearly approach to the illogical order of the dream. Art retreats before the intellect, or grows stiff and atrophied and survives only in the records of academies. But those works of art which are irrational and dreamlike—legendary myths and folk tales and the poems which embody them—these survive all economic and political changes, the transmigration of peoples and the metamorphosis of language. They are told and retold in every age and every climate, and though modified in detail, are always essentially the same, irrational and superreal, significant beyond their immediate meaning.

In a certain sense, then, the myth, and more intimately the image, makes the poem. Its vivid eidetic energy acts like a catalyst among the suspended verbal molecules and precipitates just those which clothe the image in the brightest sheath of words.

If we could *speak* our dreams we should dictate continuous poetry. But we neither speak nor even distinctly remember them, and the connections between poetry and dream must still be sought and established. It is a hazardous experiment, as I will now show.

I dreamt that I stood (I say *stood*, but one is not conscious of a physical posture—one is just present, omnipresent) by the shore of a lake or inland sea. To my right was a cliff, falling sheer into the lake, whose waters were crystal clear, so clear that I could distinctly see the rocky bed, uneven in surface and mottled in colour. As I stood there I suddenly became aware of a figure floating between the cliff and the lake. It was a naked female form, very lovely; and she held above her, like a horizontal sail, a sheet of golden silk. She floated gracefully down to the surface of the water, into which she fell without a sound or a ripple. The golden sail remained floating on the water, and in the middle of it I then observed a neat coil of rope, such as one sees on a ship or a pier. Below the sail, on the rocky floor of the lake the body of the naked girl was now extended, as if lifeless. I had a distinct impulse to dive into the lake, as if to rescue her from drowning. But as I 'registered' this impulse, at the same moment my attention was caught by the floating sail of silk and the superimposed coil of rope; and in the instant that I hesitated another figure ran across the shore and dived into the lake. As he touched the surface, I awoke.

Here is a dream of very striking imagery. From a psychoanalytical point of view it has certain obvious features, but its interpretation is a personal matter of no immediate interest. I am concerned with its literary possibilities. Can I, while the dream is still vividly impressed on my mind, convert it into a poem?

I made the attempt, and this is what I wrote:

Her angel flight from cliff to lake
sustains its poise upon the sheet of silk
she holds above her head.

The air is still in dreams
a clear and plasmic element.
No ripples dim the surface as she falls
the cold distress
of days unknown of days to be.

The lake receives her, the lake her lover.
Her ravished *flesh redeems the rocky floor.*
Still, as if asleep, *she lies*
a treasure to be salvaged *by who dares*
shatter the level mirror of the lake.

I do not dare; defeatist *I have seen*
the cloth she held relinquished on the lake;
a baldaquin *on* which *reposes*
a neatly ravelled coil of rope.

Another runs and dives and I am free
to stay a prisoner in the timeless cell of dreams.

Let me first state, to prevent a misunderstanding, that I
consider this poem a failure. It is a failure in a personal sense
because it does not nearly express the peculiar vividness and
significance of the dream. It is a failure in a general sense
because, as a consequence of its personal failure, it cannot possibly convey the quality of the dream to other people. But
most essentially it is simply a failure as poetry. It might conceivably have been a success as poetry and still not have
expressed or conveyed the quality of the dream. But actually
it fails both in creation and in communication. The experience has not adequately fused the linguistic symbols: it has not
selected them finely enough nor collocated them significantly
enough.

In seeking the cause of this failure I first notice that in the act of converting the dream into a poem I have departed here and there from the actual or manifest content of the dream. The words and phrases printed in roman type are additions of my conscious mind—critical comments or asides such as 'the air is still in dreams', or literary similes such as 'as if asleep'. Phrases like 'the cold distress of days unknown . . .' and 'a treasure to be salvaged' are poetic metaphors, and not symbols given by the unconscious, which I distinguish under the name 'images'.

These asides, similes and metaphors arise without excessive deliberation—they are spontaneous associations and as such of some psychological interest. But in their origin they are distinct from the basic symbolism of the dream itself.

I do not see how any one but the poet himself can be precise about this distinction, though I am sure it is present in all poetry. The *degree* of its presence or absence would be the basis of a very important distinction between types of poet. The degree of symbolic imagery in Shelley, for example, is much greater than in Wordsworth, who is almost entirely, like his prototype Milton, a metaphorical poet. Milton, however, is a mixed case. As his critics in the eighteenth century did not fail to point out, he is sometimes, as they would say, 'guilty' of irrational imagery. I may be expressing merely a personal preference, but I would like to suggest that the imagistic poet like Shakespeare, Shelley, and Blake is more essentially poetic than the metaphorical poet like Dryden, Pope, and Wordsworth; though admittedly this is merely one criterion. There are qualities in Dryden, for example, which compensate for his lack of imagery: there is his verbal felicity. For poetry is not only a matter of vision, but also of sound; though, as I have already suggested in their gestation the two become closely linked, so that we can scarcely see an image without immediately formulating the verbal sign for it, nor hear a sound without immediately seeing an associated image.

Do the images in a poem like 'Kubla Khan' precipitate the

verbal signs in inevitable poetry? Is the poet's dream necessarily poetic the moment it is expressed in verbal symbols?
It seems that an affirmative answer to these questions would
make poetry too easy, but actually, as my own experiment
proves, nothing is more difficult to secure than the immediate
translation of the dream into its verbal equivalents. Ignoring
the fact established by Frued, that the dream as remembered
is nearly always a fragment, and may indeed be a positive
distortion of the dream as originally dreamed, we still have
to cross the gulf between experience and expression. It can
only be done in a state of trance or automatism, in which
state the images of the dream draw words from the memory
very much as a magnet might draw needles from a haystack.
The only *proof* (it is really only pragmatic evidence) of my
conviction that these words will necessarily be poetic is a few
admittedly great poems like 'Kubla Khan' of which it is
recorded that they were written in a state of trance. It is for
poets now to test the theory by rigorous experiment. It may
take a long time to sort out the evidence—to agree on the
validity of the experience and (what should be the same thing)
the value of the poetry; but eventually the science of criticism
would be in possession of sufficient facts to settle the question.

Automatism is the phenomenon to be investigated, but I
ought perhaps to give a more precise definition of the word.
To some people it merely conveys spiritualistic procedures
which make use of instruments like the planchette, or perhaps
any form of communication made in a condition of induced
hypnosis.[1] But by automatism in the present context we mean
a state of mind in which expression is immediate and instinctive—where there is no time-gap between the image and its
verbal equivalent. Such spontaneous *utterances* are, of course,
an everyday occurrence; in fact, they are the normal utterances of joy and sorrow, of wonder and excitement, and as
such are the basic material of speech. And poetry is in this

[1] Valéry, in the passage quoted in the last essay (page 98), uses the word
in the sense of verbal habits.

sense, and for this reason, a basic form of speech—*Ursprache*. It is distinguished from the more discursive modes of conversation by its immediacy, by its expression of images which at the moment of utterance are obsessing our minds by their dramatic or lyrical importance.

D. H. Lawrence was aware of this truth. In a preface to an American edition of *New Poems* (1920) he wrote: 'One realm we have never conquered: the pure present. One great mystery of time is *terra incognita* to us: the instant. The most superb mystery we have hardly recognized: the immediate, instant self. The quick of all time is the instant. The quick of all the universe, of all creation, is the incarnate, carnal self. Poetry gave us the clue: free verse. . . . In free verse we look for the insurgent naked throb of the instant moment. To break the lovely form of metrical verse, and to dish up the fragments as a new substance, called *vers libre*, this is what most free-versifiers accomplish. They do not know that free verse has its own *nature*, that it is neither star nor pearl, but instantaneous like plasm. It has no goal in either (? time or[1]) eternity. It has no finish. It has no satisfying stability, satisfying to those who like the immutable. None of this. It is the instant; the quick; the very jetting source of all will-be and has-been. The utterance is like a spasm, naked contact with all influences at once. It does not want to get anywhere. It just takes place.'

Poetry of this instantaneous kind must necessarily be written in free verse. At the same time it tends to be strongly rhythmical, though this rhythm is also unconscious and instinctive: the pitch and interval of natural utterance. The rhythm is found just as the words are found: by the law of attraction which seems to operate in the unconscious mind, a law which selects equivalents in visual image, verbal expression, musical expression, temporal extension. There is the image like a photograph film and there is at the same time an automatically selected and adjusted sound-track, perfectly

[1] I supply two words apparently omitted from the text as printed in *Phoenix*, p. 221.

expressing and faultlessly accompanying the imagery.

I am speaking of an ideal poetry, such as has only very rarely been written in the past. Whether by research and self-control we shall ever be able to increase the quantity of such ideal poetry is a question which can only be answered at some future date when our experiments have been carried out over a sufficiently long period. It is possible that the necessary degree of concentration and of self-discipline will be beyond the capacity of the normal poet, who is after all a human being. I mean that it may possibly require a withdrawal from the normal activities of life such as the Yogi practise. But to withdraw from life is to defeat the purpose of poetry (though it may attain the purpose of religion); for the purpose of poetry is the enhancement of the enjoyment of life, either by sensuous celebration of its immediate qualities, as in lyrical poetry, or by communication of its ultimate meaning, as in epic and dramatic myths. What I am saying—the conclusion I am driven to—is that pure poetry is ideal or absolute poetry, and not real or actual poetry; that poetry is an essence which we have to dilute with grosser elements to make it viable or practicable. A poem that is pure imagery would be like a statue of crystal—something too cold and transparent for our animal senses. We therefore cloud the poem with metaphors and similes, which are our personal and human associations; we add to it sentiments and ideas, until finally the essential imagery is completely obscured and we are left with verbal rhetoric. And obviously the more rhetorical poetry is, the more popular it is; for it is then appealing to the widest range of human emotions. But just as essential music can be played on a single pipe and is by no means enriched by all the intestinal complexities of a Würlitzer organ, so essential poetry remains in the instantaneous expression of the image in 'the insurgent naked throb of the instant moment'.

To return for a moment to my own experience, I can aver that all the poetry I have written which I continue to regard as authentic poetry was written immediately, instantaneously, in a condition of trance. Now it is very difficult to hold one-self in a state of trance for any length of time; the least little noise or interruption from the outer world is sufficient to shatter it. The trance which Coleridge was in when he wrote 'Kubla Khan' was interrupted by 'a person from Porlock', and the poem could never be completed. In this particular case an American professor, Mr. Livingston Lowes, has shown that however trancelike Coleridge's condition may have been, it did nevertheless allow him to make use of fragments of know-ledge, words, and phrases, garnered during the course of his conscious reading. There is nothing surprising in this: I believe that every sound we hear and every object we see is instantaneously recorded by the brain, whether or not we consciously register the experience. Our consciousness is only a tiny aperture opening on to the wide world of the uncon-scious—a finger in an infinite range of card indexes.

The poem I am now going to quote is longer and more discursive than the dream transcript already given, and differs from it in that it had no precedent experience, such as a dream, but was itself the experience. When I began to write, my mind and my pencil worked slowly and haltingly, and there are evidences of this in the first paragraph of the poem, which I find a little too conscious or deliberate. But the rest of the poem was written automatically, without hesitation or revi-sion, in a state of trance.

LOVE AND DEATH

On a strange bed I drop my tired head
But sleep does not come—only wakeful dread.
The room was dark at first, but now
The light that filters from the street
Falls aslant the mirror, casts in my eyes
Its mildewed radiance. My limbs
That like a busy watch
Mark the seconds with their urgent twitch
Enlarge the area of my mind

GENERAL THEORIES

Keep me alert to every sound
  That echoes in the space
Around this unknown inn where I have come
  So weary and late.

The last step outside has died away.
All is quiet, the bulbs extinct
That lately glowed above the lust and stink
Of urban life. The shadows in my room
Shift like silhouettes on frosted glass,
Coagulate and tremble into shape.
The light seems now to cut across a street
Leaving an edge of darkness round which creeps
A careless figure. She stands irresolute
Her misty breath jumping like a plume
Into the icy fog. Pellicules of dew
Which catch and concentrate the light
Have settled on the fringes of her hair;
Her step is soft and soundless as she moves
Across the cobbled street whose greasy sets
Meet her worn feet like folded knuckles.
I wait in the dark, withdrawn.
But she by instinct guided comes my way
And stands before me till her silence
Is a question, and I yield
And take her hand, and lead her to my room
Which now is suddenly light and warm.

I am not curious. I see her eyes are clear
And the tresses where the hoar has formed
Are like the withered sheaths which hang from corn.
Her dress she soon discards
And falls into my arms and laughs and cries
And tells me life was sad until I came.
She sits beside the fire; her eyes, her lips, her limbs
Speak of love, a feeling I have known

But never until this moment seen
Embodied in a form not sought but found.

Between the firelight and the lamp
Her body gleams distinct, as if it had absorbed
Ethereal rays, which now give out
Their luminous response to night.
The more she gleams and grows intense
The less I know myself—until
I am not there, except that in her mind
I dwell, and look into the world through crystal eyes
And see the swelling waves break into surf
On golden sands, and birds with bright wings
Sailing the air which shakes
The fronds and ferns on wiry stalks
Against the even green
Of endless fields.

A dream,
As soon I know. For then she falls asleep
Her head upon the hearth, her limbs
Like Danaë's open to the fitful flame.
When I awake she is not there
And I am I again, a prickling frame
Of flesh and bone, gazing upon the earlier scene
Of drifting fog and artificial light.

But now there comes
Sidling round the selfsame edge of dark
Another figure, this time a boy
Dressed in rags, so thin
His shadow seems a blade
That cuts across the cobbled street.
He shuffles till he stands, a beggar, at my feet.
Then once again we are within the room
Now lit by sinking embers. Once again

The figure strips and stands
Lank and angular against the glow.
His eyes are sunk so deep I cannot see
Their colour, nor discover their intent.
His cheeks are drawn about his jaw
And every joint articulate.
He puts his bony hand against my breast.
I do not shrink—indeed, I feel
His still appeal and in his mind
Find a cool retreat.

The shore is icy, a cliff of glass
Against which the sullen waves
Slide in the distant lunar grip.
The seabirds cry in the white silence
And only cease when breaking floes
Boom like a muffled gun
Across the arctic waste.

Again I find myself
My face against the worldly scene.
But now it is no dream. The fog
Drifts over the empty street.
Sleet falls across the light.
I shudder and turn. There in my bed
The lovely girl and the destitute lad
Are lying enlaced. And I know they are dead.

It was not until I had written these lines, and read what I had written, that I realized I had invented a myth which exactly expressed Freud's theory of the two instincts which control all life—the instincts of Eros and Death. In his *Autobiographical Study* Freud describes his theory in these words:

'I have combined the instincts for self-preservation and for the preservation of the species under the concept of Eros and have contrasted with it an instinct of death or destruction which works in silence. Instinct in general is regarded as a kind of elasticity of living things, an impulsion towards the restoration of a situation which once existed but was brought to an end by some external disturbance. This essentially conservative character of instincts is exemplified by the phenomena of the *compulsion to repeat*. The picture which life presents to us is the result of the working of Eros and the death-instinct together and against each other.'

My poem is a dramatic myth, and though not very significant as poetry (I should never have ventured to publish it on its merits) it does give in visual imagery an equivalent of the abstract concepts of Freud's theory.[1] Myths, of course, were invented before theories; but the whole point of this essay is to suggest that theories are inadequate so long as they remain intellectual concepts: to dwell in the imagination of mankind they must be transformed into myths.

As a result of these experiments poetry is seen more clearly than ever as the mediator between dream and reality. For centuries philosophy has been disintegrating this concept of reality, showing what a miserable compromise of averages and probabilities it represents. Philosophy falls back upon some form of idealism—some system of intellectual absolutes which

[1] To what extent is the failure of the poem due to its automatism? To what extent could its failure have been prevented by a more conscious control of the poem in the process of creation? To these pertinent questions I can only answer: (1) that any intervention of conscious or intellectual control would have brought the process of writing to an immediate end; (2) that any but the most trivial amendments would have distorted its mythical unity; (3) that the poem must stand or fall in its integrity. It follows that a better poem could only have been produced by a different set of elements (images present on the verge of consciousness, degree of trance, state of health, physical and environmental conditions). But I do not assume, in this or any other poetic experience, that the elements are casual, or the occasion arbitrary. Automatism is not the same thing as *chance*: inspiration is not a *blind* impulse. As in a chemical experiment, for success the instruments must be clean, the quantities precise, and the temperature even. Analogous conditions in the poet are probably only secured by mental habits of a similar exactitude. It may be for this reason that good poets are usually writers of exceptionally clear prose.

gives coherence and continuity to existence; or it puts up with a provisional attitude like logical positivism, which is the contemporary form of agnosticism. But art is neither philosophy nor science, neither idealism nor agnosticism. It is an attempt to solve these existential problems by means of a living synthesis. Like the philosopher and the scientist, the poet experiences the contradictions of life, but instead of trying to solve them on the plane of inductive or deductive reasoning, solves them in the imagination. The imagination is the faculty by means of which we can encompass the antithetical terms of our experience, thus bringing the widest oppositions within a single focus, under a light which fuses them into a wholeness, a coherence, a plastic and sensuous integrity which is the work of art, that miracle which is the only objective evidence we possess of whatever superreality is cosmic and eternal.

I. THE NATURE OF POETRY

8

THE POETIC EXPERIENCE

If I am right in the general analysis of the nature of poetry which I have made in the preceding pages, it is obvious that our critical values, in relation to the poetry of the past, must be radically revised. That, however, is not a task which I propose to undertake; I have already made a first essay,[1] but not, I now recognize, with all the courage my convictions demand. But the past can wait. I am more concerned for our immediate poetic practice. If the modern poet could learn to value his 'negative capability', then something in the nature of oppression would lift from his mind and our native poetic genius might enjoy a new life. But I do not wish to end on vague notes of hope and aspiration; it is not a question of creating in the void. It is much more a question of re-establishing contact with a lost tradition, the tradition of our poetry from Chaucer to Spenser; the tradition, too, of Shakespeare. But Shakespeare is there to show us that tradition is a meaningless abstraction for the poet himself—'an irritable reaching after fact and reason'. Almost daily I lift my voice in thanksgiving for this immortal witness: a poet who was no pedant nor moralist, a man of no character nor convictions, of no caste nor culture, but just a naked sensibility living in its own gusto, reaching after nothing more distant than the impassioned accents of its own voice as it issued from

[1] *Phases of English Poetry* (London, 1928; new edn., 1950).

the 'terrible crystal' of an intuitive mind. Let me add still another quotation from Keats, who knew so well the true nature of the poet, and died on the point of revealing this knowledge in his poetry:

'As to the poetical Character itself (I mean that sort of which, if I am anything, I am a Member; that sort distinguished from the Wordsworthian or egotistical sublime; which is a thing per se and stands alone) it is not itself—it has no self—it is every thing and nothing. It has no character—it enjoys light and shade; it lives in gusto, be it foul or fair, high or low, rich or poor, mean or elevated. It has as much delight in conceiving an Iago as an Imogen. What shocks the virtuous philosopher, delights the chamelion Poet. It does no harm from its relish of the dark side of things any more than from its taste for the bright one; because they both end in speculation. A poet is the most unpoetical of anything in existence; because he has no Identity—he is continually in for[1] and filling some other Body. The Sun, the Moon, the Sea, and Men and Women who are creatures of impulse are poetical and have about them an unchangeable attribute—the poet has none; no identity—he is certainly the most unpoetical of all God's Creatures. If then he has no self, and if I am a Poet, where is the Wonder that I should say I would write no more? Might I not at that very instant have been cogitating on the Characters of Saturn and Ops? It is a wretched thing to confess; but it is a very fact that not one word I ever utter can be taken for granted as an opinion growing out of my identical nature—how can it, when I have no nature? When I am in a room with People if I ever am free from speculating on creations of my own brain, then not myself goes home to myself: but the identity of every one in the room begins so to press upon me that I am in a very little time annihilated—not only among Men; it would be the same in a Nursery of children. . . .'[2]

Along with this confession I should like to quote a similar

---

[1] Possibly Keats wrote 'informing'.   [2] *Letters*, I, p. 245.

passage from the autobiographical journal of a modern German poet, Rainer Maria Rilke:[1]

'Verses are not, as people imagine, simply feelings; they are experiences. In order to write a single verse, one must see many cities, and men and things; one must get to know animals and the flight of birds, and the gestures that the little flowers make when they open out to the morning. One must be able to return in thought to roads in unknown regions, to unexpected encounters, and to partings that had been long foreseen; to days of childhood that are still indistinct, and to parents whom one had to hurt when they sought to give one some pleasure which one did not understand (it would have been a pleasure to some one else); to childhood's illnesses that so strangely begin with such a number of profound and grave transformations, to days spent in rooms withdrawn and quiet, and to mornings by the sea, to the sea itself, to oceans, to nights of travel that rushed along loftily and flew with all the stars—and still it is not enough to be able to think of all this. There must be memories of many nights of love, each one unlike the others, of the screams of women in labour, and of women in childbed, light and blanched and sleeping, shutting themselves in. But one must also have been beside the dying, must have sat beside the dead in a room with open windows and with fitful noises. And still it is not enough to have memories. One must be able to forget them when they are many, and one must have the immense patience to wait until they come again. For it is the memories themselves that matter. Only when they have turned to blood within us, to glance and gesture, nameless and no longer to be distinguished from ourselves—only then can it happen that in a most rare hour the first word of a poem arises in their midst and goes forth from them.'

These two descriptions of the poetic process are complementary. Keats stresses the receptive nature of the poet's

[1] *The Notebook of Malte Laurids Brigge*, by Rainer Maria Rilke. Translated by John Linton. (Hogarth Press, 1930).

personality—its waywardness, its lack of fixity, its lack of solidity. Rilke shows how the experiences of such a receptive nature become a compost of his blood and being, and only then emerge fused in the poetic *word*.

We return, therefore, to our original distinction between character and personality, and the relevance of this distinction to poetic sensibility and poetic activity. I have tried to define the essential nature of poetry. I have shown how its very existence depends on the 'negative capability' of the personality, and how incompatible it is with the 'positive capability' of the character. I have shown to what extent poetry is spontaneous and intuitive rather than deliberate and ratiocinative. If I left my theory at this stage, it would, I confess, leave an impression of inadequacy. There is, one must admit, some truth in Arnold's charge of incoherence against *Endymion*. Keats was a romantic poet; so, for that matter, was Rilke. Is all the evidence I have brought forward in favour of a theory of poetry and of the poetic personality anything but a concession to the romantic theory of poetry?

I took care, it will be remembered, in the section dealing with the psychology of character and personality, to suggest a principle of coherence in the personality, and I should like in conclusion to return to this principle in the light of our subsequent discussion of the nature of poetry. Mr. Fernandez, in the passage which I quoted on page 32, and which is very significant for my whole argument, relates the coherence of the personality to the coherence of thought—thought which is guaranteed by its own laws, thought which is ever in accord with universal truth. The whole structure, not merely of this particular theory of poetry, but of the philosophy of life upon which it is based, would fall to pieces unless related to a belief in what Santayana has called a realm of essence; the highest poetry is inconceivable without the intuition of pure being as well as the sense of existence. The poet must, if my contentions are right, live in the fleeting moments of vision, but in these moments his vision penetrates very deep and far, and the degree of its penetration is measured by the range of the poet's thought or intelligence. And so, indeed, is the coherence of his personality, for 'thought is guaranteed by its own laws'. It is always an essay in order, in clarification; and that is why it cannot accept the dogmas of character, which would limit its range, or at least confine it to one direction. But the range—the ranging searchlight—of the intelligence, its essential mobility, is not to be confused with the vagaries of pseudo-romanticism, or any theory of poetry which presupposes the primacy of sentiment; poetry as the direct expression of sentiment. I do not think there is anything in these essays to countenance such a theory. It is contradicted by my insistence on the objective validity of the poetic word; it is contradicted also by the implication, everywhere present, of the objective nature of the poet's material—of the worthlessness of sentiments which are not guaranteed by experience. But more than experience is necessary, for the mind must rise above the realm of existence to the realm of essence, and this can only be achieved by intellectual vision. Santayana, my inspiration in so many loyalties, has expressed this truth with perfect eloquence:

'This incapacity of the imagination to reconstruct the conditions of life and build the frame of things nearer to the heart's desire is dangerous to a steady loyalty to what is noble and fine. We surrender ourselves to a kind of miscellaneous appreciation, without standard or goal; and calling every vexatious apparition by the name of beauty, we become incapable of discriminating its excellence or feeling its value. We need to clarify our ideals, and enliven our vision of perfection. No atheism is so terrible as the absence of an ultimate ideal, nor could any failure of power be more contrary to human nature than the failure of moral imagination, or more incompatible with healthy life. For we have faculties, and habits, and impulses. These are the basis of our demands. And these demands, although variable, constitute an ever-present intrinsic standard of value by which we feel and judge. The ideal is immanent in them; for the ideal means that environment in which our faculties would find their freest employment, and their most congenial world. Perfection would be nothing but life under those conditions. Accordingly our consciousness of the ideal becomes distinct in proportion as we advance in virtue and in proportion to the vigour and definiteness with which our faculties work. When the vital harmony is complete, when the *act* is *pure*, faith in perfection passes into vision. That man is unhappy, indeed, who in all his life has had no glimpse of perfection, who in the ecstasy of love, or in the delight of contemplation, has never been able to say: It is attained. Such moments of inspiration are the source of the arts, which have no higher function than to renew them.'[1]

Perhaps it is necessary to return in conclusion to a problem raised briefly on an earlier page: the relation of the poet to the objective values of a literary tradition. This problem depends entirely on what we mean by such a phrase. There is not one literary tradition, but many traditions; there is certainly a romantic tradition as well as a classical tradition, and, if anything, the romantic tradition has the longer history. As I see the problem, it is again a question of intelligence—of that intelligence which operates spontaneously whenever the personality is free. It is merely a lack of intelligence to refuse the experience embodied in the poetry of the past; but it shows an even greater lack of intelligence to refuse the experience embodied in the present. The only duty which the poet has in this matter is to refuse his allegiance to academic *cadres*. But if we must apply the historical distinctions to this age of ours, we shall find ourselves in a dilemma, for we shall be forced to admit that whilst it is possibly an age of satiety, it is not one of solidity; and if it is certainly an age of stress, we are more doubtful about its energy. That is to say, it is not clearly either a romantic or a classical age, nor are the categories of a romantic or a classical tradition applicable to it. In the circumstances the poet has no alternative but to rely on 'a certain inward

1 *The Sense of Beauty* (1896), pp. 261–2.

122

perspective', a coherence of the personality based on the widest evidence of the senses. I am aware that I shall be accused of merely dressing up the old romanticism in new phrases; but forced into this academic discussion I might then accept 'the rehabilitation of romanticism' as an adequate description of my aims.

2. THE NATURE OF CRITICISM

(i)

Any attempt to raise literary criticism above the vague level of emotional appreciation through the incorporation of scientific elements is sure to meet with opposition, not only from the great majority of critics, who depend on their emotions, but also from more serious people who imagine that the prescribed boundaries of decent critical activity are being broken down. To the former set we can only present our weapons; with the latter we must reason, and our task is all the more difficult for the lack, in England, of any scientific tradition. Our critics have, as a rule, resorted to nothing more distant from their subject than common sense. Perhaps the only successful attempt of a more ranging kind was that of Coleridge, who did consciously strive to give literary criticism the rank of a mental science by relating it to what he called 'the technical process of philosophy'. Unfortunately, what this technical process amounted to in Coleridge's day was a very innate kind of metaphysical speculation, speculation rather dim across an interval of more than a hundred years. We have become more empirical, and the general effect of the growth of science has been to discredit transcendental reasoning altogether.[1] Traditional criticism, therefore, in so far as it can claim to be fundamental, is a structure whose very

---

[1] I imply 'in the general mind'. That empirical science can ever dispense with all aprioristic processes is a vulgar error to which the general tenor of this book is opposed.

foundations have perished, and if we are to save it from becoming the province of emotional dictators, we must hasten to relate it to those systems of knowledge which have to a great extent replaced transcendental philosophy. Physics, demanding as it does such impressive modifications of aspect and attitude, provides the most general background for all subsidiary efforts, but for the literary critic psychology gains an intimate importance because it is so directly concerned with the material origins of art.

The critic, in approaching psychology, will not be altogether distinterested: he will merely raid it in the interests of what he conceives to be another science, literary criticism. This science—if it is permissible to call it a science—really covers a very wide field indeed. It is the valuation, by some standard, of the worth of literature. You may say that the standard is always a very definitely aesthetic one, but I find it impossible to define aesthetics without bringing in questions of value which are, when you have seen all their implications, social or ethical in nature. There is no danger, therefore (or very little danger), in the direction of a too inclusive conception of the critic's function: danger, and death, is rather to be found in the narrow drift of technical research, the analysis of the *means* of expression and so on. But it is a proper complaint against literary criticism in general that it has reached no agreed definition of its boundaries, and until it does it has no serious claim to be considered as a science. It is only because I want to distinguish one kind of literary criticism from another, even as you distingish astronomy from astrology, or chemistry from alchemy, that I resort to a pretence of science. That distinction established, there is no need to carry the pretence any further: it is not necessary, I mean, to simulate the vocabularies of science.

Another consideration meets us at the outset of this inquiry, and the more one realizes it the more it appears to put the whole utility of our discussion in doubt. I mean the very obvious difference in the subject-matter of our two sciences:

psychology is concerned with the processes of mental activity, literary criticism with the product. The psychologist only analyses the product to arrive at the process: art is, from this point of view, as significant as any other expression of mentality. But of no more significance: its significance does not correspond to its value as literature. The psychologist is indifferent to literary values (too often, alas, even in his own work), and may even definitely deplore them, especially when they represent the trimming of subjective phantasies under the influence of some objective standard or tradition. But in any case the psychologist has found and will always find a large body of material in the imaginative literature of all epochs: that side of the question is so obvious that I shall pay no more attention to it. But whether in the nature of things it is possible for such psychology to add anything positive to the principles of literary criticism is more in doubt. Analysis involves the reduction of the symbol to its origins, and once the symbol is in this way dissolved, it is of no aesthetic significance: art is art as symbol, not as sign. Alfred Adler, whom I have found, for my purpose, one of the most suggestive of the psycho-analytical school, has recognized this, pointing out that 'the attraction of a work of art arises from its synthesis, and that the analysis of science profanes and destroys this synthesis'.[1] This is perhaps too respectful an attitude; there is no need to make a mystery of art. But it is an easy and an unprofitable task to translate into crude terms of sexual phantasy a poem like William Blake's 'I saw a Chapel all of Gold'. One might as well confess that the impossibility of avoiding such a translation is a serious defect in the psychological critic; for him the naïve acceptance of such a poem is impossible; here at least there is no beauty without mystery. Luckily for the critic, few poets are so artless as Blake, and meaning and intelligence tend to be remote in the degree that they are profound.[2]

1 *Individual Psychology* (English edition, 1924), p. 268.
2 When this remoteness occurs, as in the case of Shakespeare's *Hamlet*, then I think it inevitably follows that any explanation that psychology can

I have perhaps laid sufficient emphasis on the general limitations of the psychological method in criticism. Before I begin with my main task, which is to explore the uses of psychoanalysis to literary criticism, let me deal with one of its misuses. It perhaps concerns literature rather than criticism, but we must all realize by now that no good artist exists who is not, at every point of his career, firstly a good critic. The work of art emerges within a field of critical perceptions. But, criticism apart, the author who imagines that he can start from psycho-analysis and arrive at art is making a complete mistake. No literature, not even a novel, can arise out of a schematic understanding of the phenomena of life. Art has only one origin—inspiration. It is true that art is itself a schematic construction; an order imposed on the chaos of life. As such it has its own delicate and individual laws. But to conceive art as the illustration of science, or even as the embodiment in tangible fiction of aprioristic views of the universe, is surely a final sort of degradation, a use of the imagination more finally discredited than any it is possible to think of.

That is not to say that the study of psycho-analysis is entirely without object for the would-be novelist or poet. It might at least help him to realize, more quickly and more reasonably than the normal man would realize from his own experience, such facts as the subjectivity of love,[1] and the general law of determinism in which all our emotions and ideals are bound. Again, the novelist cannot in his plot ignore with impunity what we might now call the psycho-analytical probabilities. Then surely, it might be said, the examination of such prob-

offer for the complicated strands of poetic creation tends to quicken our general sensibility. Reasoning and mechanism do not lose their value because we follow step by step the process of their operation; and a poetic process is exactly analogous. It is where you have, not a dynamic process, but a static symbol, that analysis is without any critical significance, and may be positively destructive of the aesthetic effect. I shall return to this point in dealing with Dr. Ernest Jones's study of *Hamlet*.

[1] Cf. Jacques Rivière, 'Notes on a Possible Generalization of the Theories of Freud' (*The Criterion*, vol. i, No. iv, pp. 344-5).

abilities is an opportunity for the critic well versed in psycho-analysis. But it does not follow. Here, admittedly, is the opportunity of the psycho-analyst, straying from his strict domain, eager to show what fools these artists be. But the literary critic will ignore this obvious use of psycho-analysis, if only for the sufficient reason that to a critic of any worth these psychological defects in a work of the imagination will appear as literary defects. You cannot write well—you cannot, as we say, 'create' your atmosphere—without a 'germ of the real'. Any psychological unreality will, in the end, be apparent in some insincerity of style or method.

In the endeavour to discover the critical utilty of psycho-analysis I will, merely for dialectical reasons, formulate three questions.

I. What general function does psycho-analysis give to literature?

II. How does psycho-analysis explain the process of poetic creation or inspiration?

III. Does psycho-analysis cause us to extend in any way the functions of criticism?

I ask the first question, apart from its intrinsic interest, to make sure from both points of view—that of psycho-analysis and that of criticism—that we have the same subject-matter in mind. I ask the second question—again apart from its intrinsic interest—to make sure that we have a common conception of what 'creative' literature is. We can then, without fear of misconstruction, deal with the third question—which is the question I have all the time been leading up to.

To most questions in psycho-analysis there are three answers —those respectively of Freud, Jung, and Adler—and as a mere expropriator in this territory I take the liberty to lift my material from whichever quarter suits me best. Perhaps in this matter of the general function of literature Jung is the only one of the three to work out a theory in any detail. Freud and Adler do not seem to press the question beyond its individual aspect, to which I shall come in my second question. Jung's theory springs from that general principle of contrasted attitudes which is really the characteristic method of his psychology—the contrasted attitudes which he calls introversion and extraversion, a fundamental division of the self which may be traced in every activity and which we may variously paraphrase as the opposition between subject and object, between thought and feeling, between idea and thing. Now Jung's theory is that living reality is never the exclusive product of one or the other of these contrasted attitudes, but only of a specific vital activity which unites them, bridges the gulf between them, giving intensity to sense-perception and effective force to the idea. This specific activity he calls *phantasy*, and he describes it as a perpetually creative act. 'It is the creative activity whence issue the solutions to all unanswerable questions; it is the mother of all possibilities, in which, too, the inner and the outer worlds, like all psychological antitheses, are joined in living union.'[1] Jung further differentiates *active* and *passive* phantasy—the latter a morbid state which we need not stop to consider here. Active phantasy he describes as owing its existence 'to the propensity of the conscious attitude for taking up the indications or fragments of relatively lightly-toned unconscious associations, and developing them into complete plasticity by association with parallel elements'.[2] Now although Jung remarks that this active phantasy is 'the principal attribute of the artistic mentality' he nowhere seems to have pressed home the conclusions which are surely latent in his theory, namely, that the poetic function is nothing else but this active phantasy in its more-than-individual aspect. The poet, in fact, is one who is capable of creating phantasies of more than individual use—phantasies, as we should say, of universal appeal. Thus art has for psychoanalysis the general function of resolving into one uniform flow of life all that springs from the inner well of primordial images and instinctive feelings, and all that springs from the

[1] *Psychological Types* (English edition, London, 1923), p. 69.
[2] Ibid., p. 574.

outer mechanism of actuality—doing this, not only for the artist himself, from whose own need the phantasy is born, but also, by suggestion and by symbol, for all who come to participate in his imaginative work.

And here at last the processes of psycho-analysis and literary criticism run together. 'Whether the actual social validity of the symbol', says Jung, 'is more general or more restricted depends upon the quality or vital capacity of the creative individuality. The more abnormal the individual, i.e. the less his general fitness for life, the more limited will be the common social value of the symbols he produces, although their value may be absolute for the individuality in question.'[1] Now 'the social validity of the symbol' is a phrase which I confess I would willingly annex for literary criticism, for it is to some such concept that any thorough critical activity leads us, and though I think the 'symbol' in literature (we should never call it that) is something more precise, more deliberate, something more intelligent than the normal unconscious symbol of psychology, yet, if psycho-analysis can help us to test its social validity, then it can in this respect be of some use to literary criticism.

(ii)

I come to the individual aspect: do we gain any further light from the psycho-analysis of the creative mind? How does the modern psychologist define inspiration, and does his definition bear any correspondence to our critical concepts? It is the general problem of the psychology of genius which I shall deal with in the next essay. But it will, I think, be worth while to examine here one or two relevant aspects of the question. I think that in the mind of every artist (though I think particularly of the literary artist) there are two contrary tendencies. In one direction he is impelled to shuffle off conscious control and to sink back into his primitive mind, where he knows he can find a fresh elemental imagery, a rich though

[1] *Psychological Types*, p. 380.

incoherent phantasy. It is the disjointed fortuitous world of dreams—day-dreams. In the other direction he is impelled to establish strong affective tendencies—ideals of moral beauty, of plastic form, of order and architecture. These resolve themselves into some kind of unity and form the goal towards which, consciously or unconsciously, the artist's life is turned. You get the harmony of perfect art when the two forces achieve a balance. I think this is all a matter of psychological observation, but it has a direct bearing on what we may call the central problem of literary criticism—I mean the question of romanticism and classicism. There is, therefore, a peculiar echo of reality in these words of André Gide, written from a purely literary standpoint, in reply to an inquiry on classicism:

'It is important to remember that the struggle between classicism and romanticism also exists inside each mind. And it is from this very struggle that the work is born; the classic work of art relates the triumph of order and measure over an inner romanticism. And the wilder the riot to be tamed the more beautiful your work will be. If the thing is orderly in its inception, the work will be cold and without interest.'[1]

It is this riot within that we ordinarily call inspiration, and a good deal of attention has been devoted to its description by modern psychologists. By some it is assumed to be a function of the unconscious mind, which is credited with autonomous activity, with powers of incubation and elaboration. Most people will be familiar with Poincaré's account of his own experiences in mathematical discovery (*Science et méthode*, chap. iii), where he describes how some sudden illumination would come to him after a period during which conscious application to the problem had been abandoned. Poincaré attributed these sudden illuminations to the unconscious workings of the mind, but he did not advance any explanation of the actual process. In general, psychologists explain sudden illumination or inspiration as due solely to a fortuitous entry

[1] 'Réponse à une enquête de la Renaissance sur le classicisme,' 8 Janvier 1921 (*Morceaux Choisis*, p. 453).

into activity of ideas which are immediately associated and seized upon in their happy combination.[1] What really happens may perhaps be described in the following way: you have in the first place the prevailing affectivity, the latent ideal of form or thought; what forms this ideal, what brings it into being, I shall explain in a moment. You have, next, the bringing into activity fortuitously of some image or memory which until the moment of inspiration had lain latent in the unconscious mind; this fortuitous image is as it were criticized by the excited interest; it is selected or rejected; and if selected it is developed and transformed by the ever prevalent affectivity. If the affective tendency is suddenly and strongly roused, then you get a state of emotion, bringing with it an intensity of awareness to all the images and ideas that follow in the wake of the first fortuitous image. This is the state of ecstasy. Images seem to leap from their hiding-places all fully equipped for the service of the ideal or affective tendency. But even in this state of animation or ecstasy I believe that a good deal of selection and rejection of images still goes on. However, normally a creative act occurs when the exact word or image is found. And the full creative process is but a summation of many of these primary creative moments.

The concept of inspiration must have arisen as soon as mankind began to distinguish between spirit and matter, that is to say, in prehistoric times. Life itself was then explained as matter animated by spirit, and inevitably the spirit became associated with the breath, that warm and invisible emanation of the body which ceased at death. This dynamic relationship, which was actual enough for body and soul, was also used for all other spiritual visitations; so that when a man spoke with the voice of God, it seemed that the very breath of God had entered into his mortal frame. All the Hebrew prophets were regarded as being thus breathed into, or inspired. It was, therefore, natural enough at a later stage of development to transfer this concept to the poet, for the poet, like the prophet,

[1] Cf. E. Rignano, *The Psychology of Reasoning* (London, 1923), p. 129.

seemed to speak with a more than human voice. Either the gods inspired him, or, if his utterance was too pagan, then a more sinister but still external agent was evoked—a daimon or genius. Even at its most rational extreme, the classical world could still play with the idea of a muse, whose more than human accents fell into the attentive ear of the poet.

The classical conception of inspiration or possession is beautifully illustrated by Plato, whose description of the poet in *Ion* is the final elaboration of the primitive metaphor:

'For all good poets, epic as well as lyric, compose their beautiful poems not by art, but because they are inspired and possessed. And as the Corybantian revellers when they dance are not in their right mind, so the lyric poets are not in their right mind when they are composing their beautiful strains; but when falling under the power of music and metre they are inspired and possessed; like Bacchic maidens who draw milk and honey from the rivers when they are under the influence of Dionysus but not when they are in their right mind. And the soul of the lyric poet does the same, as they themselves say; for they tell us that they bring songs from honeyed fountains, culling them out of the gardens and dells of the Muses; they, like the bees, winging their way from flower to flower. And this is true. For the poet is a light and winged and holy thing, and there is no invention in him until he has been inspired and is out of his senses, and the mind is no longer in him: when he has not attained to this state, he is powerless and is unable to utter his oracles.'[1]

It is not part of my intention to trace the history of this conception from the time of Plato—to a certain extent that has already been done by Erwin Panofsky.[2] All I would like to note here is that whilst the theory of inspiration persists in some form, at certain periods it tends to become exclusively religious. Saint Thomas Aquinas and the scholastics in general did not conceive art, whether in poetry, painting, or sculp-

[1] Jowett's translation.
[2] *Idea*, Studien der Bibliothek Warburg, v, 1924.

ture, as anything more than skill; and such inspiration as there was in the artist was in no way to be distinguished from spiritual grace. The only possible exception was demonic possession, and any form of inspiration that did not conform to the prevailing notion of Christianity probably perished as heresy or witchcraft. The attitude of the rationalists of the seventeenth and eighteenth centuries was essentially the same; the concept of inspiration was contrary to common sense and was generally condemned (in religion no less than in art) as a pernicious form of *enthusiasm*. It was only with the romantic revival that the concept was once more reinstated, and began to be seriously investigated.

Since the eighteenth century, inspiration has lost its religious significance and become almost exclusively an aesthetic term. One might almost say that the historical distinction between classicism and romanticism is determined by this concept. The classicist, and the naturalist who has much in common with him, refuse to see in the highest works of art anything but the exercise of judgement, sensibility, and skill. The romanticist cannot be satisfied with such a normal standard; for him art is essentially irrational—an experience beyond normality, sometimes destructive of normality, and at the very least evocative of that state of wonder which is the state of mind induced by the immediately inexplicable.

Classicism and romanticism are in the end temperamental attitudes, a contradiction which no argument can resolve. But whilst hitherto romanticism has had to rely on subjective convictions, and has thus earned a certain disrepute in philosophy and the science of art, it can now claim a scientific basis in the findings of psycho-analysis. That psycho-analysis itself rests under the same shadow of subjectivism is an accusation which must be dismissed, for however tentative its theoretical structure may be, the groundwork is a mass of correlated facts from which the main features clearly emerge. That the theory, even in its basic form, has a direct bearing on the problems of artistic creation has already been observed by

Freud, and Freud himself has in various places made the first approach to a solution.

Freud's study of neurosis in general soon brought the phenomena of art within the scope of his researches. He found, for example, a similarity between the phantasies which obsessed his patients and the phantasies which the artist put forth as works of the imagination. There was, however, this difference: in one case the phantasies remained mental and led eventually to a nervous breakdown; in the other case they were projected and objectified and the mind remained stable. Art, therefore, was conceived as a way back from phantasy to reality. Freud does not, of course, ignore the question of aesthetic values, and is far from suggesting that every sublimation of phantasy is a work of art. The artist has the additional ability (which Freud calls 'mysterious') of so moulding the objective form of his phantasies that the result gives a positive pleasure, which pleasure is independent of the phantasy and due to the physical proportions, the texture, the tone, the harmony, and all the other specific and objective qualities which we recognize in a work of art. The only explanation he has to offer of this objective power in the work of art is that the technique of the artist is in some way a means of breaking down the barriers between individual egos, uniting them all in some form of collective ego. He suggests that the purely formal or aesthetic elements in a work of art constitute a sort of pleasure-premium or preliminary seduction which, once it operates on our sensibilities, permits the liberation of a secondary and superior kind of enjoyment springing from much deeper levels. 'I believe', he says, 'that the aesthetic pleasure produced in us by the creative artist has a preliminary character, and that the real enjoyment of a work of art is due to the ease it gives to certain psychic tensions.'

More recently Freud has elaborated his anatomy of the mental personality, and though he does not, in this part of his work, make any direct references to the aesthetic problem, some of his observations are suggestive. As formulated in his

New Introductory Lectures (1933), we have now to regard the individual as being divided into three levels or degrees of consciousness, called the ego, the super-ego, and the id. These divisions can only be schematically represented as definite; actually they shade off into one another. The super-ego in particular is not to be imagined as something separated from the id by the ego; some of its characteristics are derived directly from the id. The id is 'the obscure inaccessible part of our personality; the little we know about it we have learnt from the study of dream-work and the formation of neurotic symptoms, and most of that is of a negative character, and can only be described as all that the ego is not. We can come nearer to the id with images, and call it a chaos, a cauldron of seething excitement. We suppose that it is somewhere in direct contact with somatic [i.e. physical or bodily] processes, and takes over from them instinctual needs and gives them mental expression, but we cannot say in what substratum this contact is made. These instincts fill it with energy, but it has no organization and no unified will, only an impulse to obtain satisfaction for the instinctual needs, in accordance with the pleasure-principle. The laws of logic—above all, the law of contradiction—do not hold for processes in the id. . . . There is nothing in the id which can be compared to negation, and we are astonished to find in it an exception to the philosopher's assertion that space and time are necessary forms of our mental acts. In the id there is nothing corresponding to the idea of time, no recognition of the passage of time, and (a thing which is very remarkable and awaits adequate attention in philosophic thought) no alteration of mental processes by the passage of time. . . . It is constantly being borne in on me that we have made far too little use for our theory of the indubitable fact that the repressed remains unaltered by the passage of time. This seems to offer us the possibility of an approach to some really profound truths. . . . Naturally the id knows no values, no good and evil, no morality. The economic, or, if you prefer, the quantitative factor, which is so closely bound up with the pleasure-principle, dominates all its processes.'

We must leave on one side the significance of the other two divisions of the mental personality—the ego and the super-ego—though their application to the sphere of criticism is not far to seek. The ego is the main agent of what Freud calls the reality-principle and its tendency is to synthetize the lawless products of the id—to bring together and unify the basic mental processes. It is in the ego that the work of art receives its formal organization, just as it is in the super-ego that it receives its moral or social aim. The super-ego is 'the representative of all moral restrictions, the advocate of the impulse towards perfection—in short, it is as much as we have been able to apprehend psychologically of what people call the 'higher' things in human life.

The work of art, therefore, has its correspondences with each region of the mind. It derives its energy, its irrationality and its mysterious power from the id, which is to be regarded as the source of what we have called 'inspiration'. It is given formal synthesis and unity by the ego; and finally it may be assimilated to those ideologies or spiritual aspirations which are the peculiar creation of the super-ego. The old metaphor underlying the word 'inspiration' is to this extent confirmed: that out of the darkness of that region of the mind we call the id, come these sudden promptings of words, sounds, or images from which the artist constructs his work of art. It is not for me to discuss at present *how* that construction is effected—to what extent, for example, it comes into consciousness ready-made. It is sufficient to note that Freud has provided a psychological explanation of the fact of inspiration. In another connection (he is discussing the phenomenon of mysticism) Freud suggests that under certain conditions 'the perceptual system becomes able to grasp relations in the deeper layers of the ego and in the id which would otherwise be inaccessible to it.' We might elaborate the metaphor and picture the regions of the mind as three superimposed strata in which a phenomenon comparable to a 'fault' in geology has taken place. As a result, in one part of the mind the layers become discontinuous, and exposed to each other at unusual levels; the sensational awareness of the ego being brought into direct contact with the id, and from that 'seething cauldron' snatching some archetypal form, some instinctive association of words, images, or sounds, which constitute the basis of the work of art. Ideas, and all the rational superstructure of the mind, can be conveyed by the instruments of thought or science; but those deeper intuitions of the mind, which are neither rational nor economic, but which nevertheless exercise a changeless and eternal influence on successive generations of men—these are accessible only to the mystic and the artist, and only the artist can give them material representation, though naturally the mystic may be, and often is, one kind of artist—a poet.

If this be a correct description of the process of poetic creation, then the part that may be played by suggestion or self-hypnosis in the encouragement of such states is obviously considerable, and I think that in time a complete technique of inspiration may be evolved. That this will result in a vast increase in the number of poets need not be feared, for nothing ever comes out of the unconscious mind that has not previously been consciously elaborated or sensibly felt: the product of the unconscious mind will always strictly correspond with the quality of the conscious mind, and dull or undisciplined intellects will find as ever that there is no short cut to genius.

It will be observed that there is nothing exceptional or peculiar in this description of the creative process: it is just what occurs in any man's mind when he is suddenly endowed with a 'bright idea'. Where then must we seek for an explanation of the abnormality of the artist? Obviously, I think, in the nature of the ideal or affective tendency to which his whole creative life is subservient.

Freud and his disciples would trace back the formation of the abnormal mentality of the artist to the period of infancy.

'Analysis of this aspiration' (for ideal beauty), says Dr. Ernest Jones, 'reveals that the chief source of its stimuli is not so much a primary impulse as a reaction, a rebellion against the coarser and more repellent aspects of material existence, one which psychogenetically arises from the reaction of the young child against its original excremental interests.'[1] The repression of such tabooed interests may indeed contribute to the details of aesthetic activity, but this particular hypothesis seems far too limited in conception, and far too poorly supported by facts, to account for the variety and profundity of aesthetic expression in general. The less specialized theory of Adler seems to offer a clearer explanation. According to the principles of 'individual psychology', 'every neurosis can be understood as an attempt to free oneself from a feeling of inferiority in order to gain a feeling of superiority'.[2] The feeling of inferiority usually arises in the family circle, and the compensatory feeling of superiority is usually a phantasy so absurd in its high-set goal of god-likeness that it remains in the unconscious; it is repressed by the communal standards of logic, sympathy, and co-operation. This buried sense of superiority is present in most of us, but the artist takes the goal of godlikeness seriously and is compelled to flee from real life and compromise to seek a life within life;[3] and he is an artist in virtue of the form and ideal perfection which he can give to this inner life. The neurotic fails to create a formal phantasy, and lapses into some degree of chaos. Now it is worth observing, as a confirmation of the truth of this theory, that the most general period for the formation of the superiority-complex coincides with the most general period for the outburst of the poetic impulse. I mean the time of the awakening of the adolescent sexual instincts, the time of the withdrawal of parental protection, the period of intense conflict between instinctive desires and

1 *Essays in Applied Psycho-Analysis*, 1923, p. 262.
2 Alfred Adler: *The Practice and Theory of Individual Psychology* (English edition, London, 1924), p. 23.
3 Ibid., p. 8.

social control. I think there can be no doubt that the artist is born of this conflict. Freud himself lends support to this view. He says: The artist 'is one who is urged on by instinctive needs which are too clamorous; he longs to attain to honour, power, riches, fame, and the love of woman; but he lacks the means of achieving these gratifications. So, like any other with an unsatisfied longing, he turns away from reality, and transfers all his interest, and all his libido too, on to the creation of his wishes in the life of phantasy.' And Freud goes on to explain how the artist can, by the expression and elaboration of his phantasies, give them the impersonality and universality of art and make them communicable and desirable to others—'and then he has won—through his phantasy—what before he could only win in phantasy: honour, power, and the love of woman'.[1]

The essential point to notice is that psycho-analysis seems to show that the artist is initially by tendency a neurotic, but that in becoming an artist he as it were escapes the ultimate fate of his tendency and through art finds his way back to reality. I think it will be seen now where psycho-analysis can be of some assistance to the critic—namely, in the verification of the reality of the sublimation of any given neurotic tendency. The psycho-analyst should be able to divide sharply for us, in any given artistic or pseudo-artistic expression, the real and the neurotic. There is much in literature that is on the border-line of reality: it would be useful for the critic to be able to determine by some scientific process the exact course of this border-line. But again I would suggest that in all probability the critic could determine this border-line by general critical principles; but psycho-analysis might be a shorter path to the test; and in any case it would supply collateral evidence of a very satisfactory kind. Psycho-analysis finds in art a system of symbols, representing a hidden reality, and by analysis it can testify to the purposive genuineness of the sym-

[1] Sigmund Freud: *Introductory Lectures on Psycho-Analysis* (English edition, London, 1922), pp. 314-15.

bols; it can also testify to the faithfulness, the richness, and the range of the mind behind the symbol.

(iii)

There still remains the third question that I propounded: Does psycho-analysis modify in any way our conception of the critic's function? The clear difference in subject-matter, already defined, makes it unlikely that we shall find any fundamental influence. It is merely a question of what kind of attitude, among the many possible to the critic within the strict limits of his function, psycho-anaylsis will stress. It does not, so far as I can see, amount to anything very definite—anything more precise than a general admonition to tolerance. Human activities are shown to be so interrelated, so productive of unrealized compensations, that any narrowly confined application of energy and intelligence results in a distortion of reality. Hence the futility of a purely categorical criticism—which may be illustrated by reference to 'the Hamlet problem'. During the past two hundred years an extensive body of criticism has accumulated around Shakespeare's cryptic masterpiece. The difficulty, for the critics, is to account within the canons of art for Hamlet's hesitancy in seeking to revenge his father's murder. Dr. Ernest Jones has given a fairly complete summary,[1] which I will summarize still further, of all the various theories advanced at different times. There are two main points of view: one, that of Goethe and Coleridge, finds a sufficient explanation of the inconsistencies of the play in the temperament of Hamlet, whom they regard as a noble nature, but one incapable of decisive action of any kind—'without that energy of the soul which constitutes the hero', as Goethe expresses it. The second point of view sees a sufficient explanation in the difficulty of the task that Hamlet is called upon to perform. Both these theories have been deci-

[1] *Essays in Applied Psycho-Analysis* (London, 1923), pp. 1–98, 'The Problem of Hamlet'.

sively refuted, time and time again, from the very facts of the play, and finally criticism has manœuvred itself into a paradoxical position, boldly asserting that the tragedy is in its essence 'inexplicable, incoherent, and incongruous'. This is the position taken up with so much force by the late J. M. Robertson. 'Robertson's thesis' (I quote from Dr. Jones's summary) 'is that Shakespeare, finding in the old play "an action that to his time discounting sense was one of unexplained delay, elaborated that aspect of the hero as he did every other", "finally missing artistic consistency simply because consistency was absolutely excluded by the material"; he concludes that Hamlet is "not finally an intelligible drama as it stands", that "the play cannot be explained from within" and that "no jugglery can do away with the fact that the construction is incoherent, and the hero perforce an enigma, the snare of idolatrous criticism".' All this can be said, and said intelligently, and with a convincing absence of emotional prejudice. But it leaves us curiously dissatisfied. We cannot dismiss so easily the personal intensity of expression throughout the play, and such intensity, such *consistent* intensity, gives the play a unity which the old academic criticism has failed to perceive. It seems that here is a case of an instrument not large enough, or not exact enough, to measure the material in hand.

Where literary criticism fails to account for its problem, what can psycho-analysis do? Dr. Jones has shown that it will claim to do a great deal, and he has elaborated in his study of Hamlet a psychological explanation of the peculiar problems of the play. He sees in Hamlet's vacillation the workings of a typical 'complex'—the Oedipus complex, as it is called by the psycho-analysts. That is to say, the mental peculiarities of Hamlet, expressed throughout the play with such vividness and actuality, can be explained as the consequences of 'repressed' infantile incestuous wishes, stirred into activity by the death of the father and the appearance of a rival, Claudius. With the use of this hypothesis Dr. Jones can explain, and explain very plausibly, all the difficulties and incoherences of the action; and he finds in the play such an exact delineation and such a rich wealth of supporting detail that he cannot but conclude that in writing *Hamlet* Shakespeare was giving expression to a conflict passing through his own mind. There is a certain amount of biographical confirmation of this further hypothesis in the circumstances of the composition of the play, but not facts enough, alas, to be of much use to any solution of the problem.

It would be interesting to follow this application of psycho-analysis to literary criticism into further detail, but perhaps I have indicated enough of Dr. Jones's theory and method to show the possibilities of this new approach to the problems of literature. Whether Dr. Jones's explanation is tenable or not, it does provide what is at present the only way out of a critical impasse, and for that reason alone it merits serious consideration. At the very least it points to a defect in our critical methods, for the failure of literary criticism to deal with *Hamlet* is largely due to its approach to the problem along too narrow a front: we must always be prepared for literature refusing to fit into our critical categories. Criticism is a process of crystallization, of the discovery and elaboration of general concepts; but we must be prepared for the voyage of discovery leading us into strange and unfamiliar tracts of the human mind.

That is one way in which psycho-analysis supplies a corrective to the narrowness of criticism. I find still another, tending to the same end. I have referred before to the eternal opposition of the classic and the romantic: to this blind difference under the influence of which even the best of critics race into untenable dogmatisms. Can psycho-analysis resolve this difficult conflict and supply us with a common standpoint?

I think it can—particularly the psycho-analysis associated with the name of Jung. Jung has devoted his best work to the analysis of psychological types. As I have mentioned before, he distinguishes between two fundamental types, the extraverted and the introverted, determined according to whether the general mental energy of the individual is directed outwards to the visible, actual world, or inward to the world of thought and imagery. These two fundamental types are further subdivided into types determined by the functions of thinking, feeling, sensation, and intuition, but the psychological types so determined do not form hard-and-fast categories into which the whole of humanity can be classified: they are merely indications of extensive divisions which merge one into another. But in our particular sphere they do supply a scientific basis for the description of literary types. You will find, for example, that the romantic artist always expresses some function of the introverted attitude, whilst the classic artist always expresses some function of the extraverted attitude. Now this suggests that the critic, like the psychologist, should take up a position above the conflict, and although his own psychological state may lead him to sympathize with one school or the other, yet as a scientific critic he must no longer be content with a dog-in-the-manger attitude. Again, he must broaden the basis of his criticism: he must see the romantic and classic elements in literature as the natural expression of a biological opposition in human nature. It is not sufficient to treat the matter one way or the other as a question of intellectual fallacy; it is a question, for the individual, of natural necessity; but criticism must find its general basis in a science of mankind.

I would like to indicate, in conclusion, what I think might be a fruitful direction for further work in the application of psycho-analysis to literature. Recent theories explain memory, and indeed most of the characteristics of mind, on a basis of physiological 'traces' left by experience. Experience may be individual or collective, and what happens individually must also happen collectively, and those instincts and experiences incidental to the struggle for adaptation and existence leave their traces on the mind when, and in so far as, it functions collectively. The accretion of innumerable traces ensures a set response to environment. A given physical structure of the brain results in certain inevitable forms of thought, and these Jung, following Burckhardt, calls primordial images. Such images eventually crystallize as myths and religions,[1] and psychology has already devoted a good deal of attention to the relation of such myths and religions to the unconscious processes of which they are the expression. Sometimes these collective ideas or primordial images find expression in literature, which, from an evolutionary point of view, has been regarded as a rational mythology.[2] Jung quotes from a letter of Burckhardt's these very suggestive sentences:

'What you are destined to find in *Faust*, that you will find by intuition. *Faust* is nothing else than pure and legitimate myth, a great primitive conception, so to speak, in which every one can divine in his own way his own nature and destiny. Allow me to make a comparison: What would the ancient Greeks have said had a commentator interposed himself between them and the Oedipus legend? There was a chord of the Oedipus legend in every Greek which longed to be touched directly and respond in its own way. And thus it is with the German nation and *Faust*.'[3]

This train of thought, allied to what we know of the possibilities of psycho-analysis in dealing with myths, seems to suggest the further possibility of relating the types actualized by the poetic imagination to their origin in the root-images of the community. In this way criticism would possess still another basic reality on which it could ground the imaginative hypotheses of art. Whether criticism, under the guidance of

[1] This process, however, should not be held to exclude the possibility of the specific origin of myths. The opposition between psycho-analysts and ethnologists on this score is largely fictitious. The origin of the myth may be a plain event devoid of psychological significance: the elaboration of this event into a mythical structure, often over a period of many years, even centuries, may all the same be a process for which we should seek an explanation in psychology.

[2] Cf. Th. Ribot: *Essai sur l'Imagination Créatrice* (Paris, 1900), p. 114: 'La littérature est une mythologie déchue et rationalisée.'

[3] C. G. Jung: *Psychology of the Unconscious* (English edition, 1918), p. 490.

psycho-analysis, could go still further and indicate the needs of the collective mind, is perhaps too venturesome a suggestion to make. But with the advance of reason we have lost the main historic content of the collective mind: the symbols of religion are no longer effective because they are no longer unconscious. We still, however, retain structural features of the mind that cry for definite satisfaction. The modern world is uneasy because it is the expression of an unappeased hunger. We need some unanimity to focus the vague desires that exist in the collective mind. Will the psychologist unite with the critic to define and to solve this problem?

Part Two

PARTICULAR STUDIES

PARTICULAR STUDIES

I

FROISSART

Sir John Froissart wrote his *Chronicles* at the very end of the Middle Ages, and in this fact more than any other lies their particular interest. Froissart is the last witness to the life of an epoch, and he wrote conscious of the fullness of that epoch— conscious, one might think, almost of its disintegration. There is something foreboding in the way this eager little man (there is perhaps no evidence for his littleness, nor yet for his lean- ness, but a man so active in body and lively in observation suggests the figure) ran up and down Europe in quest of news, anxious to be on the scene of great events, or at least to meet and interview, incontinently, note-book in hand, those who had taken part in these events. 'Sa nature vive, mobile, toujours *à la fenêtre*', is Sainte-Beuve's excellent phrase for Froissart's qualities. We get a very good picture of his methods in the first chapter of his Third Book (the twenty-first chapter of the second volume of Lord Berners' translation). Towards the end of his previous book he had been taken up with matters concerning the history of his own country, Flanders, ending with the Peace of Ghent, 1385.

'Then', writes Froissart, 'seeing the peace was made between the duke [of Burgundy] and them of Gaunt, and it greatly annoyed me to be idle, for I knew well that after my death this noble and high history should have his course, wherein divers noble men should have great pleasure and delight, and as yet, I thank God, I have understanding and remembrance of all things past, and my wit quick and sharp enough to

149

conceive all things shewed unto me touching my principal matter, and my body as yet able to endure and to suffer pain; all things considered, I thought I would not let to pursue my said first purpose: and to the intent to know the truth of deeds done in far countries, I found occasion to go to the high and mighty prince Gaston earl of Foix and of Bearn: for I knew well that if I might have that grace to come into his house and to be there at leisure, I could not be so well informed to my purpose in none other place of the world; for thither resorted all manner of knights and strange squires, for the great nobleness of the said earl. And as I imagined, so I did, and shewed to my redoubted lord the earl of Blois mine intent, and he gave me letters of recommendations to the earl of Foix. And so long I rode without peril or damage, that I came to his house called Orthez in the country of Bearn on Saint Katherine's day the year of grace one thousand three hundred fourscore and eight. And the said earl, as soon as he saw me, he made me good cheer and smiling said how he knew me, and yet he never saw me before, but he had often heard speaking of me; and so he retained me in his house to my great ease with the help of the letters of credence that I brought unto him, so that I might tarry there at my pleasure; and there I was informed of the business of the realms of Castile, Portugal, Navarre, and Aragon, yea, and of the realm of England and country of Bourbonnois and Gascoyne. And the earl himself, if I did demand anything of him, he did shew me all that he knew, saying to me how the history that I had begun should hereafter be more praised than any other; and the reason, he said, why, was this, how that fifty year past there had been done more marvellous deeds of arms in the world than in three hundred year before that. Thus was I in the court of the earl of Foix well cherished and at my pleasure: it was the thing that I most desired to know news as touching my matter, and I had at my will lords, knights, and squires ever to inform me, and also the gentle earl himself.'[1]

[1] My quotations are taken in general from the Globe edition of Berners'

FROISSART

I have quoted this passage, not only because it shows Froissart in action, but also because there are phrases which reveal his clear consciousness of the splendour of the age whose deeds he was destined to record, as well as the high conception he had of his own function in recording them. 'For I knew well that after my death this noble and high history should have his course' (*sera en grand cours* is the original, not quite exactly rendered by Berners)—we have no inclination to challenge this confident prophecy, still less inclination to question his claim to the understanding and remembrance of all things past, and to a wit quick and sharp enough (*esprit clair et aigu*) 'to conceive all things shewed unto me'. Froissart knew that he lived in a great age; did not Gaston de Foix, an earl 'in everything so perfect that he cannot be praised too much', believe 'how that fifty year past there had been done more marvellous deeds of arms in the world than in three hundred year before that'? 'Three hundred year before that' comprised the whole age of chivalry, and now for fifty years, the fifty years covered by the chronicle Froissart had already written, that age had enjoyed a settled glory. That was one consideration; further, in an age when few men were capable of writing chronicles, and those few inevitably known to each other, it was safe to conclude that he, Sir John Froissart, was, by the grace of God, destined to be the only contemporary chronicler of this marvellous age; the age and the chronicle were henceforth one inseparable glory.

Froissart in England means the Froissart of Lord Berners' version, made about a century and a half after the writing of the original. We lose little in our dependence on this translation; it is often inaccurate and obscure; it is full of omissions and paraphrases; nevertheless, it has the spirit and the style of Froissart's French—'belle, facile et abondante'. As the late W. P. Ker said in his introduction to the reprint of Berners in the Tudor Translations Series:

Froissart, but I have also consulted the more recent reprint of the full text published by the Shakespeare Head Press.

151

'It corresponds to the vocabulary of Froissart, the beauty of which, as of all good French, and not least in the French medieval prose, lies in the harmony between the single words and the syntactic idiom. The prose is not a new invention; it is natural, in the sense that it is founded upon the usages of conversation, quick and expressive, well provided with plenty of words for interesting things, unimpeded by drawling rhetoric, and free from any anxiety or curiosity about rules of good taste, because it had good taste to begin with, and did not need to think about it.'[1]

This description of the qualities of French medieval prose could not be improved on; it is, however, possible to pass beyond such an analysis and find a parallel between the qualities of this prose style and the characteristics of the age in general. The prose style was direct because the chronicler did not interpose his personality between the actuality of the event and the expression of it in narrative. 'Personality' in this sense was, indeed, a creation of the Renaissance, and if we want to see its presence clouding the clear stream of prose, we need only turn to Lord Berners' own prefaces written at the very zenith of that period. The diction there is just as involute and contorted as in Froissart it is simple. 'Personality', after the discussion in the first part of this volume, is not the word to press in this connection; but to what else, but a consciousness of self, and to an expansive desire to enlarge the impression of one's personal grandeur, can we ascribe this practice of using three words where one would do, and of generally substituting the ornate for the simple, and a multiplicity for a unity? It is dangerous to seek comparisons in other arts, but if we are careful to select parallel environments, then we may trace something like the same difference between the poetry of Chaucer and that of Spenser, between the architecture of Coucy and that of Chambord, and so on, down to the costume, armour, and all minor arts of these periods. In short, there is an essential difference, as between these periods, in the

1 *Essays on Medieval Literature*, 1905, pp. 152-3.

very way in which things are shaped in the human mind—or rather, in the way the human mind takes shape in things; and since our present tendency is away from the ornate, we cannot help having a decided sympathy for the form (as distinct from the content) of the art of the Middle Ages. Certainly, in the matter of prose style there is more essential similarity between Joinville and Froissart and the best modern narrative styles than between Froissart and the writers of any intervening age.

We began by saying that the main relevance of Froissart is that he was the best of all reporters of the pre-humanistic ideal of life; we see, therefore, in the first place that in the very act of reporting the life of his age, Froissart accomplished an art of prose which we might well desire to emulate. There is in all vigorous styles a direct reliance on an immediate observation of natural fact. This is the instinctive method of all epics, and we cannot open the Bible, or the *Iliad*, or the *Edda*, or the *Song of Roland*, without at once meeting these realistic images. There is nothing in human utterance to rival the emotional force of such vivid and elemental poetry, and though the words 'genius' and 'inspiration' may spring to our tongues ready to give an easy explanation of these magnificent virtues, we are balked by the lack of any definite individual with whom to invest such qualities: the virtue of these epics is inseparable from their anonymity. That is a theme we must not pursue at present, but the bare mention of it is sufficient to warn us that when we come to an individual like Froissart, we must be careful not to ascribe to his individuality what belongs to his age. We can give full credit to his understanding and to his wit quick and sharp enough to conceive all things shown unto him: these, however, have been the characteristics of good historians in all ages. But only in the heroic ages do these virtues conduce to a vivid and simple style, for the heroic ages are the only ages in which men live in daily contact with nature; at other times they shut themselves up in courts and corridors, and instead of force give us wit.

Froissart's chronicle is not an epic; a chronicle is only the raw material of an epic. There is a time element in the laws governing the formation of an epic: it demands distance in memory and perspective in design; it needs more than an individual point of view. As the story passes from one generation to another, it becomes more definite, more compact; what is not apt for memory gets forgotten. What remains is the eternally significant. The virtue of a chronicle, however, lies as much in its digressions as in its main theme; there are long passages in Froissart that have epic grandeur—we shall refer to them presently; there are others, like the story of the lord of Corasse and his familiar spirit Orthon, which are as fantastic as any fairy-tale; and there are many others, for the most part detailed accounts of manœuvres and campaigning, which are as tedious as the desiccated histories to which schoolboys are condemned. But the characteristic virtue of the chronicle is just in its digressions; here it takes on its particular vividness. In the following incident, which has all the qualities of a good story of adventure—speed, suspense, visibility—it is the incidental details that shine out significantly: the varlet's cloak, the poor hall 'black with smoke', the small plancher and a ladder of 'seven steps', a poor woman seated by a fire with a child in her arms, and her ready answer to the rutters of Ghent: 'I went out right now and cast out a little water and did close my door again.'

'And when the earl heard those tidings, which were right hard to him, as it was reason, he was greatly then abashed and imagined what peril he was in. Then he believed the counsel and would go no farther, but to save himself if he might, and so took his own counsel. He commanded to put out all the lights, and said to them that were about him: "I see well there is no recovery: let every man depart and save himself as well he may." And as he commanded it was done. The lights were quenched and cast into the streets, and so every man departed. The earl then went into a back lane and made a varlet of his to unarm him, and did cast away his armour, and put on an old cloak of his varlet's, and then said to him: "Go thy way from me and save thyself if thou canst; and have a good tongue, an thou fall in the hands of thine enemies, and if they ask thee anything of me, be not beknown that I am in the town." He answered and said: "Sir, to die therefor I will speak no word of you." Thus abode there the earl of Flanders all alone. . . .

'Thus about the hour of midnight the earl went from street to street and by back lanes, so that at last he was fain to take an house, or else he had been found by them of Gaunt. And so, as he went about the town, he entered into a poor woman's house, the which was not meet for such a lord. There was nother hall, palace nor chamber; it was but a poor smoky house. There was nothing but a poor hall, black with smoke, and above a small plancher and a ladder of seven steps to mount upon. And on the plancher there was a poor couch, whereas the poor woman's children lay. Then the earl, sore abashed and trembling, at his entering said: "O good woman, save me: I am thy lord the earl of Flanders. But now I must hide me, for mine enemies chase me, and if ye do me good now, I shall reward you hereafter therefor." The poor woman knew him well, for she had been oftentimes at his gate to fetch alms, and had often seen him as he went in and out a-sporting. And so incontinent, as hap was, she answered. For if she had made any delay, he had been taken talking with her by the fire. Then she said: "Sir, mount up this ladder, and lay yourself under the bed that ye find, thereas my children sleep." And so in the mean time the woman sate down by the fire with another child that she had in her arms. So the earl mounted up the plancher as well he might, and crept in between the couch and the straw and lay as flat as he could. And even therewith some of the rutters of Gaunt entered into the same house, for some of them said how they had seen a man enter into the house before them. And so they found the woman sitting by the fire with her child. Then they said: "Good woman, where is the man that we saw enter before us into this house, and did shut the door after him?" "Sirs," quoth she, "I saw no man enter into this house this night. I went out right now and cast out a little water and did close my door again. If any were here, I could not tell how to hide him. Ye see all the easement that I have in this house. Here ye may see my bed, and here above this plancher lieth my poor children." Then one of them took a candle and mounted up the ladder and put his head above the plancher, and saw there none other thing but the poor couch where her children lay and slept. And so he looked and then said to his company: "Go we hence; we lose the more for the less: the poor woman said truth; here is no creature but she and her children." And then they departed out of the house. After that there was none entered to do any hurt. All these words the earl heard right well, whereas he lay under the poor couch.' (Vol. 1, chap. cccc.)

This long passage does sufficient justice to the literary qualities of Froissart, as reflected in Lord Berners' good English. Had Froissart depended solely on his merits as a master of prose narrative, his reputation in France might have been greater than it is. As an historian he has perhaps suffered a little from the nationalistic prejudices of his readers. Froissart was not a Frenchman; he was a native of Valenciennes in Hainault. Philippa of Hainault was Queen of England, and undoubtedly English interests and English affairs loomed more largely in Froissart's understanding for that very reason. On the other hand, Froissart had exceptional knowledge of England, and of English life and character. He came to England in 1361 to present a book of his to Queen Philippa, and stayed some five years at the English Court. He travelled 'nigh over all the realm of Scotland'. He paid a second visit to England before the Queen's death in 1369, and came still again in 1394-5. It is doubtful whether nationalist sentiment was anywhere very strong in the Middle Ages; a stronger sentiment was devotion to a particular prince: the link was direct and tangible, person to person; not an abstract sentiment like patriotism. The nationality of Froissart himself is never very evident; that is part of his strength, for impartiality in the historian is not only the essential virtue of the craft; it is also the quality that endows history with one of the attributes of a universal art.

Sainte-Beuve, at any rate, has done justice to Froissart, calling his chronicle the book of honour, the bible of chivalry. It is still worth while insisting on this aspect. The philosophy of the Middle Ages is open for any one to read; the *Summa* of Saint Thomas Aquinas is a complete guide to the intellectual life of the epoch, and the ways of its imaginative life can be traced in the *Divine Comedy*. But the contemporary life of action, out of which the intellect and the imagination were fed, is more obscure. Of the records that do exist, the great chronicles of Villehardouin, Joinville, and Froissart are incomparably the most complete. Villehardouin and Joinville have their special virtues; but if only because he comes last and records most, Froissart is the most illuminating.

It is often held against the chroniclers that they were interested exclusively in the war-lords of their day, and had no thought for the common people. This complaint is rooted in a curious prejudice. Because the common people, including the burgesses who only became segregated into a class in a later age, have come to assume so important a function in the democratic state, it is assumed that the same class must have had an important function in the feudal age. As drawers of water and hewers of wood, no doubt they were essential to the economy of the country; but their status was actually that of serfdom, and to betray any particular interest in their social life is merely a backward reflection of modern humanitarian sentiment. The main stream of history in the Middle Ages passed them over; neither by virtue of economic function nor for their social significance do they deserve more attention than they actually get in a chronicle like Froissart's. They actually get a good deal. In the passage already quoted we have an intimate picture of a domestic interior. In his account of the Jacquerie revolt of 1357, and especially in the long detailed narrative devoted to Wat Tyler's insurrection, Froissart shows how ready he was to desert the chivalrous exploits of his knights to relate the history of the common people should their activities raise them out of the insignificance of serfdom. The whole story of Wat Tyler is told with such dramatic vividness that it is surprising it has not become the familiar possession of every English household. It is true that Froissart is too impartial to take a very favourable view of the rebels; they were 'ungracious' in themselves and their leaders were 'foolish'. But he presents their case with fairness and in detail, from the very words which John Ball used to preach in the cloister of Canterbury, to the final scene when the insolent behaviour of Wat Tyler in the presence of King Richard cost him his life.

Froissart might easily have taken this opportunity to contrast the characters of Wat Tyler and the boy king, the latter so fearless and capable on this occasion; but it is not part of a chronicler's business to point the moral; or perhaps Froissart takes his own code of values for granted. But at the end of his account of the Peasants' Revolt there is a paragraph about a certain knight, Sir Guichard d'Angle, which is interesting because it gives us a summary list of such values:

'And the same season there died in London a knight called sir Guichard d'Angle, earl of Huntingdon and master to the king. He was reverently buried in the Friars preachers in London. And on the day of his obsequy there was the king, his two brethren, the princess his mother, and a great number of prelates, barons, and ladies of England, and there did him great honour. And truly this gentle knight was well worthy to have honour; for in his time he had all noble virtues that a knight ought to have. He was merry, true, amorous, sage, secret, large, prewe, hardy, adventurous, and chivalrous.'

Such are the ten virtues of the medieval knight; the words are well chosen by Froissart, and each indicates an aspect of secular grace. Unfortunately some of these words have lost their meaning; the virtue, we might say, has gone out of them. How degraded the word 'merry' has become; the word 'prewe' (preux) we have lost altogether; and we are not to be trusted with the word 'amorous'. How Froissart understood some of these words is well shown in his account of Gaston de Foix:

'This earl Gaston of Foix, with whom I was, at that time he was of a fifty year of age and nine; and I say I have in my time seen many knights, kings, princes, and other, but I never saw none like him of personage, nor of so fair form nor so well made. His visage fair, sanguine and smiling, his eyen gay and amorous, whereas he list to set his regard: in every thing he was so perfect that he cannot be praised too much. He loved that ought to be beloved, and hated that ought to be hated. He was a wise knight of high enterprise and of good counsel: he never had miscreant with him: he said many orisons every day, a nocturne of the psalter, matins of our Lady, of the Holy Ghost, and of the cross, and dirige. Every day he gave five florins in small money at his gate to poor folks for the love of God. He was large and courteous in gifts: he could right well take where it pertained to him and to deliver again whereas he ought. He loved hounds of all beasts; winter and summer he loved hunting. He never loved folly outrage nor folly largess; every month he would know what he spended: he took in his country, to receive his revenues and to serve him, notable persons, that is to say twelve receivers, and ever from two months to two months two of them should serve for his receipt; for at the two months' end he would change, and put other two into that office, and one that he trusted best, should be his controller, and to him all others should account and the controller, should account to him by rolls and books written, and the accounts to remain still with the earl. He had certain coffers in his chamber, out of the which he would oft-times take money to give to lords, knights and squires, such as came to him, for none should depart from him without some gift; and yet daily multiplied his treasure to resist the adventures and fortunes that he doubted. He was of good and easy acquaintance with every man and amorously would speak to them. He was short in counsels and answers. He had four secretaries, and at his rising they must ever be ready at his hand without any calling, and when any letter were delivered him and that he had read it, then he would call them to write again, or else for some other thing.

'In this estate the earl of Foix lived; and at midnight when he came out of his chamber into the hall to supper, he had ever before him twelve torches brenning, borne by twelve varlets standing before his table at supper. They gave a great light, and the hall ever full of knights and squires, and many other tables dressed to sup who would. There was none should speak to him at his table, but if he were called. His meat was lightly wild fowl, the legs and wings all only, and in the day he did but little eat and drink. He had great pleasure in harmony of instruments: he could do it right well himself: he would have songs sung before him. He would see conceits and fantasies at his table, and when he had seen it, then he would send it to the other tables.

'Briefly all this I considered and advised; and or I came to his court, I had been in many courts of kings, dukes, princes, earls, and great ladies, but I was never in none that so well liked me, nor there was none more rejoiced [in] deeds of arms than the earl did: there was seen in his hall, chamber, and court, knights and squires of honour going up and down and talking of arms and of amours: all honour there was found, all manner of tidings of every realm and country there might be heard, for out of every country there was resort for the valiantness of this earl.' (Vol. ii, chap. xxvi.)

The story that follows, of the manner in which Gaston the earl's son died, is not so agreeable to our modern susceptibilities. The earl had refused to stand surety for fifty thousand marks to his brother-in-law, the king of Navarre. His wife had thereupon deserted him, and gone to live at her brother's court. Some years later, when Gaston the earl's son was fifteen or sixteen years old, he was allowed to go into Navarre to see his mother. When he was ready to return, the king of Navarre gave him a little purse of powder, instructing him to keep it secret, but on some favourable opportunity to put some of the powder in his father's food—the purpose being 'that your father should love again your mother'. Gaston kept the purse concealed under his clothes, but he could not hide it from his bastard brother Yvain, with whom he slept. One day Gaston and Yvain 'fell out together playing at tennis', and Gaston struck Yvain, 'and the child went into his father's chamber and wept'. He then told the earl about the purse of powder that Gaston wore concealed at his breast, and the earl told him to say nothing. But that night at dinner he called Gaston to him, discovered the purse and took it from him. He spread some of the powder on a trencher of bread and gave it to a dog; 'and as soon as the dog had eaten the first morsel, he turned his eyen in his head and died incontinent'. When the earl saw this, he took a knife and would have slain his son there and then, had not his knights and squires restrained him and beseeched him to make enquiry into the matter first. The child was thrown into a dark chamber, where he stayed ten days and refused to eat, 'and he argued in himself and was full of melancholy and cursed the time that ever he was born and engendered, to come to such an end'. Meanwhile the earl took fifteen of the squires that served his son, and on the mere suspicion that they had been cognisant of Gaston's secret, put them to death 'right horribly'—'whereof', says Froissart, 'it was great pity, for some of them were as fresh and as jolly squires as were any in the whole country, for ever the earl was served with good men'. Then it was reported to the earl that his son was starving, so the earl went to visit him; 'and in an evil hour he had the same time a little knife in his hand to pare withal his nails. He opened the prison door and came to his son and had the little knife in his hand not an inch out of his hand, and in great displeasure he thrust his hand to his son's throat, and the point of the knife a little entered into his throat into a certain vein, and said: "Ah, traitor, why dost thou not eat thy meat?" and therewith the earl departed without any more doing or saying and went into his own chamber. The child was abashed and afraid of the coming of his father and also was feeble of fasting, and the point of the knife a little entered into a vein of his throat, and so fell down suddenly and died.' The subsequent remorse of the earl does not blind us to the essential cruelty of his conduct. We cannot ignore, in fact, throughout the whole of these chronicles, the presence of what we should call a certain inhumanity. Human life was not valued highly; it was not respected as a sacred possession of the individual, coming before all other values. But before we condemn the Middle Ages for this harsh characteristic, there are several questions we might ask ourselves. We might ask: how firmly have we ourselves eradicated man's inhumanity to man? With ten million dead still mouldering in the soil of our battlefields, we can have no confident answer to that question; 'they died horribly'. There are many pettier cruelties of modern life which we might mention; but let us pass on to a more importunate question: are the positive ideals, which involve us in a righteous condemnation of the inhumanity of the Middle Ages, so much more admirable than the ideals which implied that inhumanity? More concisely, are we sure that the ideals of humanism are in any way more admirable than the ideals of chivalry?

Humanism, which in spite of its many aspects has remained a coherent tradition since the Renaissance, can be defined in many ways, but perhaps its consistency can be reduced to an essential belief in one dogma: the self-sufficiency of natural man—the belief that the only values that matter are human values. I describe this attitude as a belief, but most people would call it a fact. T. E. Hulme, in his essay on 'Humanism and the Religious Attitude' (*Speculations*, 1924), pointed out the great significance of doctrines which are thought of, not as doctrines, but as *facts*. 'There are certain doctrines which for a particular period seem not doctrines, but inevitable categories of the human mind. Men do not look upon them merely as correct opinion, for they have become so much a part of the mind, and lie so far back, that they are never really conscious of them at all. They do not see them, but other things *through* them. It is these abstract ideas at the centre, the things which they take for granted, that characterize a period.' Hulme's essay (it is hard to think of an essay which has done so much to clarify the ideas of a generation) is an attempt to distinguish the doctrinal facts of two periods, the Middle Ages and the Renaissance, the religious and the humanist periods. If, in reading medieval literature, particularly secular literature like the chronicles, we could always bear in mind this fundamental difference in the actual make-up of the world of 'facts', we should have a fairer comprehension of much that seems inhuman in the life of that time.

In the Middle Ages these 'facts' were, according to Hulme, 'the belief in the subordination of man to certain absolute values, the radical imperfection of man, the doctrine of original sin. Every one would assent to the assertion that these beliefs were held by the men of the Middle Ages. But that is not enough. It is necessary to realize that *these beliefs were the centre of their whole civilization, and that even the character of their economic life was regulated by them*—in particular by the kind of ethics which springs from the acceptance of sin as a fact'.

To read Froissart is an education in this truth. Everywhere there is evidence that life was indeed subordinate to certain absolute values. In the secular world, the lay world of knights and squires, such values are summed up in the word chivalry; and in Froissart's chronicle we have the supreme expression of these values. Hulme's mistake was to regard the ideology of the Middle Ages as exclusively religious. The ideals of chivalry and of Christianity are complementary rather than identical. The ideals of chivalry took shape under the same stress as the ideals of Christianity, but one was a philosophy of action, the other a philosophy of meditation. The knights of chivalry went on crusades to the Holy Land to rescue Christ's tomb from the hands of the infidel, but the spirit that inspired them was not specifically religious. Christ's tomb was the symbol of distress to be relieved, of honour to be redeemed. It was a cause, an oriflamme, a gage of glory. It differed only in degree from the gage of amour. It is impossible to deprive chivalry of its worldly trappings, and why should we want to? Perhaps this age was wise in thus keeping distinct the ideals of the man of action and of the man of God.

At Poitiers, as the Black Prince rode and entered in among his enemies, 'he saw on his right hand in a little bush lying dead the lord Robert of Duras and his banner by him, and a ten or twelve of his men about him. Then the prince said to two of his squires and to three archers: "Sirs, take the body of this knight on a targe and bear him to Poitiers, and present him from me to the cardinal of Perigord, and say how I salute him by that token." And this was done. The prince was informed that the cardinal's men were on the field against him, the which was not pertaining to the right order of arms, for men of the church that cometh and goeth for treaty of peace ought not by reason to bear harness nor to fight for neither of the parties; they ought to be indifferent: and because these men had done so, the prince was displeased with the cardinal, and therefore he sent unto him his nephew the lord Robert of Duras dead.'

The cardinal of Perigord had been welcomed before the battle as a mediator; he had travelled freely from camp to camp, trying in vain to make an honourable treaty between the prince and King John of France. As a clerk he was regarded by the prince as outside the strife of battle. The presence of his retainers on the French side in the battle could not be regarded as anything else but base treachery. It was a confusion of spiritual orders.

The Black Prince is the ideal man of action, the ideal of chivalry, 'courageous and cruel as a lion'. In his speech before the battle, the instinct for action lies clearly distinguished by the side of his true devotion to God; instinct and intelligence are held jointly, but not confused:

'Now, sirs, though we be but a small company as in regard to the puissance of our enemies, let us not be abashed therefor;

for the victory lieth not in the multitude of people, but whereas God will send it. If it fortune that the journey be ours, we shall be the most honoured people of all the world; and if we die in our right quarrel, I have the king my father and brethren, and also ye have good friends and kinsmen; these shall revenge us. Therefore, sirs, for God's sake I require you to do your devoirs this day; for if God be pleased and Saint George, this day ye shall see me a good knight.'

God is with the right, but it is not for man to presume to know which is the right. It is for man to fight valiantly and chase his enemies. But the passion and prejudice which endure when the battle is over, were not known then. National hatred held as a sentiment and made independent of an objective sanction seems to be a consequence of that belief in man's self-sufficiency which I have taken as the characteristic of humanism. In the age of Froissart it was different; to fight cleanly meant to fight without rancour, and afterwards to treat your enemy with all the honour due to him under the code of chivalry. After the battle of Poitiers, when the French king was brought as a prisoner before the Black Prince, 'the prince made lowly reverence to the king and caused wine and spices to be brought forth, and himself served the king in sign of great love'. And furthermore:

'The same day of the battle at night the prince made a supper in his lodging to the French king and to the most part of the great lords that were prisoners. The prince made the king and his son, the lord James of Bourbon, the lord John d'Artois, the earl of Tancarville, the earl of Estampes, the earl Dammartin, the earl of Joinville and the lord of Partenay to sit all at one board, and other lords, knights and squires at other tables; and always the prince served before the king as humbly as he could, and would not sit at the king's board for any desire that the king could make, but he said he was not sufficient to sit at the table with so great a prince as the king was. But then he said to the king: "Sir, for God's sake make none evil nor heavy cheer, though God this day did not consent to follow your will; for, sir, surely the king my father shall bear you as much honour and amity as he may do, and shall accord with you so reasonably that ye shall ever be friends together after. And, sir, methink ye ought to rejoice, though the journey be not as ye would have had it, for this day ye have won the high renown of prowess and have passed this day in valiantness all other of your party. Sir, I say not this to mock you, for all that be on our party, that saw every man's deeds, are plainly accorded by true sentence to give you the prize and chaplet." Therewith the Frenchmen began to murmur and said among themselves how the prince had spoken nobly, and that by all estimation he should prove a noble man, if God send him life and to persevere in such good fortune.' (Vol. 1, chap. clxviii.)

To distinguish between Chivalry and Christianity, between the man of action and the man of meditation, is not to lose sight of the primacy of spiritual values. The true knight was always devout. His occasional indifference to the man of God was part of that ethical realism implicit in the doctrine of original sin. No man is infallible. God is with the right. Let us put the matter to the test of our own valour, and whom God is with, will prevail.

The glory that men gained in this simple faith is the substance of Froissart's chronicle. The faith of men of action is perhaps always of this simple sort. The faith of men of meditation is more complex: it is more emotional. The fact that the chronicles are not concerned with this other faith does not mean that the chronicler was indifferent to its existence. Contemporary with Joinville, and the antitype of Froissart and all the medieval chronicles of action, is the *Golden Legend*, in which is recorded the fiercer glory of the saints. The *Summa* of Saint Thomas Aquinas, the *Golden Legend*, the *Divine Comedy* of Dante and Froissart's chronicle were all composed within about a hundred years. Together they represent the complex achievement of the Middle Ages, and individually they express the genius of that epoch in thought, word, deed, and in the love of God. Other epochs may have excelled the

Middle Ages in the expression of one of these aspects of life; none has had the necessary virtue to combine them all in such splendour.

Froissart's pages are vivid with the personal radiance of men who achieve glory. There is no question here, as in Malory's case, of an author idealizing a forgotten age. Froissart is the matter-of-fact reporter of events that happened in his own time, often under his own eyes. Naturally he was conscious of the glory of the deeds he recorded; but not as we are. For Froissart, glory was the measure of all things, the crown of all virtues. For us it has become something remote and elusive; even something romantic and literary. We have lost the sense of glory because we have lost the habit of faith. We neither love deeply enough, nor feel deeply enough, nor think deeply enough, to enjoy life's most impressive sanction.

PARTICULAR STUDIES

2
MALORY

The *Morte Darthur*, like most of the books printed by Caxton, has had an influence on the course of English literature which it would be idle to estimate; and purely as literature Malory's 'miraculous' redaction has not wanted praise. 'Miraculous' was Professor Saintsbury's word, and is to be found in that *History of English Prose Rhythm* which paid such a notable tribute to Malory's originality and mastery in the formation of an English style. Professor Saintsbury did not by any means exhaust the technical virtues of Malory's prose; and now that the spirit of the age cries out for literature visibly related to experience, we perceive more readily than ever certain subtleties of visual actuality and exact expression in the *Morte Darthur*. The last refinement of all great writing is the selection and isolation of significant detail; and no one is more triumphant in this sense than Malory. In the death scene of the Fair Maid of Astolat, for example, where for once English prose seems to out-reach the range of English verse, we see how a detail noted almost casually in the very last clause can inform the whole narrative with appropriate desolation and melancholy:

'And then she called her father, Sir Bernard, and her brother, Sir Tirre, and heartily she prayed her father that her brother might write a letter like as she did indite it: and so her father granted her. And when the letter was written word by word like as she devised, then she prayed her father that she might be watched until she were dead. And while my body is hot let this letter be put in my right hand, and my hand bound fast with the letter until that I be cold; and let me be put in a fair bed with all the richest clothes that I have about me, and so let my bed and all my richest clothes be laid with me in a chariot unto the next place where Thames is; and let me be put within a barget, and but one man with me, such as ye trust to steer me thither, and that my barget be covered with black samite over and over; thus father I beseech you let it be done. So her father granted it her faithfully, all things should be done like as she had devised. Then her father and her brother made great dole, for when this was done anon she died. And so when she was dead the corpse and the bed all was led the next way unto Thames, and there a man, and the corpse, and all, were put unto Thames; and so the man steered the barget unto Westminster, and there he rowed a great while to and fro or any espied it.'

In spite of these and other great merits, the *Morte Darthur* is to-day in a curious predicament—sometimes a butt for facetious scorn, sometimes a hobby-horse for romanticists, and when it has escaped these fates, a feast to be served in polite selections to schoolgirls. It almost seems that great books must be defamed before they can become popular; I have seen an emasculated edition of *Gulliver's Travels* sold on the bookstalls as one of a series of 'Sunny Stories for Little Folks'. Malory's genius has not been travestied in market-place and nursery in quite the same way as Swift's; but certain perversions of the spirit of his work have prevented the true appreciation of its merits.

The first of these might be called the quixotic perversion. The *Morte Darthur* is really the epitome of the literature of an age—the feudal age. It was written at the break-up of an age by one who shared in its stress and anguish with body and soul—so at least we may conclude if, as now seems likely, the author of the *Morte Darthur* can be identified with the Sir Thomas Malorie of Newbold Revel, in the parish of Monks Kirby, Warwickshire, whose name occurs among those of a number of Lancastrians excluded from a general pardon granted by Edward IV in 1468. The turbulent career of this knight has been reconstructed with a good deal of ingenuity by Mr. Edward Hicks.[1] Malory probably began his adventureous life as a member of the retinue of Richard Beauchamp, Earl of Warwick, and undoubtedly saw many years of active military service in France. Later in his life, in his native country, he became involved in adventures which we might really call 'quixotic', and was charged with insurrection, robbery, and rape. He pleaded 'in no wise guilty' of all these charges, but his plea was dismissed, and he seems to have spent the remaining twenty years of his life in prison; during which time he composed the *Morte Darthur*.

Malory was formulating for the last time a tradition which had lasted for five hundred years. He was writing of events remote enough to be legendary. The reaction was fast upon him, and when it came it fell foul of what was nearest and handiest—the *Morte Darthur*. The damosels and knights of the Arthurian cycle were fair objects and easy victims for the scorn of an age that had grown wealthy, realistic, and cynical. The legendary charm lasted until Spenser, in whom, however, romance has become too ornate and sophistical; and in a more general and yet a more profound way the spirit of Malory is the spirit of the Elizabethans, particularly of that embodiment of all most remarkable in the age, Sir Philip Sidney. But the reaction, fed by a more diffuse and bourgeois spirit, came to a head in such travesties as *The Knight of the Burning Pestle*. The world has been pleased to see this mockery sanctioned in *Don Quixote*; but that is a superficial view of Cervantes' romance. No thoughtful reader ever came from *Don Quixote* feeling cynical or ironical towards the age of chivalry. Unamuno[2] made a great protest in this sense.

[1] *Sir Thomas Malory. His Turbulent Career.* A Biography by Edward Hicks. (Harvard University Press, 1928.)

[2] *The Life of Don Quixote and Sancho according to Miguel de Cervantes Saavedra.* Expounded with comment by Miguel de Unamuno. Translated by Homer P. Earle, 1928.

'They say that thy biography, my lord Don Quixote, was written to amuse, and to cure us of the folly of heroism; and they add that the funmaker achieved his object. Thy name has come to be, for many, another name for mockery, a hocus-pocus to exorcize heroisms and belittle grandeurs. We shall not recover our manliness of yore until we resent the hoax in good earnest and play the Quixote with the greatest serious-ness and uncompromisingly.

'Most readers of thy story, sublime madman, laugh at it; but they cannot profit by its spiritual content until they mourn over it. . . . In that jocular volume is the saddest story ever written; the saddest, yes, but the most consoling to those who can enjoy, through tears of delight, redemption from the wretched practicality to which our present mode of life con-demns us.'

Don Quixote was not a mockery of the human spirit, but an affirmation of chivalry and honour. Cervantes himself had no illusions left at the end of a hard life, but he knew that the sentiment of glory was no illusion, that nothing worthy was ever done that was not done for the sake of glory. But such an interpretation of Cervantes is not the obvious one; and what we will call a facile quixotism has prevailed, many fools facetiously mouthing phrases like 'fair damsel in distress', 'the goodly Knight that pricketh on the plain', and so on, for the few graceful spirits that penetrate this perverse screen of mockery to the great morality underlying it.

The second obstacle which a reader of the *Morte Darthur* must overcome is the romantic perversion. This is more diffi-cult to avoid because ostensibly we are among friends. But Malory has had no greater enemies than his revivalists. *La Belle Dame Sans Merci* may pass as a momentary reincarnation of the magic of the *Morte Darthur*; but the travesties of Tennyson and Morris, followed by the effeminate and etiolated orna-ments of Aubrey Beardsley, have had disastrous effects. They bathe the stark narrative in an atmosphere of milk and honey; they turn romance into romanticism, muscular prose into watery verse. Such pretenders shrink from the vigorous realism of Malory. Tennyson regrets

> One
> *Touched by the adulterous finger of a time*
> *That hover'd between war and wantonness*
> *And crownings and dethronings,*

and improves on Malory by making his Arthur a king of prigs. Even the noble simplicity of Malory's style is translated into the sentimentality of a Victorian valentine. Compare Elaine's last letter:

'Most noble knight, Sir Launcelot, now hath death made us two at debate for your love. I was your lover, that men called the Fair Maiden of Astolat; therefore unto all ladies I make my moan, yet pray for my soul and bury me at least, and offer ye my mass-penny: this is my last request. And a clean maiden I died, I take God to witness: pray for my soul, Sir Launcelot, as thou art peerless.'—with Tennyson's versification of it:

> *Most noble lord, Sir Lancelot of the Lake,*
> *I, sometime call'd the maid of Astolat,*
> *Come, for you left me taking no farewell,*
> *Hither, to take my last farewell of you.*
> *I loved you, and my love had no return,*
> *And therefore my true love has been my death.*
> *And therefore to our lady Guinevere,*
> *And to all other ladies, I make moan.*
> *Pray for my soul, and yield me burial.*
> *Pray for my soul thou too, Sir Lancelot,*
> *As thou art a knight peerless.*

To romanticize and sentimentalize the *Morte Darthur* is to sacrifice its finest essence, which is action and intact honour displayed in the midst of all worldly perils—cowardice, murder, hate, and sin.

The third obstacle to the modern appreciation of Malory is in the nature of a reaction from the perversion just mentioned.

People sick of romantic transcriptions of chivalry turn away without investigating the thing itself. Anti-romantic as most of this generation must be, we imagine that all romance is romantic. It is a great error; and if the excuse is not ignorance, it is merely indifference. But an age with so few illusions, with such poor outlets for emotion and reverence, cannot afford to be either indifferent or ignorant, and must in the end go to Malory and his like to recover certain necessary virtues—virtues which Unamuno finds implicit in the figure of Don Quixote.

All such virtues are included in the sentiment of glory. It may seem odd that a generation which has lived to experience the bitterest disillusion of glory should be urged to recover that sentiment from an old romance. But glory itself has been perverted, for many centuries and from many causes. We need not be concerned with historical evidences; modern instances will suffice. The first of these is the combination of glory and nationalism, a fault from which we English can by no means hold ourselves free, though we leave to French writers like Barrès and Maurras the literary apologetics for such a misalliance. Nationalism is a deeply rooted instinct, and however irrational such instincts may be, they cannot be lightly dismissed by an appeal to absolute standards. Nevertheless, it is necessary to affirm that absolute virtues cannot pertain to an arbitrary and delimited group of men; or to a cause that is less than human: virtue is universal, and glory, which is the radiance of virtue, is only gained through universal passions. But passions pertain to the individual, and universal virtues can only be pursued by the individual mind. Or as La Rochefoucauld observed: 'Il est aussi honnête d'être glorieux avec soi-même qu'il est ridicule de l'être avec les autres.' For such reasons the most notable appeal to glory made by a moralist in our time, that of Georges Sorel in *Reflections on Violence*, must be dismissed because it too attempts to convert a disinterested and individual passion into the animating force of a faction. Sorel tried to graft on to the *idea* of proletarian revolt an *energy* which could and would achieve that idea; and he realized that the only adequate energy was a feeling for sublimity, a sense of glory. Successful tyrannies, as of a Lenin or a Mussolini, depend on the creation of such an enthusiasm, and are remarkable for nothing so much as the fact that they are individual triumphs, personal ideals maintained as much by the power of legendary inspiration as by deliberate force.

Glory has usually been associated with war, and in Malory is accompanied by what his first critic, Roger Ascham, called 'bold bawdry and open manslaughter'. That glory has no necessary connection with war is clear after a moment's reflection; for martial glory is not essential glory, and we must still distinguish glory with grace—as in Wolfe and Nelson—from glory with pride—as in Alexander and Napoleon. War occupies a privileged position because it alone has provided a large number of people with an opportunity for disinterested action. That is the burden of many apologies for war, such as those of Proudhon and Ruskin. War allows men to seek glory without pretension, in the shelter of a crowd, with the excuse of a common cause. As Vauvenargues pointed out in one of his maxims, the dominating qualities in men are not those which they willingly allow to appear, but, on the contrary, those which they hide. 'This especially applies to ambition, because it is a kind of humiliating recognition of the superiority of great men, and an avowal of the meanness of our fortune or the presumption of our spirit. Only those who desire little, or those who are on the point of realizing their pretensions, can be openly complacent about such things. What makes people ridiculous is a sense of pretensions ill founded or immoderate, and since glory and fortune are advantages most difficult to attain, they are for that reason the source of the deepest sense of ridicule in those who lack them.' Vauvenargues, to whom I devote a separate essay, has perhaps more to say of good sense on this subject than any other moralist; and because he himself was such a fine example of the pure love of glory, rather like our Sir Philip Sidney, we ought to pay special attention to his analysis. His two *Discours* expound the Greek conception of glory, and all he asks is that he may speak to his friend on this subject as he would have been able to speak to an Athenian of the time of Themistocles and of Socrates. Vauvenargues was writing in the eighteenth century in the full blast of La Rochefoucauld's cynicism, in an age whose prudent egotism found memorable expression in the verse of an English poet:

> *The paths of glory lead but to the grave.*

—a sentiment which Vauvenargues had anticipated and for which he provided the right retort:

'A la mort, dit-on, que sert la gloire? Je réponds: Que sert la fortune? que vaut la beauté? Les plaisirs et la vertu même ne finissent-ils pas avec la vie? La mort nous ravit nos honneurs, nos trésors, nos joies, nos délices, et rien ne nous suit au tombeau. Mais de là qu'osons-nous conclure? sur quoi fondons-nous nos discours? Le temps où nous ne serons plus est-il notre objet? Qu'importe au bonheur de la vie ce que nous pensons à la mort? Que peuvent, pour adoucir la mort, la mollesse, l'intempérance ou l'obscurité de la vie?'

How strange it is, he says, that we should have to incite men to glory and prove to them beforehand its advantages!

'Cette fort et noble passion, cette source ancienne et féconde des vertus humaines, qui a fait sortir le monde de la barbarie et porté les arts à leur perfection, maintenant n'est plus regardée que comme une erreur imprudente et une éclatante folie. Les hommes se sont lassés de la vertu; et, ne voulant plus qu'on les trouble dans leur dépravation et leur mollesse, ils se plaignent que la gloire se donne au crime hardi et heureux, et n'orne jamais le mérite. Ils sont sur cela dans l'erreur; et, quoi qu'il leur paraisse, le vice n'obtient point d'hommage réel.'

The *Discours* from which these passages are quoted is a noble piece of eloquence, itself expressing the noblest attitude of mind. The essential argument is that glory and virtue are

interdependent; one cannot exist without the other. The more
virtue men have, the more they are entitled to glory; and the
nearer glory is to them, the more they like it, the more they
want it, the more they feel its reality. But when virtue has
degenerated; when talent or strength is lacking; when levity
and ease govern all other passions—then glory seems a long
way off; you cannot count on it, or cultivate it, so finally men
come to regard it as a dream, and ignore it. It is much better
that we should allow ourselves to be led astray by this sentiment. What does it matter if we are deceived since in the process we gain talent, feeling, sensibility? What does it matter
if we never attain our end, if on the way we gather such noble
flowers, if even in adversity our conscience is serener than that
of men merely viciously happy? We are reminded again of
Unamuno, who expresses almost precisely similar thoughts in
the book from which I have already quoted:

'Heroic or saintly life has always followed in the wake of
glory, temporal or eternal, earthly or celestial. Believe not
those who tell you they seek to do good for its own sake,
without hope of reward; if that were true, their souls would
be like bodies without weight, purely apparitional. To preserve and multiply the human race there was given us the
instinct and sentiment of love between man and woman; to
enrich it with grand deeds there was given us the thirst for
glory.'

Again and again these two authors, so typical of the spirit
of their diverse countries, reinforce one another. In the *Introduction à la Connaissance de l'Esprit Humain* Vauvenargues
speaks of this same sense of the ineluctability of glory:

'La gloire nous donne sur les cœurs une autorité naturelle
qui nous touche sans doute autant que nulle de nos sensations,
et nous étourdit plus sur nos misères qu'une vaine dissipation:
elle est donc réelle en tous sens.

'Ceux qui parlent de son néant inévitable soutiendraient
peut-être avec peine le mépris ouvert d'un seul homme. Le
vide des grandes passions est rempli par le grand nombre des

petites: les contempteurs de la gloire se piquent de bien danser, ou de quelque misère encore plus basse. Ils sont si aveugles qu'ils ne sentent pas que c'est la gloire qu'ils cherchent si curieusement, et si vains qu'ils osent la mettre dans les choses les plus frivoles. La gloire, disent-ils, n'est ni vertu, ni mérite; ils raisonnent bien en cela: elle n'est que leur récompense; mais elle nous excite donc au travail et à la vertu, et nous rend souvent estimables afin de nous faire estimer.'

Vauvenargues then compares the love of glory with the love of knowledge. They are alike in principle, for both spring from a sense of our imperfection. But glory tries as it were to create a new being from without, the love of knowledge to extend and cultivate the being within.

The glory which Vauvenargues saw in the clear light of reason, and which Cervantes saw in the gentler light of a profound sympathy, Malory saw as the mainspring of action. Vauvenargues finds it necessary to defend glory; Cervantes must approach it obliquely, smother it in hocus-pocus; but Malory takes it as a matter of course: it is the natural thirst of all 'men of worship'. Worship ('worth-ship') is a word which recurs many times throughout the *Morte Darthur*; the glossaries usually give its meaning as 'honour', but from the context it is evident that it means something more definite. It means active honour, magnanimity, *grandeur d'âme*, glory gained. The tale of Sir Gareth of Orkney, 'that was called Beaumains'—a part of the *Morte Darthur* which seems to be dependent to an unusual extent on Malory's own genius—illustrates the concept of worship more clearly than most of Malory's tales. Three men and a dwarf arrived at King Arthur's Court, and when they had alighted from their horses, 'right so came into the hall two men well beseem and richly, and upon their shoulders there leaned the goodliest young man and the fairest that ever they all saw, and he was large and long, and broad in the shoulders, and well visaged, and the fairest and largest handed that ever man saw, but he fared as though he might not go nor bear himself but if he leaned upon their shoulders'. This was Sir Gareth in disguise, and he asked of the King three gifts, one to be given then, and the other two on that day twelvemonth. The first request was that he should be given meat and drink for that twelvemonth. The King judged his man to be 'of right great worship', and though the request surprised him, he did not refuse it. He handed the stranger over to his steward, Sir Kay, to be treated as though he were a lord's son. Subtleties of conduct and bearing were beyond Sir Kay, and he was for not treating the stranger so grandly, 'for I dare undertake he is a villain born, and never will make man, for an he had come of gentlemen he would have asked of you horse and armour, but such as he is, so he asketh. And sithen he has no name, I shall give him a name that shall be Beaumains, that is Fair-hands, and into the kitchen I shall bring him, and there he shall have fat brose every day, that he shall be as fat by the twelvemonth's end as a pork hog.' Sir Gawaine and Sir Launcelot protested against this treatment of one who they thought would prove 'a man of great worship'. 'Beware, said Sir Launcelot, so ye gave the good knight Brewnor, Sir Dinadan's brother, a name, and ye called him La Cote Male Taile, and that turned you to anger afterwards. As for that, said Sir Kay, this shall never prove none such. For Sir Brewnor desired ever worship, and this desireth bread and drink and broth; upon pain of my life he was fostered up in some abbey, and, howsomever it was, they failed meat and drink, and so hither he is come for his sustenance.' And Sir Kay got his way; and Beaumains 'set him down among boys and lads, and there he ate sadly'. At the twelvemonth's end there came a damosel, asking for succour, but because she would not tell her name, the King would not allow any of his knights to go with her. Then Beaumains stepped forward and asked for the two gifts that had been promised him, and he asked that he should be granted this adventure of the damosel, and that he should be knighted by Sir Launcelot for this purpose. The King granted him these gifts, but 'Fie on thee, said the damosel, shall I have none but one that is your kitchen page? Then was she wroth and took her horse and departed.' After jousting with Sir Launcelot, and having obtained the order of knighthood, Beaumains set off in pursuit of the damosel, who received him with high spirit and undisguised scorn. Malory here shows his admirable sense of humour:

'When he had overtaken the damosel, anon she said, What dost thou here? Thou stinkest all of the kitchen, thy clothes be bawdy of the grease and tallow that thou gainest in King Arthur's kitchen; weenest thou, said she, that I allow thee, for yonder knight that thou killest. Nay truly, for thou slewest him unhappily and cowardly; therefore turn again, bawdy kitchen page, I know thee well, for Sir Kay named thee Beaumains. What art thou but a lusk and a turner of broaches and a ladle-washer? Damosel, said Beaumains, say to me what ye will, I will not go from you whatsomever ye say, for I have undertaken to King Arthur for to achieve your adventure, and so shall I finish it to the end, either I shall die therefore. Fie on thee, kitchen knave, wilt thou finish mine adventure? thou shalt anon be met withal, that thou wouldest not for all the broth that ever thou suppest once look him in the face. I shall assay, said Beaumains.'

That quiet, confident reply takes us back once more to Don Quixote, with his equally quiet and confident 'Yo sé quién soy'. And Unamuno's comment is once again apt for the English epic:

'In saying, "I know who I am", Don Quixote said only, "I know what I will be!" That is the hinge of all human life: to know what one wills to be. Little ought you to care who you are; the urgent thing is what you will to be. The being that you are is but an unstable, perishable being, which eats of the earth and which the earth some day will eat; what you will to be is the idea of you in God, the Consciousness of the universe; it is the divine idea of which you are the manifestation in time and space. And your longing impulse toward the one you will to be, is only homesickness drawing you toward your divine home. Man is complete and upstanding only when he would be more than man.'

The subsequent adventures of Beaumains show how, after many arduous encounters with obstreperous knights, he at last overcame the repugnance of the damosel, whose name was Linet, but not before an illuminating conversation had taken place on the subject of 'worship'. After his fourth encounter, Sir Beaumains and the damosel set forth again, 'and ever she rode chiding him in the foulest manner':

'Damosel, said Beaumains, ye are uncourteous so to rebuke me as ye do, for me seemeth I have done you good service, and ever ye threaten me I shall be beaten with knights that we meet, but ever for all your boast they lie in the dust or in the mire, and therefore I pray you rebuke me no more;—and when ye see me beaten or yielden as recreant, then may ye bid me go from you shamefully; but first I let you wit I will not depart from you, for I were worse than a fool an I would depart from you all the while that I win worship. Well, said she, right soon there shall meet a knight shall pay thee all thy wages, for he is the most man of worship of the world, except King Arthur. I will well, said Beaumains, the more he is of worship, the more shall be my worship to have ado with him.'

It is easy now to identify Malory's 'worship' with Vauvenargues's and Unamuno's sentiment of glory. The further exploits of Beaumains show how he won greater worship, and how he rescued and wedded Dame Lionesse of the Castle Perilous. But one thing is to be observed as typical of this 'path of glory': each triumph is made to contribute to the greater glory of King Arthur; the defeated knights are one by one made to swear fealty to Beaumains' overlord. This, however, is not in any way to be interpreted as an abstraction of the sentiment of glory: the worship is definitely personal to Arthur himself. The King is a knight of knights, a great leader like Charlemagne, but not a symbol; king by the magic test of Excalibur, but not by divine right; king in virtue of his great worship only.

The mention of Charlemagne calls to mind the *Song of Roland*, which might well be named the 'Song of Worship', for in that great epic human glory shines out in pure masculine beauty. In this the *Song of Roland* is superior to the *Morte Darthur*, which pays as the price of its enhanced romance all the confusion and disaster of sexual passion. A militant religion is the mainspring of action in the *Song of Roland*, but the sense of glory is still the individual sense. There is no suggestion of gaining glory for a particular body like Church or State; glory is pursued at the expense of flesh:

Dieu! dit le Roi, que ma vie est peineuse!

There is base treachery in the *Song of Roland*, but the *Morte Darthur* is dark with sexual intrigue. The morals, to an ascetic like Ascham, or to a conventionalist like Tennyson, could not appear as anything but queer. Malory himself excuses the adulterous conduct of Launcelot and Queen Guenever with the naïve remark: 'For love that time was not as is nowadays.' This makes all the more curious the last chapter of Book xviii, with its lament for love in the old way. True love is compared to the month of May:

'For then all herbs and trees renew a man and woman, and likewise lovers call again to their mind old gentleness and old service, and many kind deeds that were forgotten by negligence. For like as winter rasure does always erase and deface green summer, so fareth it by unstable love in man and woman. For in many persons there is no stability; for we may see all day, for a little blast of winter's rasure, anon we shall deface and lay apart true love for little or nought, that cost much thing; this is no wisdom nor stability, but it is feebleness of nature and great disworship, whomsoever useth this. Therefore like as May month flowereth and flourisheth in many gardens, so in like wise let every man of worship flourish his heart in this world, first unto God, and next unto the joy of them that he promised this faith unto; for there was never worshipful man or worshipful woman, but they loved one better than another; and worship in arms may never be foiled, but first reserve the honour to God, and secondly the quarrel must come of thy lady; and such love I call virtuous love.

'But nowadays men cannot love seven night, but they must have all their desires; that love may not endure by reason; for where they be soon accorded and hasty heat, soon it cooleth. Right so fareth love nowadays, soon hot soon cold; this is no stability. But the old love was not so; men and women could love together seven years, and no licours lusts were between them, and then was love, truth, and faithfulness; and lo, in like wise was used love in King Arthur's days.'

Malory is here moralizing, and expressing his own spirit rather than the spirit of his narrative. He seeks, like Don Quixote, to identify love and glory. It was a paradox more evident to the age of Malory and of Cervantes (for theirs were essentially the same age) than to the legendary age in which Malory found the sources of his romance. We might say that in the interval the moral sense had become finer, that manners had improved, and that a code of honour had been established; we might say such things did not a deeper instinct tell us that mankind has always been the same in such matters, beneficent and cruel by turns, in love chaste and stable one day, harsh and adulterous the next; the true life being lived only by those who, like Sir Beaumains and Don Quixote, see beyond the futility of what is to the glory of what might be.

PARTICULAR STUDIES

3
DESCARTES

The Abbé Baillet, in his life of Descartes, relates how one day in November 1628 a small company was gathered together in the house of the Papal Nuncio, Guido di Bagno, to listen to the discourse of a certain Sieur de Chandoux, who had a new philosophy which he wished to substitute for the outworn doctrines of scholasticism. Among the company were Descartes and the Cardinal de Bérulle, founder of the Congregation of the Oratory and a Catholic diplomat whose hand may be traced in many affairs of the first part of the seventeenth century. The Sieur de Chandoux was perhaps a charlatan; at any rate, he was later convicted and hanged on a charge of forging money, though it is just possible that his crime was no more than an indiscreet devotion to experimental chemistry. However that may be, it is certain that on the occasion of which we speak he made a brave show of eloquence and plausibility. Every one there seemed to be carried away by his arguments—every one except Descartes. He remained silent and, when de Bérulle invited him to express an opinion, made a pretence of modesty and unwillingness. But pressed by the Cardinal, he quickly but quietly demolished the feeble structure of Chandoux's neo-scholasticism. He did not, for the moment, enter upon an exposition of the new thoughts which had begun to ferment in his own mind; but he did indicate, at the end of his speech, his possession of a method whereby it would be possible to establish in philosophy certain principles

183

so clear and indubitable that all the processes of nature would become explicable. The curiosity of the assembly was aroused, and de Bérulle went so far as to invite Descartes to pay him a visit so that the new method might be explained to him in more detail. Descartes was greatly flattered (for socially he was never lacking in a profound respect for those in authority), and a few days afterwards he had given to the Cardinal a more intimate account of his discovery.

The encounter was decisive for Descartes; it was a significant moment in the history of modern thought. De Bérulle was a great organizer; not only had he founded the Congregation of the Oratory, but just at this time was recruiting a new society, the Company of the Holy Sacrament, which was to be a vast army of devout Catholic laymen, mobilized for the struggle against Protestantism and free thought. For this organization he needed, above all, a corps of controversialists —men apt for the destruction of heresies and the demonstration of the true faith. In Descartes he immediately perceived his man; and there is no doubt that then and there a definite relationship was established between the two. M. Alfred Espinas, in the extremely interesting study which he has devoted to the development of Descartes's ideas,[1] would go further and impute to de Bérulle a complete dominance over the conscience and practical activities of Descartes; and certainly Baillet implies as much. Nor is such a relationship in conflict with what else we know of Descartes's personality. It was a strange mixture of mental acuteness and natural piety; and it is really in the persistence of these two strains that we must seek for an explanation of the enormous paradox of his philosophy.

Baillet tells us that Descartes looked on M. de Bérulle as, after God, 'le principal auteur de ses desseins et de sa retraite hors de son pays'. Descartes's life becomes settled from this moment. He retired to Holland to escape the importunate

[1] *Descartes et la Morale* (Études sur l'Histoire de la Philosophie de l'Action). By Alfred Espinas. Two volumes. (Paris, 1925.)

society of his countrymen, and there set about, deliberately and solemnly, to execute the great task with which he had been entrusted, which was to apply his infallible method to the sphere of natural theology.

'The Cardinal', says Baillet, 'was not slow to see the importance of the project, and judging Descartes as very capable of carrying it out, used the authority which he possessed over his mind to persuade him to undertake this great work. He even put it to him as an obligation of conscience, in that having received from God an ability and insight in these matters not accorded to others, he should render to Him an exact account of the use of his talents, and should be responsible to this sovereign judge of men for the wrong he would do to mankind should he deprive them of the fruit of his meditations. He went so far as to assure Descartes that with such pure intentions, and with such a wide intelligence as he knew him to have, God would not fail to bless his work and to crown it with all possible success.'

From the Cardinal de Bérulle to M. Jacques Maritain is not so long a step as might appear. M. Maritain would have made an admirable auxiliary for the 'Cabale des Dévots' (as the Company of the Holy Sacrament was called by its adversaries). He is the great lay-apologist for the neo-Catholics in France to-day. His published works are already considerable in number, and not negligible in force and cogency. They include a long and careful examination of the philosophy of Bergson, a criticism of the basis of the modern theory of knowledge (*Réflexions sur l'Intelligence*), and various essays on those aspects of modern life and literature which bring most into question the nature of our own beliefs. He is an eager and active controversialist, and exercises a considerable influence on contemporary French writers—an influence that sometimes reveals itself in most unexpected quarters. It gives us, then, a measure of the immense divagation that somehow or other was caused by this innocent enterprise of Descartes to find him ranged with Luther and Rousseau as the inspiration of that modernity to which M. Maritain addresses his hostile rhetoric.[1]

Of the innocency of Descartes there can be no doubt. His recently discovered correspondence with Constantyn Huygens[2] reveals him in his retirement preoccupied with the avocations, not of an heresiarch, but of a God-fearing student whose only desire is to have liberty to pursue his studies. This correspondence is the record of a perfect intellectual friendship, and the revelation of a mind in all things serene, considerate and earnest. His faith is secure, his spirit unperturbed; only the intelligence is busy, probing into the mechanism so carefully dissociated from the being of God. But he worked among unseen springs and endless reverberations. The doubts dismissed from his own mind were not so easily dislodged from places where the prior faith was lacking.

From the first the new method gave rise to anxieties, but its success was never in doubt. The history of modern philosophy is a history of the development of Cartesianism in its dual aspect of idealism and mechanism. Only within recent years has that triumphant progress been checked. The manifold errors of the system have always been obvious and freely criticized. But only now have we begun to realize how totally wrong are its very first assumptions; only now have we begun to see in this simple and direct philosophy the source of all the great intellectual sophisms of our age.

This fatal criticism comes from two quite different camps; it is a corollary of the most recent advances of science, and it is a doctrine of that revival of scholasticism represented in France by M. Maritain. It would be interesting to inquire how far these two quite different schools of thought coincide—how near, that is to say, they approach each other in their metaphysical assumptions. Their terminology might well be

[1] *Trois Réformateurs, Luther, Descartes, Rousseau.* By Jacques Maritain. (Paris, 1926.)

[2] *Correspondence of Descartes and Constantyn Huygens, 1635–47.* Edited by Leon Roth. (Clarendon Press, 1926.)

quite different, one being derived from an ancient tradition, the other from a new science, and it is very hard to strip a system of thought of its slowly evolved mode of expression. But if, on further research, it appears that the differences of religion (of *a* religion, it is true), and of science are merely logical, differences of mode rather than of mood, then the situation becomes tremendously significant. Obviously we exist, as an age or an epoch, in a state of indecision; the easy assumption is that we exist in a state of despair. But the facts equally suggest that we may be on the boundaries of a new life. The modern atmosphere is much the same as that in which the party met three hundred years ago in the *salon* of Guido di Bagno. There is the same condition of stalemate, the same agitation of minds, all eager for a new light. And it is not difficult to find protagonists who would fit the roles of the Sieur de Chandoux and Descartes; perhaps M. Maritain would do for one and Professor Whitehead for the other— though which for which is difficult to determine. Only it should be noted that on that famous occasion Descartes confessed to a whole-hearted sympathy with the aims of de Chandoux: he merely begged to offer a different—a more infallible—method of procedure.

To bring the Abbé Baillet's ingenuous account of Descartes's departure to his philosophical retreat, there to renovate the natural theology of the Church, into opposition with M. Maritain's bitter and ably destructive analysis of that renovation, perhaps savours of ironic facility. But it is the irony of events. M. Maritain goes so far as to say that the Cartesian reform is the one great sin committed by the French in the history of modern thought. Its devout originator, who believed in nothing so much as the goodness of God, who was passionately attached to the practice of his religion, and who, even in the act of formulating his philosophy, made a pilgrimage to Loretto—by what strange chance has this man come to assume the satanic dignity accorded to him by a modern Catholic? It is only done, of course, by strictly dissociating the philosopher from his philosophy; and this M. Maritain makes his first task:

'Tête superbement lourde et violente, front bas, œil prudent, obstiné, chimérique, bouche d'orgueil et de terre; étrange vie secrète et cauteleuse, mais tout de même forte et grande, de par un seul dessein poursuivi sans répit de bout en bout, et de par une compréhension singulièrement lucide et précoce de la première condition de la vie intellectuelle parmi les hommes, qui est de les fuir; obscur déclenchement, bref comme un battement d'ailes, du songe dans le poêle d'Allemagne, et de l'appel à philosopher jusqu'à la mort, pour le renouvellement de l'humanité: il nous servirait peu d'étudier la carrière et la physionomie morale de Descartes. C'est son système qui importe; c'est en lui qu'il noue son destin.'

The mistake—the 'sin', in fact—of Descartes was, quite simply, according to M. Maritain, that he conceived human thought as of the type of angelic thought: Descartes made thought independent of things—intuitive as to its mode, innate as to its origins, autonomous as to its nature. But these, in the Catholic theocracy and in the philosophy of Saint Thomas Aquinas, are the attributes of angelic knowledge. The confusion is not merely theocratic: it is intellectual and logical. It leads, in the first place, to a denial of the syllogism. The famous 'method' of Descartes is not properly a method at all, but merely an impatient rejection of the essentially discursive nature of human reasoning. For M. Maritain it is a curious fact that the first event in the history of rationalism was a misconception of reason and a renunciation of the normal conditions of its activity.

The difference between discursive and intuitive reasoning, which M. Maritain would make a difference between human and angelic nature, is only a temporal difference. According to Descartes, our understanding has only one sure mode of operation: to see. Knowledge is immediate: a clear and untrammelled vision of the intellect, apart from and independent of the perceptive faculties of the body. This knowledge Descartes calls 'intuitive', and by 'intuition' (*intuitus*) he means 'not the fluctuating testimony of the senses, nor the misleading judgement that proceeds from the blundering constructions of imagination, but the conception which an unclouded and attentive mind gives us so readily and distinctly that we are wholly freed from doubt about that which we understand'. And he continues:

'Or what comes to the same thing, intuition is the undoubting conception of an unclouded and attentive mind, and springs from the light of reason alone; it is more certain than deduction itself, in that it is simpler, though deduction cannot by us be erroneously conducted. Thus each individual can mentally have intuition of the fact that he exists, and that he thinks; that the triangle is bounded by three lines only, the sphere by a single superficies, and so on. Facts of such a kind are far more numerous than many people think, disdaining as they do to direct their attention upon such simple matters.'

The process of deduction is reduced to the mere manipulation of intuitions; as a process it can discover no truths: it can only present them. From this it follows that knowledge is necessarily an individual experience: it cannot accumulate or be carried on from any given point. Tradition is discredited and learning as such despised. 'There is no more need', said Descartes, 'for an honest man to know Greek and Latin than Swiss or Low Breton.' And this is M. Maritain's great score against Cartesianism; it is the foundation of the characteristic *inhumanity* of modern science. It ignores all that wisdom which is the work of generations; it does not understand the essential role of time in the development of human wisdom.

There is another aspect of the Cartesian method equally repugnant to the modern Catholic. The corollary of a mind independent of matter is matter independent of mind. The world becomes a mechanism, and as such only needs to be taken to pieces to be comprehended. And comprehension is easy for the angelic mind. This aspect of Cartesianism is rightly conceived by M. Maritain as the source of that facile rationalism of which we have now reached the absurd limit; it is responsible for the 'immense futility of the modern world, and for that strange condition in which we now see humanity —as powerful over matter, as apt and cunning to dominate the physical world, as it is helpless and dismayed before those intellectual realities to which formerly it was linked by the humility of a wisdom subordinate to existence. To struggle against the body it is equipped like a god; but against the spiritual world it has lost all its weapons and the pitiless laws of the metaphysical world crush it derisively.'

The mind no longer measured by things becomes irresponsible: reason has no criterion. 'Under pretext', wrote Bossuet in a letter from which M. Maritain quotes, 'that you can only admit what you understand clearly—which within certain limits is very true—any one is at liberty to say: I understand this, but I do not understand that; and on this basis you can approve or reject whatever you like.' This freedom of the mind from external measures results in every kind of liberty: in the liberty to be carried away by any plausible wind of doctrine: 'La raison désarmée perd sa prise sur le réel, et après un temps de présomption elle est réduite à abdiquer, tombant alors dans le mal contraire, anti-intellectualisme, volontarisme, pragmatisme, &c.'

The separation of the mind from the material world was in effect the divorce of science and philosophy; and it is from this point of view that Professor Whitehead, in his *Science and the Modern World*, has brought to a head the scientific reaction against Descartes. This is not a fashionable nor an emotional change: Descartes still remains of significance, even for the general reader, as I shall attempt to show presently. And even for the scientist his genius still remains 'worthy of the century in which he writes, and of the clearness of the French intellect. Descartes in his distinction between time and duration, and in his way of grounding time upon motion, and in his close relation between matter and extension, anticipates, as far as it is possible at his epoch, modern notions suggested by the doctrine of relativity, or by some aspects of Bergson's doctrine of the generation of things'.

Then follows the charge made by this modern scientist against Cartesianism: it will be seen not to differ widely in its expression from the charge of M. Maritain:

'But the fundamental principles are so set out as to pre-suppose independently existing substances with simple location in a community of temporal durations, and, in the case of bodies, with simple location in the community of spatial extensions. Those principles lead straight to the materialistic, mechanistic nature, surveyed by cogitating minds. After the close of the seventeenth century, science took charge of the materialistic nature, and philosophy took charge of the cogitating minds.'

It is perhaps easy to find in certain general ideas the determining forces in the history of mankind. It is easier still to ignore such abstract entities. In any case, the development of Cartesianism is clear enough. It begins with the pious aim of demonstrating the certain existence of God; it ends by denying all spiritual values whatsoever. 'The independence ascribed to bodily substances carried them away from the realm of values altogether. They degenerated into a mechanism entirely valueless, except as suggestive of an external ingenuity. The heavens had lost the glory of God.' Professor Whitehead goes on to show that the doctrine of minds as independent of substances leads directly, not only to private worlds of experience, but also to private worlds of morals. It involves the break-up of all values that cannot be proved within the strictly private world of psychological experience—and that involves, not only all ethical values, but also all aesthetic values (for there is no beauty without an objective and material form). This basic dualism in Cartesianism has often, of course, been contested on metaphysical grounds. But it is only within recent years that science itself has come to realize the insufficiency of a mind independent of objects, and of a theory of objects independent of mind. Professor Whitehead, more definitely than any one else, has demonstrated the fundamental unity of relationship which exists between mind and matter, and has attempted to embrace within one world-picture the elements of experimental and intuitive knowledge.

In one of his essays M. André Suarès remarks that nothing was lacking in Descartes except poetry; and he probably means the judgement to be purely descriptive. It is, however, capable of extension, for Descartes's method or system of reasoning is non-poetic in a very profound sense. We have already seen that his first principle of dualism leads to a denial of aesthetic values. Beauty can only be a mechanical harmony, devoid of spiritual animation, deficient in the sense of glory. Such a concept of beauty has, in fact, satisfied certain schools of aesthetic theory. But it has not satisfied the poet himself, who realizes that the forms of his art are part of some larger reality, of some glory beyond the activity of the senses. This universality is precisely what the Cartesian philosophy could not attain, and precisely for that reason no great art has prevailed during the domination of the Cartesian spirit. 'La grande vanité de ceux qui n'imaginent pas', wrote Vauvenargues in this connection, 'est de se croire seuls judicieux.' The real concomitant of Cartesianism is Puritanism, as Professor Whitehead suggests. M. Espinas reached similar conclusions, drawing a parallel between the ideas of Descartes and the paintings of Poussin, the drama of Corneille, and the architecture of the age of Richelieu. All knowledge becomes an invention, an experimental discovery, and all invention a structure of some kind. Poussin's landscapes are 'fabrications', vast assemblages of stage machinery; Corneille's plays are symmetrical arrangements of artificial elements, and even the most moving scenes in his tragedies are draped on the obvious framework of a system.

But to make explicit the non-poetic nature of Descartes's philosophy we must scrutinize a little more closely his use of the term 'intuition'. We have already quoted Descartes's own definition, and this is so admirably precise and clear that it leaves us in no doubt as to the faculty's mode of operation. It is, for Descartes, the only instrument of understanding: it is the light of reason itself. And for a modern reader nothing is so valuable in Descartes as this concentration on the problem of the mind and its machinery. It may be true, as M. Espinas claims, that the Cartesian concept of intuition owes much more to Platonism than has generally been recognized, and is, in fact, but a development of a theory of memory advanced by Saint Augustine in his *De Ordine*. It would be possible, thought Saint Augustine, to replace memorized facts by visual images. The inward eye could order before it all objects that the intelligence could conceive. This idea Descartes seized upon and made the basis of his method. First arrange your images, he said, in a mutual dependence, and then, from this chain of images, select groups which offer a certain unity, and of these make another image, common to the group and in relation to the whole series. Such is the method that was to replace the syllogism; such is Cartesian intuition. This method failed, not from any inherent fallacy, but because it was compelled to operate in a dualistic universe. A mind quite independent of the objects of the senses could only know itself. This Descartes thought sufficient; I think, therefore I am. But it is not sufficient merely to affirm existence. We must prove it in detail and in action. Thought is only valid when, like faith, it can move mountains. We are always under the necessity of finding our place within the world of objective facts; and this is precisely what the Cartesians could never do.

We may now push our scrutiny a little further. The mind, we now realize (and perhaps the medieval philosophers realized it too), has certain fixed states of belief which have little to do with the actual process of the understanding: *fides praecedit intellectum*. Such fixed states may be innate ideas, they may be merely ingrained habits of thought. More likely still, for a modern psychologist, they are unconscious rationalizations of personal experience. Now a theory of intuition which presumes, as does the Cartesian theory, that the understanding may proceed from the perception of images to the perception of concepts embodying these images must obviously be in danger of easily accepting for such concepts the promptings of a state of belief. How, that is to say, on such a theory, are you to distinguish between the inspirations of faith and the perceptions of the intuitive faculty?

It is doubtful if they ever were distinguished, and it is possible that we need a new definition and a further limitation of the meaning of the word 'intuition'. This can be secured by limiting the sense of the process to objective apprehension, and this, in its turn, means identifying intuition with the poetic process. For poetry is the apprehension or verbalization of an objective world. The poet must even, as Keats was the first to understand, objectify his own emotions before he can make poetic use of them. Perception is of things, not of abstractions, and intuition is a perceptive process—the only process that perceives things in nakedness rather than in a cloak of second-hand words.

But the world is not a concourse of particulars, and it may be doubted whether intuition can stop at particular things. Its range is not only immediate, but also universal. And for a concept of this wider reality we must return to Professor Whitehead. 'We have to admit that the body is the organism whose states regulate our cognisance of the world. The unity of the perceptual field therefore must be a unity of bodily experience. In being aware of the bodily experience, we must thereby be aware of aspects of the whole spatio-temporal world as mirrored within the bodily life.' Further, Professor Whitehead's theory of organic mechanism asserts that 'an individual entity, whose own life-history is a part within the life-history of some larger, deeper, more complete pattern, is liable to have aspects of that larger pattern reflected in itself as modifications of its own being'.

This new concept of pattern is very suggestive for a possible theory of intuition. Pattern is an event evolved in time. It is spatially 'now', but only by virtue of its endurance over a definite lapse of time. To express the same idea inversely, 'endurance is the repetition of the pattern in successive events'. And 'pattern' must in some way be correlated with 'value'. Value is the outcome of limitation. It is the definition of the particular pattern. It constitutes the intrinsic reality of an event. We may visualize an object with 'an unclouded and attentive mind'. Such is perception. We may discover relations between the visual images thus provided. That is the faculty of imagination; in poetry it is the invention of metaphors. There is then a further process and a higher faculty, and there is at present no better way of describing it than by saying that it is the sudden perception of a pattern in life: the sudden realization of the fact that an organic event, of which we are a part, is in its turn the part of a greater unity, of a unity limited in time and space, formal and harmonious. This further perception or realization is the process to which we might perhaps limit the term 'intuition'; and it is, under the aspect of expression, the process of poetry. In this way poetry involves everything: it is the sense of integral unity without which, not only no poetry, but no philosophy—even no religion—is ever possible.

PARTICULAR STUDIES

4
SWIFT
(i)

There is a general difficulty in any critical approach to Swift's work which this note is only intended to raise, not to solve: the temerity of any purely literary judgement. If we make a distinction between contingent literature and absolute literature—between authors who only write when there is a public and external stimulus and authors whose stimulus is subjective, who write because they enjoy writing as a free and creative activity—then we shall see that the whole of Swift's work is contingent. He is, on a grand scale, an occasional writer; even *Gulliver's Travels*, the most absolute of his works, is determined by his political experience; it is a final judgement on humanity, but not on the abstract humanity of history and philosophy, but on the mass of human beings contemporary with the author. All that Swift wrote is empirical, experiential, *actuel*. It is impossible to detach it from circumstances; we must consider each book or pamphlet in relation to its political intention. It is true that the world has refused to do this in the case of *Gulliver*, but the world's appreciation of *Gulliver* is not critical, not exact. We cut the slings and blunt the arrows of that angry onslaught; we dull the deadly mirror with the moist breath of our complacency.

Nevertheless, though none of Swift's works can be separated from its historical occasion, historical considerations cannot usurp aesthetic judgement. Nor are we at liberty to assume that Swift himself would have resented the application of a purely literary standard to his writings. In a 'Letter to a Young Gentleman lately enter'd into Holy Orders', Swift laid the greatest emphasis on literary accomplishment. In that pamphlet occurs his famous 'true definition of style'—'proper Words in proper Places'; and there he urges the study of the *English* language—'the neglect whereof is one of the most general Defects among the Scholars of this Kingdom'. After warning the novice against pedantry and vulgarity, he selects two especial defects for mention:

'The first is the Frequency of flat unnecessary Epithets, and the other is the Folly of using old threadbare Phrases, which will often make you go out of your Way to find and apply them, are nauseous to rational Hearers, and will seldom express your Meaning as well as your own natural Words. . . . When a Man's Thoughts are clear, the properest Words will generally offer themselves first, and his own Judgement will direct him in what Order to place them, so they may best be understood. . . . In short, that Simplicity without which no human Performance can arrive to any great Perfection, is nowhere more eminently useful than in this.'

All this shows a high literary conscience; and the same quality is betrayed in the very interesting references to the composition of *Gulliver's Travels* which occur in his letters to Ford.[1] On 19th January 1723–4, he writes: 'My greatest want here is of somebody qualified to censure and correct what I write, I know not above two or three whose Judgement I would value, and they are lazy, negligent, and without any Opinion of my Abilityes.' Then in a letter of 20th November 1733, referring to Motte's edition, he writes: 'Had there been onely omissions, I should not care one farthing; but changes of Style, new things foysted in, that are false facts, and I know not what, is very provoking. . . . Besides, the whole Sting is taken out in severall passages, in order to soften them. Thus the Style is debased, the humor quite lost, and the matter

1 *The Letters of Jonathan Swift to Charles Ford.* Edited by David Nichol Smith. (Clarendon Press, 1935.)

insipid.' Other references to the composition of *Gulliver* show that it was first written in rough draft, then amended, and finally completely transcribed by the author.

Swift's literary conscience thus established, we might next inquire whether he considered himself as primarily a writer, as an author rather than a clergyman or a politician; whether he considered himself as of the same 'trade' as his cousin Dryden or his friends Pope and Gay. Such an inquiry touches on one of the mysteries of Swift's life—his attitude towards religion in general and his holy orders in particular. That difficult problem must for the present be evaded,though incidentally a sentence in a letter to Ford of 22nd June 1736 should be noted: 'I have long given up all hopes of Church or Christianity.' The problem can be evaded because a career as author is not inconsistent with a career in the Church—both ends can be pursued concurrently, as many careers testify (Newman's, for example). If we are charitable, and assume that Swift took orders for more than worldly motives; if we make the still more generous assumption that his political activities were based on a disinterested idealism; even then we can still ask: Did Swift consider himself as first and foremost an author? Was his highest ambition literary—was he, not merely a clergyman, but also, in the medieval sense of the word and in Julien Benda's modern sense, a clerk?

It is at any rate illuminating to reconstruct Swift's life from this point of view—to regard him as essentially what we should call an 'intellectual', and to see in his various strivings nothing but the desire of an intellectual to secure himself an economic competency and an assured position on which he could base a life of disinterested intellectual activity—a life of scholarship, as he would probably have called it. It will be remembered how much he hankered after the post of Historiographer Royal, and how scornful he was when it went to an obscure (though competent) archaeologist. In a letter to Lord Peterborough, written in 1711 when his political career was yet full of promise, Swift said: 'My ambition is to live in

England, and with a competency to support me with honour', and there is no reason to doubt the sincerity of that modest ambition. But some of his letters to Ford, written with more obvious sincerity, are still more revealing. Later in this same year 1711 he wrote:

'Now to your former Letter, where you say the Publick requires my Leisure. The Publick is a very civil Person, and I am it's humble Servant, but I shall be glad to shake hands with it as soon as I can.... You are in the right as to my Indifference about Irish affairs, which is not occasioned by my Absence, but contempt of them; and when I return my Indifference will be full as much. I had as live be a Beau in Dublin as a Politician, nay, I had as lieve be an Author there; and if ever I have any thoughts of making a Figure in that Kingdom, it shall be at Laracor. I will talk Politicks to the Farmers, and publish my Works at Trim.'

Later, in 1719, when his high ambitions for place and power had been disappointed, when he was irrevocably condemned to a deanery in Dublin, he wrote to his friend a little more ruefully, but still in the same strain:

'You know I chuse all the sillyest Things in the World to amuse my self, in an evil age, and a late time of life, ad fallendam canitiem quae indies obrepit. Little trifling Businesses take up so much of my time, that I have little left for speculation, in which I could gladly employ my self, for my Eyes begin to grudge (that I may speak in Royall Style) me reading, and the Pen is not half so troublesom. But instead of that, I do everything to make me forget my self and the World as much as I can.'

About a month later he confesses to Ford that 'it would be an admirable Scituation to be neither Whig nor Tory. For a Man without Passions might find very strong Amusements.' A Man without Passions—party passions, national passions, religious passions—that is the definition of the true clerk, the intellectual, the scholar. One can admire Swift only this side idolatry and still regret that this 'indifference', this sublime

199

rational sentiment, had been his earlier in life. For he found that 'the turn of Blood at fifty' disposed him strongly to fears; he had lost his equanimity, as Wood's halfpence were soon to prove. But in the midst of his fears he was struggling for serenity, and through the course of *Gulliver's Travels* we see him gradually achieving it. They were finished, revised, and transcribed in his country cabin at Quilca, among the bogs and rocks. His last Voyage was to a race 'whose grand Maxim is, to cultivate *Reason*, and to be wholly governed by it'. 'Neither is *Reason* among them a Point problematical as with us, where Men can argue with Plausibility on both sides of a Question; but strikes you with immediate Conviction; as it needs must do where it is not mingled, obscured, or discoloured by Passion and Interest.' But it was a man already broken in health, weary of nerve, and empty of love, who made this discovery; leaving us to wonder that in such extremity such a masterpiece could be written.

(ii)

The prodigious succeess that awaited *Gulliver's Travels into several Remote Nations of the World* on its first appearance towards the end of the year 1726 came as a great surprise to both author and publisher. The publisher's hasty shifts have been revealed in recent years by various ingenious bibliographers; they have compared page with page, line with line and word with word, and in the end shown not only that three editions were published within a few weeks but that each of these editions was wholly or partly reset, and that Benjamin Motte, the publisher, unable to meet the demand single-handed, was compelled to utilize the services of more than one printing-house.[1] The first edition, apparently of several thousand copies, seems to have been sold out in about a week. The second edition was published about the middle

[1] A full account of all that concerns the Motte editions of *Gulliver's Travels* has been given by Mr. Harold Williams in the *Library* for December 1925.

of November, and the third possibly early in December. Two further editions were published by Motte in 1727, and still another in 1731; and in addition to these there had been two Irish editions and a serial publication in *Parker's Penny Post*. But it is of no account to pursue this enumeration; what matters is the revelation of the immediateness and completeness of the popularity of this extraordinary book.

Swift himself was not the man to lose his head over such good fortune; fourteen months after the event, in a letter to his publisher, he remarks in his detached way that 'the world glutted itself with that book at first, but now it will go off but soberly; but I suppose will not be soon worn out'. Not so soon, nor so soberly, as is suggested. *Gulliver* has sold year in year out; it stands with the Authorized Version and *The Pilgrim's Progress* as one of the three great precipitants of modern English usage, and rivals *Robinson Crusoe* in the amplitude of its secular appeal. It will perhaps be profitable to enquire into the causes which underlie this popularity—and this literary appeal; for the first step in any analysis is to realize a distinction here. There have always been two classes: those who are like the old gentleman who went to his map to search for Lilliput (or, more subtly, the bishop who hardly believed a word of it) and those who are like Pope and Arbuthnot and from the first see what the author is driving at. We shall not be far wrong if we ascribe the popularity of the book to the first class, and its position in English literature to the second. For of the first class are all children—of all sizes, ages, and epochs—who are open to be beguiled, innocently or ignorantly, by a tale of adventures. It is such as these, whose numbers are legion, that have kept the printing presses busy with these *Travels*: no other proposition is tolerable. For once to look into the dark pain and dreadful bitterness which lie beneath the verisimilitude of *Gulliver* is to resign the cloak of innocence and the mask of ignorance. Those who have found themselves so naked as this in the world are, for good or ill, too few to ensure the popularity of a book.

The critic, of course, must plunge into this harsher element, though he need not stay there: he will find a critical problem in the very popularity of Gulliver. We want to know what the elements are that in this book appeal so infallibly to some instinct within us. It is obvious, of course, that we like to be beguiled—to be taken out of ourselves, to forget ourselves in another world of fancy. It is a mental playtime, the daydream of our senses, and there is physical ease and rest in the process. But what in *Gulliver* secures this effect? That is the first question to ask, and it is decidedly to the point in any literary enquiry. For it will be found that effects of this kind are purely effects of style. In *Gulliver* we shall find two such distinctive features: the expression is direct and unobstructed, and the development of the narrative is continuous. As for the first of these, Johnson went to the heart of the subject, as he so often did in anything that concerned the technique of writing, when he wrote:

'His style was well suited to his thoughts, which are never subtilized by nice disquisitions, decorated by sparkling conceits, elevated by ambitious sentences, or variegated by far-sought learning. He pays no court to the passions; he excites neither surprise nor admiration; he always understands himself: and his reader always understands him: the peruser of Swift wants little previous knowledge: it will be sufficient that he is acquainted with common words and common things; he is neither required to mount elevations, nor to explore profundities; his passage is always on a level, along solid ground, without asperities, without obstruction.'

This is the perfect definition of a popular style, whose essence, apart from the unqualifiable merit of grammatical righteousness, lies in that simplicity which Johnson elsewhere characterized in the remark, 'the rogue never hazards a metaphor'. The appeal that is latent in all poetry and eloquence is an appeal to a higher and a rarer sensibility; and it was just this appeal which Swift could afford to neglect. He could venture in this way because he was supported by that other feature of his style—the economy and coherence of the narrated action. Of this Johnson's famous remark was, 'when once you have thought of big men and little men, it is very easy to do all the rest'. But that is a spiteful sally, unworthy of its author. The actual performance is more wonderful, and amounts to an extraordinary logic in which, once a few premises are granted, a whole fabric of history is created, seemingly accurate in its verisimilitude and action. Logic here becomes a substitute for imagination. In imagination the writer moves from a foundation of experience to a fictive evocation whose touchstone is the original experience: the process is logical in a way. But in *Gulliver* Swift's whole erection is based on fictive elements; and the verisimilitude is not due to his selection of the various elements, but to the way in which many particulars are deduced from a few general premises. The make-believe is not one of fancy, but of effect: we are gulled by the implacable machinery of the narration, and our interest is not at all an interest of passion or surprise (to use Johnson's words), but rather of curiosity and constructiveness.

In such a manner we can explain the popularity of *Gulliver*; for these elements—of simplicity, of make-believe, of 'constructive' rather than of 'creative' elaboration—are the elements which appeal to any mind irrespective of its sensibility or, in a certain sense, its intelligence. But *Gulliver*, of course, does not owe its singular position in the history of English literature to any such adventitious causes: they were quite beside the author's intention in writing the book, and have nothing to do with its implications. Of Swift's purpose we are assured in unequivocal terms that it is solely to vex the world. 'Drown the world! I am not content with despising it, but I would anger it, if I could with safety.' In these words he exposed his spleen to Pope towards the end of 1725, just about the time he was 'finishing, correcting, amending, and transcribing' his *Travels*. And it was in this splenetic mood that the book was born, though it is possible that it was conceived in a

PARTICULAR STUDIES

happier state. The first hint of the project goes back to 1714, the year of the Scriblerus Club; and there is now no doubt that the actual writing was begun by the spring of 1721.[1] The date is significant; for it was at this time that the drama of his relations with Stella and Vanessa was drawing him into a condition of insupportable anguish, and the state endured until it reached its climax in the death of Vanessa, which was in 1723. We may well believe that the circumstances of her death left Swift in mental anguish greater than any caused by the dilemma of her love for him during her life. But the tremendous distraction of Wood's halfpence and *The Drapier's Letters* came mercifully at this juncture and occupied his mind the greater part of the succeeding year. But, this incident over, Swift turned once more to the *Travels*, to prolong them and deepen them into that darkness of despair which is their final quality.

It is to the precise definition of this quality that we must now turn. It has commonly been described as irony; and Swift himself gave countenance to the term:

> *Arbuthnot is no more my friend*
> *Who dares to irony pretend*
> *Which I was born to introduce,*
> *Refin'd it first, and shew'd its use.*

And Mr. Charles Whibley, in his essay on Swift (the Leslie Stephen Lecture for 1917), which is perhaps the most understanding of modern interpretations of the man, strongly underlines this quality, describing Swift as 'a great master of irony—the greatest that has ever been born in these isles. Great enough to teach a lesson to Voltaire himself, and to inspire the author of *Jonathan Wild*'.

There exist in the English language a group of terms which, though precise enough when pondered sufficiently, describe subtle variations of temper, and are therefore frequently con-

[1] See Mr. Harold Williams' Introduction to the text of the first edition published by the First Edition Club, 1926.

fused in writing. These are satire, sarcasm, irony, cynicism, and the sardonic. It is not suggested that it is possible to define Swift's quality by any one of these terms: it would he possible to find in his writings specimens of them all. But if we consider *Gulliver*, and *Gulliver* is the most significant of all his works, we find in it an obvious consistency of mood which must be designated by a single term. Mr. Whibley (like Swift himself) would say irony. But there has been a general tendency to reject this term as too smooth, too suave in its connotation, to fit the savagery of *Gulliver*. Accordingly, the common voice has taken up cynicism. But one of the most convincing passages in Mr. Whibley's essay is devoted to a refusal of this term and to a refutation of the charge implied in it:

'Now the cynic may be defined as one who looks upon life and morals with an indifferent curiosity, whose levity persuades him to smile upon the views of others, and to let them go to destruction each his own way. Of this kind of cynicism Swift was wholly innocent. He may be absolved also of that cynicism which the dictionary defines as 'captious fault-finding'. The heart that was torn by *saeva indignatio*, to use a phrase from the epitaph he composed for himself, was no cynic's heart. The truth is that he was a born idealist, with no desire either to snarl or to smile at life. The master-passion of his mind was anger against injustice and oppression.'

This is valid criticism, and the only comment necessary is in the nature of a limitation of the word 'idealist'. For there are idealists of fancy and idealists of fact; idealists who would make the world consonant with their abstractions, and idealists who begin with a knowledge of cause and effect, and whose vision is a progressive sense of the issue of trial and error. These latter are better called rationalists; and reason was a very real term with Swift. The grand maxim of his beloved Houyhnhnms was 'to cultivate reason, and to be wholly governed by it'. The whole basis of the positive part of *Gulliver*, as implied, for example, in the criticisms of the King of Brobdingnag, is rational in the extreme. But this rational idealism was, from a cause which we shall proceed to investigate, brought to nothing by the prevalent pessimism of its author's mind.

Of satire and sarcasm there is, of an incidental kind, more than enough in *Gulliver*. These elements, we may again conjecture, go back to the early days of the conception; they come earliest in the book, and Arbuthnot and Pope were right in considering them the weakest part of it. The College of Projectors is the most obvious case in point. But if we reject satire and sarcasm as of no real account, and have disposed of cynicism, must we after all fall back on irony, or is there hope in the final term of our list—the sardonic?

All these terms have been clearly defined in Mr. Fowler's *Dictionary of Modern English Usage*. The definitions are there arranged in a tabular form, giving separately the motive or aim, the province, the method or means, and the audience, which each word should connote. Of satire the motive is given as 'amendment', the province as 'morals and manners', the method as 'accentuation', and the audience as 'the self-satisfied'. Similarly, sarcasm has for aim 'inflicting pain', for province 'faults and foibles', for method 'inversion', and for audience 'victim and bystander'. These definitions are obvious in their rightness, and the definition of cynicism only shows how justly Mr. Whibley has dismissed it from the province of Swift's writings. Its motive is 'self-justification', its province 'morals', its method 'exposure of nakedness', and its audience 'the respectable'. The motive is sufficient to exempt Swift here, however near the method be to that of *Gulliver*. The definition of irony is even more decisive, but, on the other hand, it is perhaps the least adequate of any in Mr. Fowler's table. The motive is given as 'exclusiveness', the province as 'statement of facts', the method as 'mystification', and the audience as 'an inner circle'. It is the motive again that defeats any application to Swift; but in this case the audience too is inadequate—or, if not inadequate, too ample. There was, indeed, an inner circle, but it was contracted nearly to a point.

We look finally at the definition of the sardonic. It has for motive 'self-relief', for province 'adversity'; its method is 'pessimism', and its audience 'self'. There is no evidence that the author of this definition had Swift in mind when he made it; but the conjunction of the two brings with it a sense of illumination, and the use of the word in this connection cannot ever again escape us. *Gulliver* responds in all its particulars when once it is considered as the release of a mind from the strain of an intense emotion. It is, perhaps, only too easy to be sentimental about Swift's curious love affairs. The facts are far from complete, and in the absence of facts, to sentimentalize is the easiest course. But the reality of Vanessa's passion is inescapable; and this passion was insinuated, with Swift's complicity, into the rather base and inhuman tyranny of his love for Stella. It is doubtful if any useful analysis can be made of the complex state of Swift's mind at this juncture; what might, by such means, be reduced to a pettiness in his character might equally well be revealed as a tragedy. Signs are not wanting of both possibilities; but, on either supposition, that mind had as issue from its intolerable strain the sardonic pages of *Gulliver*.

The application of these terms cannot be exclusive, and the more precise we make them the less generally can they serve us. But if it be admitted that the special quality of *Gulliver* is sardonic, and that this quality arises out of the special stress of mind under which the work was composed, then it is still possible that the term 'irony' might be of use in the description of a more normal condition of the same mind. The sardonic, that is to say, might presuppose the ironic. This is only true, however, if we abandon the special definition of irony which has been quoted; and this is legitimate because that definition has a special application to literature, being, in fact, the definition of a *genre*. But there is a wider connotation of the word which implies the general sentiment of mockery; and from this sense Swift can hardly be exempted. It would not generally be considered necessary so to exempt him; irony is a fashionable mode, and has to-day an esteem such as it also had in the eighteenth century. It is in this sense the hall-mark of an insincere age; and though Swift is the last man to be accused of a lack of sincerity, yet this provocative display of indirectness is the counterpart of a certain defect of character. This we may illustrate by reference to another age, when a sensitive nature might more honestly express its consciousness of this defect. The following extract is from Renan's intimate account of the life of his sister Henriette—a work surcharged with a kind of beauty totally foreign to the previous century:

'Sa religion du vrai ne souffrait pas la moindre note discordante. Un trait qui la blessa dans mes écrits fut un sentiment d'ironie qui m'obsédait et que je mêlais aux meilleures choses. Je n'avais jamais souffert, et je trouvais dans le sourire discret, provoqué par la faiblesse ou la vanité de l'homme, une certaine philosophie. Cette habitude la blessait, et je la lui sacrifiai peu à peu. Maintenant je reconnais combien elle avait raison. Les bons doivent être simplement bons; toute pointe de moquerie implique un reste de vanité et de défi personnel qu'on finit par trouver de mauvais goût.'

Any ironic attitude implies a sense of superiority, which is perhaps the same thing as the 'exclusiveness' of Mr. Fowler's definition. And though a sense of superiority may be well grounded in fact, it seldom takes the form of 'ironic philosophy' without involving the possessor of it in a certain vulgarity of sentiment hardly consistent with the right kind of superiority. Renan achieved the right kind precisely for the reason for which his detractors despise him. He came to recognize, as he so frankly states in this passage which we have quoted, that the good is *simply* good, and is not enhanced by oblique or indirect expression. Perhaps in his intimate moods even Swift recognized something of this—the *Journal to Stella* is the best evidence of certain moments of simple goodness; but his general lack of equanimity and directness is bound up with a certain weakness in his character which he was continually betraying. This is the unmeasured vanity of his ambitions and the insistent rancour of his disappointment:

'My greatest misery', he wrote to Bolingbroke in 1729, 'is recollecting the scene of twenty years past, and then all of a sudden dropping into the present. I remember, when I was a little boy, I felt a great fish at the end of my line which I drew up almost on the ground, but it dropped in, and the disappointment vexes me to this very day, and I believe it was the type of all my future disappointments.'

We might have sympathized more fully if the fish had been a less appropriate metaphor; but it is the type of the very worldly success which Swift always had in mind. Wealth was the immediate object of his desire, and if he could not obtain it by direct means he would have its equivalent in another way:

'All my endeavours from a boy, to distinguish myself, were only for want of a great title and fortune, that I might be used like a Lord by those who have an opinion of my parts—whether right or wrong, it is no great matter, and so the reputation of wit or great learning does the office of a blue ribbon, or a coach and six horses.'

This is from a letter to Pope, and there is no reason to doubt the essential truth of the confession. But even this prostitution of his talents might in a sense be condoned if we could be sure that success would have brought him the happiness he longed for; but the innate parsimony of his character forbids that assumption.

There is no evidence to show that Swift entered the Church with any other purpose than the calculating purpose of a careerist. Once committed to that way of life, he seems to have decided that what he could not gain by the talents appropriate to his calling (which he did not possess) he might gain by political intrigue. But at the height of his influence—and no man ever went higher—he found himself waiting in vain for his reward and a bishopric. The dilatoriness of his patrons need not, perhaps, be ascribed to the highest motives—it may be that Swift had made himself too useful a tool to be dispensed with, or too dangerous a one to be released. But it is also conceivable that Harley and Bolingbroke had more judgement than they were credited with, and more respect for the Church; and that they hesitated to confer the dignity of a see on one whose character they knew too well. They, or other advisers of the Queen, may have considered that the author of the *Tale of a Tub*, though endowed with wit, was lacking in learning. And this is the plain truth, if by learning we mean the appropriate mind.

Swift could write quizzically of Dr. George Berkeley, as he did in an otherwise kindly letter of recommendation to Lord Carteret; but if he had had more of Berkeley's humility he might have had some of his success. Berkeley is one of the contrasts that best illuminate Swift; for Berkeley had qualities of imagination and speculative intelligence which were totally wanting in the genius of Swift. It was this lack which justified to some extent Dryden's observation, which I shall deal with presently, that Swift was no poet. Whether we consider him as a writer or as a prospective bishop, this is a drastic limitation. It is not that it implies a lack of intellectual energy (Swift was inventive enough), but it does qualify the nature of that energy, making it operative on a lower plane and with a narrower range. The poet, who in this sense is not confined to verse, sees beyond his 'separate fantasy'; he perceives the 'clear universe of things around', and from this perception he derives a sense of sublimity and an eloquence to which Swift was a total stranger.

There is a very significant passage, in one of the letters to Pope which has already been quoted, in which Swift owns La Rochefoucauld as his 'favourite'—'because I found my whole character in him'. This is not the only reference to La Rochefoucauld in Swift's correspondence; and from another passage it would seem that he had made Vanessa read his favourite. This direct connection is worth emphasizing; for, though Swift pretended to base his view of human nature on his own observations, it is possible that his mortification was soothed

by no other influence so agreeable as the disconsolate philosophy of the French maxim-writer—a philosophy which, like
Swift's, was derived from the limited field of Court intrigues
and politics rather than from the world at large. Now La
Rochefoucauld has his perfect foil and critic in Vauvenargues;
and what Vauvenargues wrote of La Rochefoucauld very
perfectly fits the case of Swift:

'Le duc de La Rochefoucauld a saisi admirablement le côté
faible de l'esprit humain; peut-être n'en a-t-il pas ignoré la
force; peut-être n'a-t-il contesté le mérite de tant d'actions
éblouissantes, que pour démasquer la fausse sagesse. Quelles
qu'aient été ses intentions, l'effet m'en parait pernicieux; son
livre, rempli d'invectives contre l'hypocrisie, détourne, encore
aujourd'hui, les hommes de la vertu, en leur persuadant qu'il
n'y en a point de véritable.'

This is merely an introduction to a note in which Vauvenargues does full justice to the real greatness of La Rochefoucauld. He does, however, add a qualification relating to
the latter's style: La Rochefoucauld 'n'était pas peintre, talent
sans lequel il est bien difficile d'être éloquent'—and with
Vauvenargues, as we shall see in the next essay, eloquence is
the sign of true greatness (*granduer d'âme*). It is to Vauvenargues's very character, indeed, that we should go for a further
contrast; for Vauvenargues in his unhappy life suffered disappointments quite comparable with Swift's, but from his
state there issued one of the most equable and courageous
views of life that has ever found expression. Vauvenargues
tried to show that the *grandeur d'âme* which was for him the
greatest of realities was something as natural as bodily health:
it was the power to be superior to one's misfortune and the
power to control other men by virtue of one's patience, deeds,
or counsels. The error of Swift's philosophy lies in the unifor-
mity and perfection of its pessimism; and the best answer to
the misanthropy of *Gulliver* is to be found in these lines of
Vauvenargues:

'Les inégalités de la vertu, les faiblesses qui l'accompagnent, les vices qui flétrissent les plus belles vies, ces défauts inséparables de notre nature, mêlée si manifestement de grandeur et de petitesse, n'en détruisent pas les perfections. Ceux qui veulent que les hommes soient tout bons ou tout méchants, absolument grands ou petits, ne connaissent pas la nature. Tout est mélangé dans les hommes; tout y est limité; et le vice même y a ses bornes.'

Style is the touchstone of all these matters; and though Swift's style cannot be sufficiently praised for its vigour, clarity, and economy, yet it must be recognized that here too Swift has the limitations that belong to his character. Johnson was again percipient in a matter of technique. 'For purposes merely didactic' this style is the best of all. 'But against that inattention by which known truths are suffered to lie neglected it makes no provision; it instructs, but it does not persuade.' Vauvenargues would say it lacks eloquence—not that eloquence of words, which is better called invective, and in which Swift excelled, but the eloquence of ideas and sentiments. In this sense 'l'éloquence vaut mieux que le savoir'.

'Tout ce qu'on a jamais dit du prix de l'éloquence n'en est qu'une faible expression. Elle donne la vie à tout: dans les sciences, dans les affaires, dans la conversation, dans la composition, dans la recherche même des plaisirs, rien ne peut réussir sans elle. Elle se joue des passions des hommes, les émeut, les calme, les pousse, et les détermine à son gré: tout cède à son voix; elle seule enfin est capable de se célébrer dignement.'

Eloquence in this sense is mind's highest reach and widest conquest. It is the creative energy of life itself, manifested on those frontiers which we call variously religion, philosophy, and poetry. But in all these forms eloquence was denied to Swift; and without eloquence he was at the mercy of his passions. For a time he could temporize, and so give us *Gulliver's Travels*; but the disruptive forces could not for ever be held in check; and then, as Thackeray said, 'thinking of him is like thinking of an empire falling'.

(iii)

That the author of *A Tale of a Tub* and *Gulliver's Travels* should also be a considerable poet upsets the neat classifications of the literary historian; and even his contemporaries were not willing to admit his claim. On this subject every one knows Dryden's famous remark, repeated by Johnson: 'Cousin Swift, you will never be a poet.' This was justly inspired by a certain Pindaric Ode written to the 'Athenian Society', which begins in this strain:

> As when the deluge first began to fall,
>   That mighty ebb never to flow again,
> When this huge body's moisture was so great,
>   It quite o'ercame the vital heat;
> That mountain which was highest, first of all
> Appear'd above the universal main,
> To bless the primitive sailor's weary sight;
> And 'twas perhaps Parnassus, if in height
>   It be as great as 'tis in fame,
>   And nigh to Heaven as is its name;
> So, after the inundation of a war,
> When Learning's little household did embark,
> With her world's fruitful system, in her sacred ark,
>   At the first ebb of noise and fears,
> Philosophy's exalted head appears. . . .

There is no sensible quickening of this pedestrian pace anywhere else in the Ode, which is long and desperately wearisome; there is not a single line with which a partisan of Swift could challenge Dryden's judgement. But the Ode was written by a young man of twenty-four; the Pindaric style was imposed upon him by the fashion of the time; and had he never written in another style, he would never have outlived Dryden's damnation.

But we cannot be sure that this side of Swift's genius is properly appreciated even now, with the whole bulk of his verse before us. That bulk is considerable (more than 1,000 pages of the Oxford edition edited by Mr. Harold Williams), and there is no doubt that Swift was a poet in his own estimation. In the estimation of others he has not fared so well. Goldsmith was willing to place him for poetic genius in the same rank as Milton, Dryden, and Pope; but the more representative estimate for the eighteenth century is that of Johnson:

'In the Poetical Works of Dr. Swift there is not much upon which the critick can exercise his powers. They are often humorous, almost always light, and have the qualities which recommend such compositions, easiness, and gaiety. They are, for the most part, what their author intended. The diction is correct, the numbers are smooth, and the rhymes exact. There seldom occurs a hard-laboured expression, or a redundant epithet; all his verses exemplify his own definition of a good style, they consist of *proper words in proper places*.'

The only critic who has since dared to qualify this Johnsonian estimate is Taine, whose nationality perhaps secured for him the necessary detachment. Taine, it is true, is still impeded by a certain presupposition about the nature of poetry: but who, among the critics of a romantic age, is free? 'Ce qui manque le plus à ses vers c'est la poésie. L'esprit positif ne peut ni l'aimer ni l'entendre; il n'y voit qu'une machine ou une mode, et ne l'emploie que par vanité ou convention. . . . Je ne me rappelle pas une seule ligne de lui qui indique un sentiment vrai de la nature; il n'apercevait dans les forêts que des bûches et dans les champs que des sacs de grain.' But if he could fall into this error (which we shall comment on presently) Taine could in return appreciate those aspects of genius which transcend academic distinctions, and cry out his admiration in these magnificent terms:

'Mais, dans les sujets prosaïques, quelle vérité et quelle force! Comme cette mâle nudité rabaisse l'élégance cherchée et la poésie artificielle d'Addison et de Pope! Jamais d'épithètes; il laisse sa pensée telle qu'elle est, l'estimant pour elle-même et pour elle seule, n'ayant besoin ni d'ornements, ni de préparations, ni d'allongements, élevé au-dessus des procédés métier, des conventions d'école, de la vanité de rimailleur, des difficultés de l'art, maître de son sujet et de lui-même. Cette simplicité et ce naturel étonnent en des vers. Ici, comme ailleurs, son originalité est entière et son génie créateur; il dépasse son siècle classique et timide; il s'asservit la forme, il la brise, il y ose tout dire, il ne lui épargne aucune crudité. Reconaissez la grandeur dans cette invention et dans cette audace; celui-là seul est un homme supérieur qui trouve tout et ne copie rien.'

Magnificent? But not altogether true. For this picture of a giant breaking through all bonds, scorning all obstructions, master of his subject and of himself, is a romantic half-truth. In reality, before he can be master of himself and of his subject this giant must forge new chains. He cannot break an old form without finding himself under the necessity of creating a new one; and the grandeur and audacity of the poet Swift lies not in his lack of all convention, but in his discovery of his own. He found the Pindaric style uncongenial to the substance of his inspiration; for him it had no meaning and no sympathetic appeal. If he had meekly accepted Dryden's reproof he would never have written another verse. But he realized that although he might not be a poet in Dryden's sense, the poetry within him was too real to be refused expression.

Dryden died when Swift was only thirty-three. It is just possible that he may have seen 'Mrs. Frances Harris's Petition', which is one of the first of Swift's poems in an original manner. If so, it is difficult to believe that in his wise tolerance he would not have recognized its kinship with Chaucer, whom he praised so greatly. Mrs. Harris is as vivid as the Wife of Bath, and the verses in which she li es are a miracle of humorous invention. It must be admitted that we never find in Swift that 'rude sweetness of a Scotch tune' which Dryden rather grudgingly allowed to Chaucer, but in the poems which we would make the basis of an apology for him, the very accents of human speech are imposed upon the rhythm, giving it an

PARTICULAR STUDIES

actuality in which mere sweetness is transcended. It is doubtful whether Dryden would have admitted this quality into his poetic code, for with all his tolerance he reverted always to certain abstract categories against which he judged present performances. Of his English predecessors he was always ready to insist 'the times were ignorant in which they lived'. Of much of Shakespeare that we habitually admire, he would remark: 'What a pudder is here kept in raising the expression of trifling thoughts.'

Dryden's is the finest expression in English criticism of what we may term a traditional classicism. But there is another type of classicism, not necessarily an alternative type, which must be briefly delineated before we can justify Swift's right to the name of poet. We would call it a natural classicism, and it arises precisely from that effort to find new forms to match new substances for which Swift is notable. Dryden's abstract categories of verse were based on the best classical models; the problem was, how to mould our rough island speech into these golden numbers. But it is possible to conceive another kind of abstraction which is based on the inherent qualities of the poetic substance: the form is inherent in the substance, and the problem is one of elucidation.

There is no evidence that Swift ever posed the problem in this categorical manner, but the moral of 'The Battle of the Books', if it has one, tends in this direction. Ancient and Modern are terms conveying no necessary virtue; all alike must be submitted to a clear judgement, and the same judgement prevails in the act of composition. It is the presence of judgement, with the purpose of fitting form to substance, that determines the classical quality of the poet's work. The first instructions which Swift gives to 'a young beginner' in that ironic masterpiece, 'On Poetry—a Rhapsody', are meant seriously enough:

> Consult yourself; and if you find
> A powerful impulse urge your mind,

Impartial judge within your breast
What subject you can manage best;
Whether your genius most inclines
To satire, praise, or humorous lines,
To elegies in mournful tone,
Or prologue sent from hand unknown.
Then, rising with Aurora's light,
The Muse invoked, sit down to write;
Blot out, correct, insert, refine,
Enlarge, diminish, interline;
Be mindful, when invention fails,
To scratch your head, and bite your nails.

There can be no doubt that Swift found in himself a powerful impulse to write verse, and though at first, as we have seen, he attempted a form not suited to his genius, he soon abandoned these artificial exercises. The forms that he then adopted he made essentially his own. In his introduction to the essay which he devoted to Swift's verse[1] the late Dr. Elrington Ball remarked that 'no exact prototype is to be found for Swift's style of versification. It has been described as Hudibrastic, but the influence of Samuel Butler was only partial. In its construction Swift laid under contribution all classes of metrical composition from the Elizabethan age to his own, ephermeral songs and ballads no less than the standard writings of poets and dramatists.' We have already quoted Johnson's testimony to the technical perfection of Swift's verse, and indeed that has never been in question. It is the substance which we are called upon to justify.

Goldsmith said that Swift was the first poet who dared to describe nature as it is with all its deformities, and to give exact expression to a turn of thought alike dry, sarcastic, and severe. It was for this courage that he placed him in the same rank as Milton, Dryden, and Pope. This shows that the poet

[1] *Swift's Verse.* An Essay, by F. Elrington Ball, Litt.D. (London: Murray, 1929.)

of 'The Deserted Village' had none of the prejudices about the
nature of poetry which have distinguished many other poets
and critics in the presence of Swift's verse. The assumption of
such people is that poetry connotes but one half of life—things
of beauty, sentiments of pleasure, innocence of experience.
This is the attitude represented by *The Golden Treasury*, a
justly famous anthology which has nevertheless done more
to prevent a catholic appreciation of English poetry than any
other single book or influence. Its sub-title 'Of the best Songs
and Lyrical Poems' is always ignored; 'Lyrical' is silently
equated with 'poetical'. There is an ironic justice in the fact
that the only poem in the volume which reflects in any
realistic manner the darker aspects of life should contain the
lines:

> *Make no deep scrutiny*
> *Into her mutiny.*

But that is just what Swift was bent on doing. His whole life
was one long mutiny—mutiny against the darkness of fate,
the injustice of men, the baseness of our natural instincts, the
indignity of our bodily functions—and his work is a deep
scrutiny into these depths. It is possible to say that Swift's
reaction to life was morbid. Mr. Ellis Roberts once expressed
this point of view in an interesting essay which he published
with a selection of Swift's poems.[1] He said:

'In this matter Swift exhibits all the signs of an enormous
neurasthenia. To the neurasthenic anything which comes
regularly and in routine is liable to become intolerable. Not
all of life, fortunately, will so change its character. Different
sufferers will become victims of different fears. . . . With
Swift it was, at last, always this one thing. The boudoir, the
closet, the double bed . . . his fancy only has to stray to one
of them—and it strayed far too often—and he writhes helpless,
indignant, outraged, in pangs which make him for ever of the

[1] *Miscellaneous Poems*, by Jonathan Swift, D.D. Edited by R. Ellis
Roberts; decorated with Engravings on Wood, by Robert Gibbings.
(The Golden Cockerel Press, 1928.)

company of those artists who pace, like the damned souls whom Vathek saw on the fiery and reverberating pavements of hell, each with his hand over his heart, and each with a heart of burning flame.'

Mr. Roberts in another place in his essay says of Swift that 'he does not delight in filth, as Rabelais: nor has he the curiosity, intellectual, sombre, enragedly humorous, into sexual life which marks Mr. James Joyce's work; Swift's attitude is one of plain, simple, immediate reaction.' Both these statements are true in intention, and so far illuminating; their fault is that they conjure up, in a slight degree, the romantic giant of Taine's invention. They do not, that is to say, sufficiently convey the cool deliberateness of Swift's pen. The man who wrote 'A Beautiful Young Nymph Going to Bed', 'The Progress of Marriage', 'The Lady's Dressing Room', 'Strephon and Chloe', and other such grim pieces was certainly indignant, but he was not helpless. He was always, in Taine's words, 'maître de son sujet et de lui-même'. If he had a tendency to be neurasthenic (and what man of sensibility is free from it?), then it is more than likely that in his poetry he purged himself of this anguish. But is it possible, the reader of *The Golden Treasury* may ask, to dignify with the name of poetry such dross of a diseased sensibility?

To this question we must answer, that the relations of art to life are so intricate that they do not permit of a neat separation into categories. It is impossible to define art by its substance; it is impossible to define it by its form. All we can say is that substance determines form, and that if from the substance we can proceed to the form, then the work of art is in being. The power needed to pass from substance to form, from matter to essence, is the specific creative impulse, an intense awareness of sensibility in the individual. The direction of this power is arbitrary; that is to say, it depends on the particular environment or constitution of the individual, and one might as well complain of the varieties of colour given by the light of the sun, as of the varieties of art reflected by the mind of man.

PARTICULAR STUDIES

5
VAUVENARGUES

'Revenons avec Vauvenargues à la pureté de la langue, à la
sérénité des pensées et à l'intégrité morale'—these words, with
which Sainte-Beuve opened his essay on Vauvenargues, an-
nounce the three essential aspects of one of the most interesting
figures in the history of French literature. Sainte-Beuve saw in
Vauvenargues a return, after a period of frivolity and insincerity, to the seriousness of the seventeenth century; he found
in his work a presentiment of the new seriousness that was to
distinguish the remainder of the eighteenth century. Vauvenargues was born in 1715 and died in 1747; in 1715 Fénelon
had died; Bayle had died nine years earlier; Bossuet died in
1704, and Pascal, who was of the same generation, preceded
Bossuet by more than forty years. The world in 1715 seemed
as empty as it did in 1915, and continued to be empty during
Vauvenargues's life as it continues in ours—empty of grace, of
faith, of fervour, and magnanimity. It is because Vauvenargues
revolted against the shallowness of his age that he has a peculiar
value for ours, not only because that shallowness has something in common with ours, but more particularly because
the experiences of Vauvenargues, and the events which brought
about his disillusion and caused his fervour, were very similar
to the common experiences and universal events of our own
time. His actuality arises from the fact that on the basis of his
experiences and out of the depth of his disillusior.ment he
built up a possible philosophy of life.

VAUVENARGUES

There is a certain obvious parallelism between the historical situation as it existed at the end of the seventeenth century and beginning of the eighteenth century and the situation that has faced us at the end of the nineteenth century and beginning of the twentieth. A century of genius is behind us as it was behind the contemporaries of Vauvenargues. Genius cannot be manufactured at will, but its works may be made the basis of a tradition. Instead of a tradition, however, the reaction to a period of self-confidence usually takes the shape of a resignation to despair; and just as Vauvenargues's contemporaries turned for their mortification to a typical prophet of despair like La Rochefoucauld, so nowadays, lacking a La Rochefoucauld, we exalt a company of minor prophets. The *Maximes* had the inestimable advantage of precision: to-day our introspective energies must be expended on drearier wastes of self-analysis.

Vauvenargues was the eldest son of an impoverished aristocrat of Aix in Provence. He was destined for the Army because the Army was the only career that a man of his birth and his poverty could honourably embrace. We gather from his letters and from many observations in his writings which bear on his own character that he was by temperament and physique ill suited to the conditions of army life. This does not mean that he despised the profession of arms or deplored the necessity of wars: he rather tended to idealize military virtues and to see in heroic deeds the only sanction of glory. 'Il n'y a pas de gloire achevée sans celle des armes' is one of his own maxims. He saw immediate active service in the War of the Polish Succession, which broke out between France and the Empire in 1733. But it was one of the most uninspiring campaigns in history; and though we have no personal records for this period, we can be sure that it offered Vauvenargues few opportunities of testing his idealism. His regiment spent two years in Italy, with little fighting and long intervals of demoralizing idleness. The campaign was a farce, but it took the five years of peace that followed it to complete the disillusionment of a spirit strong enough to survive the disappointments of an inglorious war. For this period we have the evidence of a number of letters written by Vauvenargues to his friends at Aix, the Marquis de Mirabeau and Jules François Paul Fauris de Saint-Vincens. We gather that he had little in common with his fellow-officers, and hated the distractions with which they whiled away their time. Vauvenargues was gentle by nature, plain looking, weak-sighted, and, though not spiritless, timid in physique. He laid himself out to be popular, but he was too diffident to secure that social prestige upon which peace-time promotion depends. Perhaps he took life too seriously: we may be sure that he aroused distrust and suspicion in his companions by his occasional solemnity, his self-consciousness and by all the little awkwardnesses inseparable from a sensitive and reflective habit of mind. The result of the conflict between such a mind and its environment is invariable: the mind retires on itself, idealizes itself and formulates those introverted fantasies which are the material of an imaginative life.

The campaign in Italy had been a farce, but Vauvenargues was not destined to escape the grimmer realities of war. The Bohemian campaign of 1741-3 was one of the most distressful in European history; with the exception of intensive shelling, poison gas, and stagnant trenches, it is doubtful if modern war could excel its horrors. Vauvenargues left France with his regiment in July 1741 as part of an army under the command of the Maréchal de Belle-Île. In November the French troops assaulted and captured Prague with an ease that proved fatal. For, once ensconced there, they found themselves deserted by their allies the Prussians and surrounded by the hostile Austrians. They were trapped in the city they had so easily captured. The winter went by, and then month by month the following year, with no sign of relief. Supplies became very scarce. By August the French were killing their horses for food, and suffering terribly from want of salt. Rumours of relief, as ever, proved false, and as another winter approached the Army began to despair. Belle-Île grew desperate, and on the night of December 16th secretly left Prague with fourteen thousand men, and by forced marches hastened across country towards Bavaria. It was the Retreat from Moscow on a smaller scale, but the quality of the misery was the same. Hundreds of men died on the wayside, overcome by fatigue and the intense cold. When the Army after ten days reached friendly territory at Eger, it is related that many of the men collapsed and died, some of them 'through having gone too close to the fire'. Belle-Île's forces did not finally reach France until the spring of 1743. There they remained at rest until June, when once again they crossed the Rhine and took part in the battle of Dettingen.

But Vauvenargues was now a broken man. He was permanently injured by frost-bite and had contracted a lung disease of which he was to die four years later. He was weary in spirit too. At Prague he had lost a young friend, Hippolyte de Seytres, in whose ardour and intelligence Vauvenargues saw the very qualities he had idealized made actual. Here again Vauvenargues seems to anticipate one of the bitterest of our recent experiences: we read of Hippolyte de Seytres and think of Wilfred Owen, of Otto Braun, of Charles Péguy, and of many others, their names not recorded in elegies. Vauvenargues's *Discours sur les Plaisirs, Discours sur la Gloire,* and *Conseils à un Jeune Homme,* were all written for de Seytres; and the fervour of their idealization gives us a measure of the pathos which lies hidden under the rather formal periods of the actual 'Éloge funèbre' which Vauvenargues wrote on his friend. Vauvenargues now began to seek a different path to glory. On his return from Bohemia he had applied for an appointment at Court, or in the Diplomatic Service, but without receiving any acknowledgement. After Dettingen he renewed his application, none too tactfully. He waited in vain for a reply, growing more impatient every day. Finally, in January 1744 he resigned his commission, and completely spoilt any chances he had of other employment by the tone of righteous indignation with which he invested his action.

He had no money—not even enough to take him to Paris. He negotiated a loan and reached the capital in February. He was not entirely without hope, for during this post-war period he had formed a connection with the most famous writer of the day. This new friend was no less a person than Voltaire, and there is nothing prettier in the history of literature than the way in which the elder man from the first gave understanding and encouragement to this strange aspirant to literary fame. In 1743 Voltaire was already famous throughout Europe. He received from an unknown officer in the Army an essay on the respective merits of Racine and Corneille. Not a very original theme, and not one which was likely to kindle the weary eye of a busy man of letters. But Voltaire read the essay and was impressed. He made enquiries about the social standing of the young officer who had written to him, and was flattered. Miss Wallas in an interesting study which she has devoted to the life and thought of Vauvenargues,[1] gives a good description of what happened:

'Voltaire was pleased by what he heard and pleased by what he had read in Vauvenargues's letter. He loved admiration and gratitude, he was fond of giving literary advice, and he was genuinely kind. He had already given help and criticism to a number of struggling young writers, and the idea of adding an intelligent Army officer to the mixed collection of his admirers delighted him. The comparison between Corneille and Racine, which reflected the usual eighteenth-century preference for Racine, was not very interesting in itself; and the essay as a whole was slight and loosely constructed. But Voltaire discerned, and the fact does honour to his critical powers, the traces of a fine intelligence in some of Vauvenargues's general reflections on literary "taste". The remark that "good taste" is "a quick and true feeling for natural beauty", and a passage at the end of the letter describing the differences in

[1] *Luc de Clapiers, Marquis de Vauvenargues.* By Mary Wallas. (Cambridge University Press, 1928.)

taste which result from individual differences in intelligence and sensitiveness were a proof that the writer possessed that veiled and discreet type of originality which the French call "finesse", and which even the eighteenth-century critics were not afraid to admire. ". . . Depuis que j'entends raisonner sur le goût", wrote Voltaire, "je n'ai rien vu de si fin et de si approfondi que ce que vous m'avez fait l'honneur de m'écrire."'

Vauvenargues, in common with the aristocrats of his time and in spite of his genuine urge to express himself, had hitherto despised the profession of letters, and earlier in his life had rejected with scorn the suggestion that he should adopt it. Even now, encouraged by the serious consideration which Voltaire gave to his apprentice essay, he only thought of using his literary gifts to make sure of his diplomatic mission. Voltaire, who was in favour at this time, no doubt helped his cause considerably, and Vauvenargues seems to have been definitely promised some employment. He went home to Aix to await his call, and while there met with a last malign stroke of fate. He caught the smallpox, which left him weaker than ever—his sight almost gone, his face disfigured. A diplomatic career was now out of the question. He was reduced to the last and most despised instrument of glory—the pen. He felt he had very little longer to live (actually he only lived two more years); but this time he resolved to devote to the perfection of a philosophy of life, observing his own maxim: That to accomplish anything worth while, a man must always live as if he were never going to die.

The conversion of a man of action into a man of letters is a difficult process. Perhaps Vauvenargues was never essentially a man of action—only such by necessity. The problem in that case becomes the merely technical one of the conversion of experience into expression. The problem is made none the easier if experience has led to disillusionment. Vauvenargues was disillusioned and sick in body and mind, but he differed from most of his modern counterparts in not being deprived of some kind of faith in life. Integrity and courage are useless without this simple faith. The case of Vauvenargues is all the more interesting because the basis of his faith in life was not religious: it was a kind of stoicism. He would probably have accepted the doctrine of original sin in all its essentials, but he refused to convert that dogma into a fatalistic drama, as Pascal did. Original virtue was just as patent to him as original sin; man was stretched between the polarity of good and evil, and not the gift of grace, but the practice of courage, was necessary for salvation. Nevertheless, Vauvenargues is in many senses a disciple of Pascal; Pascal's thought acted as a continual inspiration to him. 'He moves the mind,' he wrote of Pascal, 'startles it and illuminates it and forces it to feel the power of truth'; and this was a deliberate opinion held in the face of Voltaire's derision.

Miss Wallas, in her criticism of Vauvenargues's thought, makes too much of its incompleteness and confusion. She has perhaps fallen into the common error of imagining that the construction of a system of philosophy is a proof of systematic thought; it is more often an elaborate façade designed to hide a structure of meaner dimensions. Sainte-Beuve was nearer the truth when he said that Vauvenargues in his modest fashion brings to morals something of the universal and all-embracing genius of a Leibniz—that what he lacked was no more than time to develop. In his maxims and scattered fragments we can recognize not a wayward and merely inquisitive mind but a universal vision.

'Vauvenargues a l'âme antique'—that is another of Sainte-Beuve's decisive phrases. Like so many great men, Vauvenargues had been profoundly influenced by the reading of Plutarch's *Lives*, as well as by Seneca and the supposed letters of Brutus to Cicero. There is an enlightening passage in one of his letters to his friend Mirabeau:

'I used to weep with joy when I read those *Lives*; I could never spend a night without speaking to Alcibiades, to Agesilaus and others; I used to go into the Forum at Rome to harangue with the Gracchi, or to defend Cato when he was being stoned. . . . There fell into my hands about the same time, I don't know by what chance, a volume of Seneca; and later, some letters which Brutus wrote to Cicero at the time he was in Greece, after Caesar's death. These letters are so full of dignity, fine feeling, passion and courage, that I found it quite impossible to read them in cold blood; I read these three books together, and I was so moved that I could no longer restrain the feelings they aroused in me; I choked, I left my books, I tore out like a man in a rage, and ran as hard as I could several times up and down a fairly long terrace, until at last tiredness put an end to my agitation.'

Such is the true mode of initiation into the power of eloquence. It is the true initiation into the reality of glory.

'Nowhere else but in those fortunate centuries', Vauvenargues wrote in the same letter to Mirabeau, 'does one so well get the measure of the strength and magnitude of the human heart and spirit; liberty reveals, in the very excess of crime, the real greatness of our soul; there the forces of Nature shine out in the depths of corruption; there you have virtue without limits, pleasures without infamy, intelligence without affectation, dignity without vanity, vice without baseness and without disguises.'

Vauvenargues was twenty-five when he wrote this letter; the Bohemian campaign was still in front of him, but his analysis of the Roman virtues shows even at that time a certain realism and a recognition of natural imperfections which experience was to confirm. But neither in history nor in life did Vauvenargues find any justification for despair.

Instead of admitting despair, he sought glory. Glory is now a discredited word, and it will be difficult to re-establish it. It has been spoilt by a too close association with military grandeur; it has been confused with fame and ambition. But true glory is a private and discreet virtue, and is only fully realized in solitariness. It is not Vauvenargues, but Traherne in his *Centuries of Meditations*, who has given us the true definition of glory:

227

'The noble inclination whereby man thirsteth after riches and dominion is his highest virtue, when rightly guided; and carries him as in a triumphant chariot, to his sovereign happiness. Men are made miserable only by abusing it. Taking a false way to satisfy it, they pursue the wind; nay, labour in the very fire, and after all reap but vanity. Whereas, as God's love, which is the fountain of all, did cost us nothing; so were all other things prepared by it to satisfy our inclinations in the best of manners, freely, without any cost of ours. Seeing therefore that all satisfactions are near at hand, by going further we do but leave them; and wearying ourselves in a long way round about, like a blind man, forsake them. They are immediately near to the very gate of our senses. It becometh the bounty of God to prepare them freely: to make them glorious, and their enjoyment easy. For because His love is free, so are His treasures. He therefore that will despise them because he hath them is marvellously irrational: the way to possess them is to esteem them. And the true way of reigning over them is to break the world all into parts, to examine them asunder. And if we find them so excellent that better could not possibly be made, and so made they could not be more ours, to rejoice in all with pleasure answerable to the merit of their Goodness. We being then Kings over the whole world, when we restore the pieces to their proper places, being perfectly pleased with the whole composure. This shall give you a thorough grounded contentment, far beyond what troublesome wars or conquests can acquire.'

Vauvenargues often tries to reach such a definition of glory, but its real nature eludes him; it is for him something indefinable. In its essence it is a thing intangible, like light, and light and glory have always been associated together—Heaven, for example, being a City of Light and Glory. In Vauvenargues's sense, glory is the radiance in which virtues flourish. The love of glory is the sanction of great deeds; all greatness and magnanimity proceed not from calculation but from an instinctive desire for the quality of glory. Glory is distinguished from

228

fortune, because fortune exacts care; you must connive with your fellows and compromise yourself in a thousand ways to make sure of its fickle favours. Glory is gained directly, if one has the genius to deserve it: glory is 'sudden. If we despise glory, it is because we lack virtue.

For Traherne, on the other hand, glory was the sum of all things tangible and concrete:

'By the very right of your senses you enjoy the World. Is not the beauty of the Hemisphere present to your eye? Doth not the glory of the Sun pay tribute to your sight? Is not the vision of the World an amiable thing? Do not the stars shed influences to perfect the Air? Is that not a marvellous body to breathe in? To visit the lungs, repair the spirits, revive the senses, cool the blood, fill the empty spaces between the Earth and Heavens, and yet give liberty to all objects? Prize these first, and you shall enjoy the residue: Glory, Dominion, Power, Wisdom, Honour, Angels, Souls, Kingdoms, Ages.'

For such glories man is insatiable, and insatiableness is good. 'It is of the nobility of man's soul that he is insatiable.' Perhaps the difference between Traherne and Vauvenargues in this respect is that Vauvenargues, like Malory before him and in common with the whole tradition of chivalry, saw in glory a reflection of the esteem of other men; whereas Traherne, more profoundly, found glory not in the active pursuit of worship but in the quiet possession of the objective world. 'The service of things and their excellences are spiritual, being objects not of the eye but of the mind; and you are more spiritual by how much more you esteem them.' And further:

'Till your spirit filleth the whole world, and the stars are your jewels; till you are as familiar with the ways of God in all Ages as with your walk and table; till you are intimately acquainted with that shady nothing out of which the world was made; till you love men so as to desire their happiness, with a thirst equal to the zeal of your own; till you delight in God for being good to all: you never enjoy the world. Till you more feel it than your private estate, and are more present

229

in the Hemisphere, considering the glories and the beauties there, than in your own house: till you remember how lately you were made, and how wonderful it was when you came into it: and more rejoice in the palace of your glory, than if it had been made but to-day morning.'

Traherne's doctrine proceeds from metaphysical meditation, Vauvenargues's from action; but both are spiritual. But Vauvenargues's doctrine is more limited, its sources being in individual experience rather than in universal knowledge. In so far as his faith was reinforced by reading, it was such as Plutarch provided, and in Plutarch glory is the reward only of heroes. Perhaps this was Vauvenargues's fundamental belief. But he had already discerned, in his *Introduction à la Connaissance de l'Esprit humain*, an essential connection between glory and eloquence. There are two kinds of eloquence—the eloquence of words, which consists in saying with ease and aptness whatever comes into one's head; and the eloquence of ideas or sentiments, which force their own appropriate expression. The latter kind is true eloquence, and it is a characteristic of all great men, not merely of great writers. Eloquence is the expression of glory: glory in words, not of words.

Vauvenargues's own experience tended to show that action alone could not encompass glory; that fate and the imperfections of fortune easily overwhelm the strongest will. Any career involving relations with other men is impure to that extent. All virtue is the outcome of a solitary strife. Glory is solitary. All that can be gained openly is the fame that is dependent on fortune. Glory must be sought in the interior court of Traherne's great asseveration: 'To think well is to serve God in the interior court.' There the act is direct eloquence. Sensation and idea unite to create the exact image of truth. Vauvenargues himself said:

'Those who are born eloquent speak with such great clearness and brevity on great subjects, that most other people do not realize that they are speaking with profundity. Sophists and cold calculating spirits fail to recognize philosophy when eloquence gives it a universal appeal, daring to paint the truth in bold and vigorous strokes. They treat as superficial and frivolous this splendour of expression which is in itself the hall-mark of great thoughts.'

There is, in this and in all Vauvenargues's observations on truth, a feeling for what later in the century came to be known as 'sentiment'. He distrusted the 'reason', both in the seventeenth-century sense of austerity, severity, and repression, and in the eighteenth-century sense of scientific materialism. 'La raison nous trompe plus souvent que la nature' was one of his maxims. Vauvenargues let some personal quality, which we can only vaguely call 'tenderness', colour his thoughts. 'Les grandes pensées viennent du cœur' is one of his most famous sayings, but it is meant in no sentimental fashion. He anticipates Rousseau, but not Rousseau's abasement of the intellect. There is a saving virtue in Vauvenargues's epithet 'grandes'. It implies eloquence, and eloquence, as we have seen, is glory sublimated. Glory is far from any conception we may have of Rousseau. The tenderness of Vauvenargues is no more than a sense of the instinctive basis of so much of our life. Miss Wallas remarks:

'There existed in Vauvenargues's mind a distinction, inherited through centuries from the earliest Greek thinkers, between the 'natural' or instinctive and the acquired or artificial elements in human behaviour. He felt that 'passion' was one of the most unalterable elements in man because it was one of the most 'natural', and that the 'reason' of the Stoics and the Cartesians was something fundamentally artificial, imposed upon man from without.'

Miss Wallas, in her final judgement of Vauvenargues, makes this quality at once his advantage and his shortcoming:

'The permanent value, not only of Vauvenargues's psychology of thinking, but of his whole literary work, depends on the degree to which his inborn power of sensitive and vivid observation was brought into play, and the extent to which it was either intensified or blurred by the angry feelings aroused by his experience. His attempt to construct a new ethic was, taken as a whole, a failure, because, whereas sensitive introspection is the most valuable of all qualities to a psychologist, we ask of the moralist who undertakes to judge the permanent value of varied human experience, that he should possess, besides psychological accuracy, singleness of purpose, breadth of understanding, and intellectual consistency. Vauvenargues's ethical purpose was confused by the tumult of his feelings, and by a half-conscious desire to justify the actions and motives of his own life. He could not form a consistent ethic for other men, because he was incapable of reconciling the conflict between the motions of ambition, timidity, and kindness in his own soul.'

This is excellent criticism, but is the judgement quite fair? Nothing is more true, and no truth more in need of enforcement to-day, than that the spheres of pure thought and of emotion should be kept distinct. Our philosophy suffers from emotional bias, and our religion from a mistaken attempt to rationalize it. But Vauvenargues was concerned with neither religion nor with pure thought. He saw quite clearly that religion is an affair of the emotions, and he left it at that. To pure thought he had no pretensions. Perhaps he thought of it as a phantom category, for in one of his maxims he says: 'On ne s'élève point aux grandes vérités sans enthousiasme; le sang-froid discute et n'invente point; il faut peut-être autant de feu que de justesse pour faire un véritable philosophe.' Apart from pure thought and religion, what is left? Miss Wallas mentions ethics, morals, and those calvinistic virtues, singleness of purpose, breadth of understanding, and intellectual consistency. Every system of ethics that has been inspired by such aims as these lies like a heap of bleached bones in the waste of time. The code of human behaviour is an illusion; there is only the science of individual behaviour, which is psychology; and Vauvenargues is a superb psychologist. So is Pascal. Miss Wallas's strictures apply equally to that other genius in many ways so complementary to Vauvenargues.

Pascal and Vauvenargues—between them they embrace all the variations of the human soul, from its deepest subjection in emotion to its highest intellectual glory. Vauvenargues confesses in one place, that if such talents could exist side by side, he would like to think like Pascal, to write like Bossuet, and to talk like Fénelon. Perhaps he did none of these things in the degree of his exemplars, but perhaps he added another talent to these three; so that now we can wish to think like Pascal, to write like Bossuet, to talk like Fénelon, and to live like Vauvenargues.

PARTICULAR STUDIES

6

TOBIAS SMOLLETT

It has long been a commonplace of criticism that Smollett is the most neglected of our eighteenth-century authors, and it may be that the gradual emergence of a freer sensibility in manners and literature makes it possible for us to redress our judgements. It is not a question of recovering from the reaction of a generation that has grown tired of the habit of praise; nor is there the excuse of original obscurity, as in the case of Blake or Melville. We have rather a series of carelessly propagated clichés, derived perhaps from Sir Walter Scott, and given general critical currency by Hazlitt and Thackeray; and these clichés, not carrying conviction, are disregarded. The traditional view of the man and his work takes two parallel courses —it expatiates on his humour and deprecates his indecency. But the truth is that Smollett was not essentially a humorist, and that the charge of indecency is, if not meaningless, at least misleading.

The early conditions of Smollett's life were such as to induce a spirit of self-reliance in a temperament of sensibility and pride. He was left without a father while still an infant, and though his relations were in fair enough circumstances to give him a good education, they did not consult his wishes to the extent of his ambitions. At the age of fifteen he found himself apprenticed to a surgeon, but without any real enthusiasm for that calling. His interest tended rather to literature and the humanities, though this interest, we can see, was not of the tender-minded sort. That is to say, Smollett did not seek intellectual accomplishments as a compensation for physical deficiencies, but, like Goethe, as evidence of the possible normality of genius.

He left Glasgow at the age of eighteen and made his way to London, fully confident that a tragedy he had written, *The Regicide*, would be an Open Sesame to fame and fortune. This play is a wretched affair, pompous, insipid, and at times positively ludicrous. It has neither poetry nor wit; and it is astonishing that any one of Smollett's practical temperament could have made it the occasion for so much resentment and false pride. He was incensed at his failure to provoke the least interest in his production and at his wit's end for a living. He finally secured a position as surgeon's mate in the Navy, and in this capacity he took part in the war against Spain. Of this experience he has left us an account, not only in *Roderick Random*, but also in a characteristic but neglected narrative called 'The Expedition against Carthagena'. This was first published in 1756 in Smollett's *Compendium of Authentic and Entertaining Voyages*, and though not of any great length is distinguished by its direct realism and fearless censure. A passage like the following shows that warfare in the eighteenth century had horrors to equal the scientific barbarisms of our more antiseptic age:

'As for the sick and wounded, they were next day sent on board of the transports and vessels called hospital-ships, where they languished in want of every necessary comfort and accommodation. They were destitute of surgeons, nurses, cooks, and proper provision; they were pent up between decks in small vessels where they had not room to sit upright; they wallowed in filth; myriads of maggots were hatched in the putrefaction of their sores, which had no other dressing than that of being washed by themselves with their own allowance of brandy; and nothing was heard but groans, lamentations, and the language of despair invoking death to deliver them from their miseries. What served to encourage this despondency was the prospect of those poor wretches who had strength and opportunity to look around them; for there they beheld the naked bodies of their fellow-soldiers and comrades floating up and down the harbour, affording prey to the carrion crows and sharks, which tore them in pieces without interruption, and contributed by their stench to the mortality that prevailed.'

Smollett left the Fleet at Jamaica; and there he seems to have stayed two or three years, in the society of a congenial Scottish colony. And while there he fell in love with the daughter of a planter, Nancy Lascelles, and to her he was married on his return to London. It is a curious but undeniable fact that this author whose books have for a century or more been surrounded with an aura of infamy, and whose very name was mentioned only in the smoking-room, lived all his life a faithful husband and devoted father. Upon his return from the West Indies he set up a practice as surgeon in Downing Street; but he is said to have lacked an agreeable bedside manner, and in any case he was no success in the profession. He was still intent on literary fame—still confident, in fact, of the merits of *The Regicide*. But in the hands of Richardson and Fielding the novel was just at that time in the ascendancy, and Smollett resolved to try his fortune with this form. The result was *Roderick Random*. Its success was immediate, and Smollet from that moment determined to make his living by his pen.

We need not follow any further the immediate course of his career, but should rather pause to take stock of the qualities he had exhibited in his first novel. We may in the first place dissociate his work almost entirely from Fielding's. *Joseph Andrews* was perhaps an economic cause of Smollett's work, but it had nothing to do with its internal inspiration. For that it had nearer sponsors in Defoe and Le Sage. And though in general we cannot claim for Smollett anything like the profound humanism of Fielding, yet in point of style Smollett, as Hazlitt acknowledged, was the better man. In this particular he was more allied to Swift, and cultivated a clean impersonal mode, devoid of mannerisms. His sentences flow with the even rhythm of economy and ease. For incidents (we can scarcely speak of plot) he relied mainly on his experiences, and the imagination he expends on these is mainly visual. His mind is innocent of ideas, and indeed of abstractions of any sort, and he is at the best but an arranger of the objective facts of existence. Such an imagination is not necessarily of an inferior order, and indeed may achieve a clarity hardly possible to minds of a more intuitive or speculative order. Smollett never indulges in introspection of any sort, and the only subjective feeling he ever gives the rein to is the *saeva indignatio* of the satirist—too often, in his case, a mere reaction to the peevish nature of his constitution (the *systema nervosum maxime irritabile* of his own diagnosis).

Roderick Random certainly determined Smollett's career, but it does not reveal, any more than *Peregrine Pickle* or *Humphrey Clinker*, the true quality of his talent. Smollett's was a logical and sequestered mind; and of the two strains—rationality and artificiality—whose inter-play makes for the peculiar complexity of the eighteenth century, he at least was an unconfused exponent of reason. *Roderick Random* was published in 1748; *Peregrine Pickle* and *Ferdinand, Count Fathom* followed fairly quickly, in 1751 and 1753. There then ensued a period of seventeen years during which Smollett produced no fiction, with the exception of *Sir Launcelot Greaves*, a *feuilleton* of the most haphazard origin. But these seventeen years were years of the most unremitting literary labour, and to omit to reckon them in any estimate of Smollett is as though we were to ignore in Milton's case the twenty years that elapsed between *Lycidas* and *Paradise Lost*. In that interval Smollett translated *Don Quixote*, edited a famous literary review, wrote a *History of England* in four quarto volumes, brought out a farce, edited the *Compendium of Voyages* already mentioned (a work in seven volumes), organized and partly wrote a 'universal history'; revised his history of England and published it in sixpenny weekly parts, was imprisoned for libel, carried on a second magazine, edited a translation of the complete works of Voltaire in thirty-eight volumes, published a *Continuation of the History of England* (five volumes), as well as a work entitled *The Present State of All Nations*, a geographical compendium in eight large volumes. Finally, he threw himself into political journalism as a champion of Bute's administration; and this last venture led to a breach with Wilkes, a politician he really admired. Worn out with vexations of every kind, his health ruined by the long sedentary labours he had undergone, he was already a broken man when the death of his only daughter in 1763 came as a final blow and compelled him to resign everything and go abroad in search of life itself.

We have as a record of this journey the *Travels through France and Italy*—certainly the most important source of our understanding of the man Smollett. His temperament as there revealed is mainly a compost of superficial irascibility and fundamental good nature—the *bourru bienfaisant* of Austin Dobson's phrase. But what is of more interest is the revelation of Smollett's mind—its independence, its complete freedom from the second-hand claptrap which almost every traveller repeats from his guide-book, and its complete disregard for the fashionable and dilettante opinions of his contemporaries. This frankness is best expressed in his aesthetic judgements, and these have been the laughing-stock of the world ever since Sterne made fun of them in the famous passage about Smelfungus. How many readers of Sterne's ridicule of Smollett, particularly of his judgement of the Venus de' Medici, have ever cared to refer to the original, and to consider Smollett's actual words? Sterne's is a good joke, not to be denied at any cost; but is Smollett so absurd after all?

'With respect to the famous Venus Pontia, commonly called *de Medicis*, which was found at Tivoli, and is kept in a separate apartment called the *Tribuna*, I believe I ought to be entirely silent, or at least conceal my real sentiments, which will otherwise appear equally absurd and presumptious. It must be want of taste that prevents my feeling that enthusiastic admiration with which others are inspired at sight of this statue; a statue which in reputation equals that of Cupid by Praxiteles, which brought such a concourse of strangers of old to the little town of Thespiae. I cannot help thinking that there is no beauty in the features of Venus; and that the attitude is awkward and out of character. It is a bad plea to urge that the antients and we differ in the ideas of beauty. We know the contrary, from their medals, busts, and historians. Without all doubt, the limbs and proportions of this statue are elegantly formed, and accurately designed, according to the nicest rules of symmetry and proportion; and the back parts especially are executed so happily as to excite the admiration of the most indifferent spectator.'

Smollett, it will be seen, moves heavily in this unfamiliar ground of aesthetic appreciation; but there is an honest attempt to come to terms with truth, and it may be doubted whether any modern traveller of average sensibility would express himself with an equal disregard for 'the ridicule of the virtuosi'. This, too, can be said for Smollett: he was aware of the limitations of common sense; elsewhere in his *Travels* he writes: 'I am used to speak my mind freely on all subjects that fall under the cognizance of my senses; though I must as freely own, there is something more than common sense required to discover and distinguish the more delicate beauties of painting.' His mind, of course, was not quite free; it was under the dominion of those classical prejudices which make most eighteenth-century aesthetic criticism intemperate. But within his limits Smollett shows a good deal of penetration. At Pisa he was charmed with 'the brass gates, designed and executed by John of Bologna, representing, embossed in different compartments, the history of the Old and New Testament. I was so charmed with this work that I could have stood a whole day to examine and admire it.' And when he got to Florence, in front of Ghiberti's doors, he 'still retained a greater veneration for those at Pisa—a preference which either arises from want of taste, or from the charm of novelty, by which the former were recommended to my attention'. If Smollett were to revisit the scene to-day, he might find even certain of the virtuosi sharing his want of taste! His remarks on Giotto are intelligent for his time, and in this judgement of a 'basso relievo' he saw in the Campo Santo at Pisa there is a freshness worth many of the expansive similes of less phlegmatic travellers:

'I was struck with the figure of a woman lying dead on a tombstone, covered with a piece of thin drapery, so delicately cut as to show all the flexures of the attitude, and even all the swellings and sinuosities of the muscles. Instead of stone, it looks like a sheet of wet linen.'

His criticism of Michelangelo's Pietà at Saint Peter's is surprising in an author of his reputation: he found 'something indelicate, not to say indecent, in the attitude and design of a man's body, stark naked, lying upon the knees of a woman'; and before the 'Last Judgement' in the Sistine Chapel he uttered this remark, which has more acuteness in it:

'Michelangelo, with all his skill in anatomy, his correctness of design, his grand composition, his fire, and force of expression, seems to have had very little idea of grace.'

It was necessary to expatiate a little on these aesthetic judgements of Smollett's because they show a side of his mind in sharp contrast with the ordinary conception of his personality. Of the same tendency are his views on religion, which are rationalistic (he compared Catholicism and Calvinism to the comic and tragic masks of the human drama); his serious antiquarianism (he measured the arena of the amphitheatre at Cemenelum with packthread); and his curious philological digressions, introduced on the least provocation.

But we must now turn to consider the nature of Smollett's humour, which is, when all is said and done, the true basis of his claim on modern readers. We use the word 'humour' without any hesitation, for no one ever accused Smollett of wit. The distinction between wit and humour is one of the favourite exercises of philosophical critics and serious psychologists; but perhaps Hazlitt's distinction, having our immediate subject-matter in mind, is most apt:

'Humour is the describing the ludicrous as it is in itself; wit is the exposing it, by comparing or contrasting it with something else. Humour is, as it were, the growth of nature and accident; wit is the product of art and fancy. Humour, as it is shewn in books, is an imitation of the natural or acquired absurdities of mankind, of the ludicrous in accident, situation and character; wit is the illustrating and heightening the sense of that absurdity by some sudden and unexpected likeness or opposition of one thing to another, which sets off the quality we laugh at or despise in a still more contemptible or striking point of view.'

We may add a modern *nuance* to these distinctions by showing how well they fit in with those distinctions in the human personality elaborated by modern psychology. Humour is descriptive, external, accidental, imitative—that is, an objective faculty. Wit is introspective, comparative, analytical—that is, a subjective faculty. And the exercise of these faculties is appropriate to temperaments that correspond—to the objective man, or extravert, in the one case; to the subjective man, or introvert, in the other case. Now Smollett, as we have seen, was essentially an extravert; and his mind, full of the observation of events rather than the consideration of ideas, naturally expressed itself in terms of humour rather than of wit.

The originality of Smollett's humour lay not so much in its character as in the mode of employment. He took over a form of prose fiction established by Le Sage and Scarron, and introduced it to English literature; he infused it with a certain element of humour which we like to consider distinctively English, and which we trace to Shakespeare. As a matter of fact, Smollet is, for an eighteenth-century writer, oddly conversant with Shakespeare; *Count Fathom* especially is sprinkled with quotations from the plays. It seems that he takes a certain element direct from Shakespeare—the element of Falstaff and

Bardolph—and extends it with his peculiar talent for imagination extension. The words that greeted Fathom as he entered the 'mansions of misery' are very Elizabethan:

'You, Bess Beetle, score a couple of fresh eggs, a penny-worth of butter, and half a pint of mountain to the king; and stop credit till the bill is paid: he is now debtor for fifteen shillings and sixpence, and damn me if I trust him one farthing more, if he was the best king in Christendom; and d'ye hear, send Ragged-head with five pounds of potatoes for Major Macleaver's supper, and let him have what drink he wants; the fat widow gentlewoman from Pimlico has promised to quit his score. Sir Mungo Barebones may have some hasty pudding and small beer, though I don't expect to see his coin, no more than to receive the eighteen pence I laid out for a pair of breeches to his backside—what then? He's a quiet sort of body and a great scholar, and it was a scandal to see him going about in that naked condition.'

But Commodore Trunnion's ride to church, and the entertainment in the manner of the ancients, in *Peregrine Pickle*, are something more. We pass from realism to phantasy, and the phantasy is, as Hazlitt objected, rather vulgar. Some one in the character of clown has entered the arena of literature, and the fun is never quite the same thereafter. Though we are diverted well enough on the first occasion, we may well be appalled by the surfeit that follows. Many of us might prefer to come first to Mr. Pickwick or Mr. Jorrocks, instead of Commodore Trunnion and Lieutenant Lismahago, and so get our vulgarity neat. But in the mass these humorists fairly do away with the English reputation for wit. How could we answer a charge that we have seen in this array of grotesques a sufficient apology for our want of intelligence and subtlety? In our right senses we cling more desperately to Sterne. He had few of the civic virtues of Smollett, but his grace was a guardian angel for all occasions. Sterne, indeed, is the right foil for Smollett; bring these two in opposition and all the richest lights and colours emerge on each in admirable contrast. But then Sterne is incomparable. Goethe called him the freest spirit of his century; and Nietzsche, in the profoundest criticism ever written of Sterne,[1] took up Goethe's words and called him the freest writer of all time.

'Compared with him all other writers are stiff, clumsy, intolerant and absolutely boorish. He is to be praised, not for his clear, finished form, but for his "infinite melody"—if by such a phrase we can give a name to a style in art where the selected form is continually broken, disregarded, thrust back into the indeterminate, so that it signifies one thing and at the same time another thing.'

Midway between Sterne and Smollett is Diderot. The bare recital of Smollett's professional activities will have suggested a comparison with the great 'father of the encyclopaedia'; and in their rational temperaments these authors had much in common, though Diderot's was a more inquiring mind, and a mind, of course, much more introspective and philosophical. But in the superficial aspect of their careers these two correspond; and there is even a possibility that the author of *Le Neveu de Rameau* and *Jacques le Fataliste* owed something to the author of *Roderick Random* and *Peregrine Pickle*. But perhaps he owed more to the author of *Tristram Shandy*; for the French, as Nietzsche observes, are too serious for humour—above all, for this humoristic fashion of exploiting humour. Smollett's humour, however, was not all pure buffoonery, and he himself at any rate would have maintained that it was inspired by a satirical intention. That intention could, if need be, blaze out without any equivocation whatsoever; and *The Adventures of an Atom* is too savage for most people's taste. It is even too much for the sober critic, who sees in satire something closely bound to the real. Once it transcends the real it enters another category—that of humour in Smollett's case. His caricatures of humanity—Uncle Bowling, Strap, Peregrine, Trunnion, Fathom, Tabitha, and the rest—are too

[1] *Menschliches, allzumenschliches*, vol. ii. ('Vermischte Meinungen und Sprüche,' Aph. 113, Der freiste Schriftsteller).

extravagant to affect the conscience of a public; yet that is the function of satire. We immediately feel that we ourselves live in a different world, less fantastic, less amusing. We do not have the same agreeable illusion about the Yahoos.

Finally, there is the question of indecency. Smollett himself, in the first chapter of *Count Fathom*, was at some pains to defend himself against this charge:

'Have a little patience, gentle, delicate, sublime critic; you, I doubt not, are one of those consummate connoisseurs, who, in their purifications, let humour evaporate, while they endeavour to preserve decorum, and polish wit, until the edge of it is quite worn off; or, perhaps, of that class, who, in the sapience of taste, are disgusted with those very flavours in the productions of their own country, which have yielded infinite delectation to their faculties, when imported from another clime; and damn an author in despite of all precedent and prescription—who extol the writings of Petronius Arbiter, read with rapture the amorous sallies of Ovid's pen, and chuckle over the story of Lucian's ass; yet, if a modern author presumes to relate the progress of a simple intrigue, are shocked at the indecency and immorality of the scene—who delight in following Guzman d'Alfarache through all the mazes of squalid beggary; who with pleasure accompany Don Quixote and his squire, in the lowest paths of fortune; who are diverted with the adventures of Scarron's ragged troop of strollers, and highly entertained with the servile situations of Gil Blas; yet, when a character in humble life occasionally occurs in a performance of our own growth, exclaim, with an air of disgust, "Was ever anything so mean? sure, this writer must have been very conversant with the lowest scenes of life"; who, when Swift or Pope represents a coxcomb in the act of swearing, scruple not to laugh at the ridiculous execrations; but, in a less reputed author, condemn the use of such profane expletives; who eagerly explore the jakes of Rabelais for amusement, and even extract humour from the dean's description of a lady's dressing-room; yet, in a production of these days, unstamped with such venerable names, will stop their noses, with all the signs of loathing and abhorrence, at a bare mention of the china chamber-pot; who applaud Catullus, Juvenal, Persius, and Lucan, for their spirit in lashing the greatest names of antiquity; yet, when a British satirist, of this generation, has courage enough to call in question the talents of a pseudo-patron in power, accuse him of insolence, rancour, and scurrility.'

That defence may still speak for itself; and though, like Smollett, we must refrain from discussing the ethics of the question, we might at least make one or two distinctions which are of its essence. Indecency is of many sorts; and though we need not extenuate the ethical condemnation of any of them, we must insist that there is a scale of values in this as in all other matters of conduct. Distinct words, like obscenity, eroticism, blasphemy, pornography, and coprology (or scatology) do not exist without a purpose; but this subject is so often treated with a lack of frankness that their connotation is always uncertain, and a writer like Smollett is in danger of having any or all of these opprobrious terms heaped upon him without discrimination. As a matter of fact, Smollett is never obscene or blasphemous, nor in any but a limited sense pornographical or erotic. The 'Memoirs of a Lady of Quality' in *Peregrine Pickle*, which Robert Chambers described in his biography of Smollett as 'a recital which could not show face in any decent company' (and perhaps for that reason he always refers to them as the 'Memoirs of a *Woman* of Quality') is, nevertheless, a recital absolutely free from the sensuality that would inevitably distinguish such a narrative in modern hands. Smollett is not sensual; it is almost our complaint that he is not sensual enough. In short, his indiscretions are confined to the coprological kind: that is to say, they hover round certain daily physical acts to which we are all subject, but of which only the neurotic are ashamed. It may be that such acts are not a proper subject for humour; but humour being by definition an imitation of the ludicrous in nature, and nothing being

245

more ludicrous than a dignified human being's submission to these necessities, it is difficult to escape from, at any rate, a logical defence of coprological humour. It may be objected, however, that realism is not of the essence of indecency, but that everything is determined by the manner of it. There is every difference, for example, between the plain realism of Rabelais's coprology and the subjective disgust of Mr. Joyce's. There is also every difference between the matter-of-fact narrative of Smollett and the equivocal suggestions of Sterne. But this all redounds to the credit of Smollett: he is everywhere masculine and healthy, direct and unfurtive. *Humphrey Clinker* is the epitome of all these qualities. This admirable book came in the twilight of Smollett's life—he only just lived to see its appearance—and it has a serenity and harmony fitting to the time of its origin. The humour is quieter, the pace is unforced; there is no pretence of plot, no unction of satirical purpose, but, as Professor Saintsbury once noted, 'an almost Shakespearean touch of sureness, completeness, self-sufficingness'. Matt Bramble is the centre of this unflurried stage; and Matt Bramble is Smollett himself, mellow, loquacious, quizzically surveying at a distance the manners and economy of his native land. And at bottom the work is still serious; the book is rational despite its immense fund of humour; for all its types and oddities are ranged like puppets against a clean curtain of common sense. In this manner Smollett took his leave of a scene where he had lived dangerously and met defeat—but a defeat of the body, not of the spirit. He once anonymously described himself as 'one of those few writers of the age that stand upon their own foundation, without patronage, and above dependence'. There are few self-opinions that posterity can so agreeably confirm.

PARTICULAR STUDIES

7

STERNE

'If they have a fault', Sterne said of the French, 'they are too *serious*.' The Count in *A Sentimental Journey* received this statement as a pleasantry, but, says the author, 'it was my most settled opinion'. The Count could not wait for reasons, and this we must regret, for probably Sterne would have enforced the corollary of his statement, namely, that if you would know the wittiest, most whimsical and most humorous nation in the world, seek the English. It is a great pity that Sterne did not make this claim for us, for no one since has had the courage. We have found it more profitable to keep up a pretence of native phlegm and melancholy—Bagehot described our greatest political asset as stupidity. In literature we admit 'homely humour', but if by any chance we find ourselves blessed with an author remarkable for wit, we search hastily for some foreign strain in his ancestry. We are never happy until we have made him an Irishman, or better still, if he is really wicked, a Frenchman. This has been Sterne's fate. He is very droll, it cannot be denied; the drollest of all our writers. But then he was born in Ireland of a mother who may have been partly French and of a father who was mainly a Yorkshireman. What, then, was Sterne? Nothing that can be measured. An individual is born as a merely potential quality: both before and after his birth the possible variations in his development are determined by a thousand chances. A work of art, on the other hand, is born to a finite shape. Its growth

247

is completed at birth, and for that reason it is much more to the point to enquire into the birth and parentage of a work of art than into those of its author. The significant fact is that *Tristram Shandy* was written by a Yorkshire parson who had never moved far from his parish for more than twenty years. We might go further and say that it was written by a man whose interests and passions were purely local, and that it was, primarily, written for a local public. Its close relation to its immediate predecessor, the satire on local affairs known as *The History of a Good Warm Watch-Coat*, should be borne in mind. *Tristram Shandy* is an epic of Yorkshire life, and this fact is only an illustration of the profound truth that all the great epics of the world are local epics. From the *Iliad* to *Don Quixote* they were all generated in a small society, and took on their universality by virtue of the genius that enabled each of their authors to see a world in his particular grain of sand. It is almost possible to say that an epic needs for its creation the all-inclusive self-consciousness of a small community. The ideal conditions exist when you have a community large enough to employ all the capacities and exhibit all the passions of mankind, yet small enough to be within the knowledge and observation of one man. Such a community existed in York in the eighteenth century. It was an autonomous society, independent of London. As a city it was a centre of social life, with its own learned societies and coffee-houses, its theatre, and race-course. Its ancient history, its ecclesiastical pre-eminence, and its civic dignities: these endowed it with the necessary density of tradition. Life was seen against a background. A prebendary of the cathedral church, such as Sterne, with a parish within an easy amble, was at the heart of this miniature world, and could watch, and take part in, the variety and intensity of its serio-comic life. He could compass the whole scale between the yokels of his own parish at Sutton and the Archbishop in his palace at Bishopthorpe. And within this compass lies the comic world of *Tristram Shandy*.

Sterne is a popular author—surely more popular than

Fielding or Richardson or Smollett, though not, alas, so popular as Dickens. But in a critical sense English authors are neglected in the measure of their popularity. English critics seem to assume that because an author is accepted, there is no need to explain his achievement. So most of the essays which have been written on Sterne are lacking in interest or freshness: they are confined to admirable acquiescence in his sense of humour and fierce denunciation of his impropriety. Thackeray's lecture is positively splenetic in tone, and seems to possess a violence and a baselessness more worthy of psychological than critical attention. Here are some of the epithets hurled at Sterne or his work in the course of a few pages: 'Coward'; 'wretched'; 'worn-out old scamp'; 'vain, wicked, witty, and false'; 'this actor, this quack'; 'an impure presence'; 'foul satyr'; 'poor wretch'; 'horrible baseness of blasphemy'; 'cheap dribble'; and so on. A critic who uses such thoughtless expletives is obviously not going to bother much about the extenuating genuineness of his subject; it is not easy, even for an unprejudiced mind, to balance morality against art. Walter Bagehot made a better attempt: his view is not unprejudiced —whose could be in that circumspect age?—but there is genuine insight in a passage like the following:

'The real excellence of Sterne is single and simple: the defects are numberless and complicated. He excels, perhaps, all other writers in mere simple description of common sensitive human action. He places before you in their simplest form the elemental facts of human life; he does not view them through the intellect, he scarcely views them through the imagination; he does but reflect the unimpaired impression which the facts of life which does not change from age to age make on the deep basis of human feeling, which changes as little though years go on. . . . Sterne's feelings in his higher moments so much overpowered his intellect, and so directed his imagination, that no intrusive thought blemishes, no distorting fancy mars, the perfection of the representation. The disenchanting facts which deface, the low circumstances which debase the simpler feelings oftener than any other feelings, his art excludes. The feeling which would probably be coarse in the reality is refined in the picture. The unconscious tact of the nice artist heightens and chastens reality, but yet it is reality still. His mind was like a pure lake of delicate water: it reflects the ordinary landscape, the rugged hills, the loose pebbles, the knotted and the distorted firs perfectly and as they are, yet with a charm and fascination that they have not in themselves. This is the highest attainment of art, to be at the same time nature and something more than nature.'

That is excellent criticism, vividly written and definitely illuminating. But the fuss Bagehot makes about the indecency of *Tristram Shandy* and its general unfitness for young ladies would make modern young ladies open their eyes with wonder. What the Victorian critics did not realize—could not realize, because of their lack of frankness in sexual matters—was the triviality of the question on which they expended so much energy. Coleridge alone leads us to the essentials of the theme. There is more real criticism in his fragmentary notes on Sterne than in the whole body of anything else written on the same subject. It is true that at first sight he would seem to feel as strongly as Thackeray or Bagehot on the question of Sterne's licentiousness—but with this difference: he not merely condemns it, but also analyses it. It is his analysis of the question that more than ever reveals its essential triviality. And when Coleridge says that 'Sterne cannot be too severely censured for using the best dispositions of our nature [he is thinking of the characters of Mr. Shandy, Uncle Toby, and Trim] as the panders and condiments for the basest', he thereby suggests the possible defence that these dispositions gain by their juxtaposition with a shade of evil. Uncle Toby is not so much a butt to this kind of wit, as the illustration of its insufficiency.

Coleridge in his lecture 'on the nature and constituents of humour' distinguishes humour from the different kinds of wit. Wit is impersonal, consisting wholly in the understanding

STERNE

and the senses. It is a play with words, or with thoughts, or with images. But 'no combination of thoughts, words, or images will of itself constitute humour, unless some peculiarity of individual temperament and character be indicated thereby, as the cause of the same'. And Coleridge, to illustrate his meaning, compares the comedies of Congreve with Falstaff, and with Sterne's Corporal Trim, Uncle Toby, and Mr. Shandy. That is the first point established by Coleridge's analysis—the dependence of humour upon personality. The second point is equally important. In Coleridge's own words: 'there always is in a genuine humour an acknowledgment of the hollowness and farce of the world, and its disproportion to the godlike within us'. If we combine these two observations we might say that humour is an exposure of the contrast between the godlike and the trivial exhibited in a personality. But Coleridge probed deeper still, to ask: 'Is there some one humorific point common to all that can be called humorous?' He thought there was and that it consisted in 'a certain reference to the general and the universal, by which the finite great is brought into identity with the little, or the little with the finite great, so as to make both nothing in comparison with the infinite. The little is made great, and the great little, in order to destroy both; because all is equal in contrast with the infinite. "It is not without reason, brother Toby, that learned men write dialogues on long noses."' And Coleridge adds: 'Humorous writers, therefore, as Sterne in particular, delight, after much preparation, to end in nothing, or in direct contradiction.'

Coleridge makes one further and more subtle distinction in the case of Sterne which must be referred to before returning to Sterne himself. He puts as first among the excellences of Sterne his ability 'in bringing forward into distinct consciousness those minutiae of thought and feeling which appear trifles, yet have an importance for the moment, and which almost every man feels in one way or another. Thus is produced the novelty of an individual peculiarity together with

251

the interest of a something that belongs to our common nature. In short, Sterne seizes happily on those points, in which every man is more or less a humorist. And, indeed, to be a little more subtle, the propensity to notice these things does itself constitute the humorist, and the superadded power of so presenting them to men in general gives us the man of humour. Hence the difference of the man of humour, the effect of whose portraits does not depend on the felt presence of himself, as humorist, as in the instances of Cervantes and Shakespeare—nay, of Rabelais too; and of the humorist, the effect of whose works does very much depend on the sense of his own oddity, as in Sterne's case, and perhaps Swift's: though Swift again would require a separate classification.'

Coleridge gives us here a very clear indication of the singularity of Sterne's genius. If there is one characteristic which distinguishes Sterne from his fellow humorists, it is certainly the 'felt presence' of the man in his work: the author himself is the real hero of *Tristram Shandy*. And in this matter Sterne was very much of his age. He was born within a year of the birth of Rousseau, and though it would be difficult to maintain that there was any direct communication of ideas, yet there were common influences at work, and these influences produced similar fruit. There are, of course, many differences: there is nothing of Rousseau's romantic naturalism about Sterne, and he is too much a creature of common sense to discard the rational framework of religion and society. But when all these differences have been discounted there remains a common doctrine of sensibility which is fundamental to both men. It was the same doctrine, but very differently interpreted. In Rousseau the doctrine was applied inwardly, to his own feelings, until his own sensibility became the only value and his own sanctity the predominating illusion. But in Sterne the doctrine is applied outwardly: it is sympathetic: it is a measure, not merely of the intensity of his own feelings, but of the definite reality of his fellow men. Spontaneity is perhaps the only word which can be applied without qualification to both Rousseau and Sterne: that quality they had in common. It only became differentiated when, in Rousseau's case, it was corrupted by egoism. But incidentally we may note that this freedom of sensibility, this spontaneity, had quite parallel effects in the development of prose style in France and in England. In this matter Rousseau and Sterne occupy almost precisely similar positions. They break down the dignity, the orotundity and the volubility of their predecessors and give us instead a prose that is vivid, nervous, and swift.

The nineteenth-century conception of Sterne as a ribald prelate has quite blinded us to the truth that he was in reality a writer with a purpose, a moral preceptor, a subtle intelligence that masked beneath his humour and licentiousness the kindly philanthropy of his age—the age of Shaftesbury and Hutcheson. Coleridge asked his audience to note 'Sterne's assertion of, and faith in, a moral good in the characters of Trim, Toby, etc., as contrasted with the cold skepticism of motives which is the stamp of the Jacobin spirit'. And in an Advertisement to his sermon on the Abuses of Conscience—Yorick's sermon in *Tristram Shandy*, but published separately in 1766—Sterne himself referred to *Tristram Shandy* as 'a moral work, more read than understood'. This perfectly serious claim on his part is borne out by another equally serious reference to the *Sentimental Journey* made in a letter of 12th November 1767, addressed to Mr. and Mrs. James: 'My design in it was to teach us to love the world and our fellow-creatures better than we do—so it runs most upon those gentle passions and affections, which aid so much to it.'

This paradox of a moral Sterne will be found more acceptable when the world begins to read that neglected half of Sterne's genius—his Sermons. There is no inconsistency—in style, in manner, and in sincerity and aim—between the Sermons and *Tristram Shandy* or the *Sentimental Journey*. Since their first success no one seems to have bothered to read the Sermons; certainly Thackeray had not seen them, and Bagehot does not seem to have considered them for long. It is unfortunate because there, more explicitly than in his works of fiction, Sterne reveals his approach to life. In the opening passage of his sermon on the Prodigal Son he makes this very significant statement:

'I know not whether the remark is to our honour or otherwise, that lessons of wisdom have never such a power over us, as when they are wrought into the heart, through the groundwork of a story which engages the passions. Is it that we are like iron, and must first be heated before we can be wrought upon? or, Is the heart so in love with deceit, that where a true report will not reach it, we must cheat it with a fable, in order to come at truth?'

The preacher does not stop to answer his questions: they are rhetorical. But he answered them in his works, which are, as he meant them quite simply to be, stories which engage our passions and by that experience teach us 'to love the world and our fellow-creatures better than we do'—such love being, Sterne ever maintained, the beginning and the end of all wisdom.

This metaphor of the iron heated until it can be wrought upon, this stress upon the passions and affections, was not with Sterne the commonplace that it might seem to us. There was, at the back of it, the groundwork of a philosophy, and though it may be freely admitted that no one is on the surface less philosophical than Sterne, yet when we dive below the surface we find that he was everywhere indebted to philosophy, and in particular to the philosophy of John Locke.

In his *Life and Times of Laurence Sterne* Professor Wilbur Cross has drawn attention to an interesting volume of memoirs published in Paris in the year 1820—*Mémoires historiques sur la Vie de M. Suard, sur ses Écrits, et sur le XVIIIe siècle* by Dominique Joseph Garat, where there is to be found a long and extremely interesting account of Sterne, based on the recollections of M. Suard. Suard was later a famous Academician —it was due to his efforts that the Academy survived the Revolution. In his youth he became friendly with Sterne

during the latter's stay in Paris, and had read and appreciated
Tristram Shandy. He had intimate discussions with Sterne on
many subjects, and on one occasion asked him what were the
influences which had determined the cast of his genius.
Sterne's reply is extremely illuminating. There is no question
of Suard's embroidery: the self-analysis is too exact, too penetrating, for any one but Sterne himself to have expressed it.
The first source of his originality, he said, was 'an organization
in which predominated the sacred principle which forms the
soul, that immortal flame which nourishes life and yet devours
it, which suddenly exalts and modifies all sensations, and
which we call *imagination* or *sensibility*, according as it is used
to depict scenes or to portray passions; the second source of
his originality was the daily reading of the Old and New
Testaments, books which were as agreeable to his taste as they
were necessary to his profession; and the third source was the
study of Locke, which he had begun in his youth and continued through all his life; those who knew the philosopher
well enough to recognize his presence and his influence will
find them or sense them on every page, in every line, and in
the choice of all his expressions; this philosopher, who was too
religious to want to explain the miracle of sensation, but who,
with this miracle which he does not dare to question but
accounts to God, unfolds all the secrets of the understanding,
avoids all errors, and arrives at positive truths; a holy philosophy, without which there will never be on earth either a
true universal religion or a true system of morals or man's
complete power over Nature'.[1]

We have in this confession a most important clue to the real
understanding of Sterne. Now, of the three explanations which
Sterne gives of his genius, the first and the third have a direct
connection. The doctrine of sensibility in which Sterne found
an explanation of his creative energy, and to which he made
his writings subservient—this doctrine arises out of the philosophy of Locke. The main object of Locke was to destroy the

[1] Garat, op. cit., vol. ii, pp. 149–50.

scholastic dogma of innate principles and to explain all knowledge as the product of sensation or reflection. The emphasis
was very much on the sensations, and sensation, with its
related word 'sensibility', was very much on men's lips during
the first half of the eighteenth century. It was the catchword of
that age, in the way that 'relativity' is the catchword of ours.

I must digress at this point into that very interesting pursuit
—the history of words. There is nothing more salutary, both
for our self-esteem and our critical rectitude. The particular
group of words we are concerned with—those originating
out of the word 'sense'—have a most complicated history, and
might very well be made to illustrate the whole development
of philosophy and taste since the seventeenth century. But for
the moment we are concerned only with the word 'sentimental'. It is a word which, though not invented by Sterne, was
nevertheless given universal currency by him. The date of the
first use of the word recorded by the *Oxford English Dictionary*
is 1749.[1] Lady Bradshaigh writes to Samuel Richardson:

'What in your opinion is the meaning of the word *sentimental*, so much in vogue among the polite. . . . Everything clever
and agreeable is comprehended in that word. . . . I am frequently astonished to hear such a one is a *sentimental* man; we
were a *sentimental* party; I have been taking a *sentimental* walk.'

This shows us the word in its first usage. It meant 'characterized by sentiment' and 'sentiment' meant sensation—
Locke's sensation—in its personal aspect. But as the word got
bandied about among the illiterate, or at any rate among the
unphilosophical, it lost the definiteness of its impress and came
to signify something at once more limited and less exact. A
sentiment was, by the middle of the eighteenth century, any
refined or tender emotion, especially those portrayed in literature and art. But the emphasis was on the refinement, as we
see from Lady Bradshaigh's letter, and this was the implication

[1] I have discussed in an Introduction to an edition of the *Sentimental
Journey* published by the Scholartis Press (London, 1929) the possibility
that Sterne himself used the word as early as 1740.

of the word as used by Sterne. The *Sentimental Journey* (1768) was one involving and exhibiting delicate feelings. That these delicate feelings sometimes lead us into indelicate situations does not alter the meaning of the word. But the word did alter in meaning, though not in the direction of indelicacy. In 1823 Southey wrote: 'Rousseau addressed himself to the sentimental classes, persons of ardent or morbid sensibility, who believe themselves to be composed of finer elements than the gross multitude.' The word is already, more than a hundred years ago, beginning to imply something excessive. In 1826 Disraeli speaks of 'a soft sentimental whisper'; in 1827 Scott of 'a sentimental tear'. And so the degeneration of the word proceeds, until in 1862 we have Miss Braddon writing: 'You have no sentimental nonsense, no silly infatuation . . . to fear from me.' Nowadays it can be used for the extreme stages of emotional deliquescence.

It cannot be doubted that Sterne's reputation has suffered unjustly from this degeneration of the word 'sentimental'. In the modern sense, Sterne is not sentimental; he is almost cynical, which is the opposite quality. But he is not really cynical; he is just humorous. It must be admitted that there are passages in *Tristram Shandy* and *A Sentimental Journey* which border on the modern sense of sentimentality. But they keep beyond the border. Sterne's intelligence is always there, ready to play with, to play on, your 'gentler passions and affections'; but he always saves himself, either by a perfect control of expression (that is, by the technique of his style), or, more remarkably, by a sudden humorous recovery—as in his famous encounter with the disconsolate Maria:

'They were the sweetest notes I ever heard; and I instantly let down the fore-glass to hear them more distinctly—'Tis *Maria*, said the postillion, observing I was listening—Poor *Maria*, continued he (leaning his body on one side to let me see her, for he was in a line betwixt us), is sitting upon a bank, playing her vespers upon her pipe, with her little goat beside her.

'The young fellow uttered this with an accent and a look so perfectly in tune to a feeling heart, that I instantly made a vow I would give him a four-and-twenty sous piece when I got to *Moulins*—

'—And who is *poor Maria*? said I.

'The love and piety of all the villages around us, said the postillion—it is but three years ago that the sun did not shine upon so fair, so quick-witted and amiable a maid; and better fate did *Maria* deserve than to have her Banns forbid by the intrigues of the curate of the parish who published them—

'He was going on, when *Maria*, who had made a short pause, put the pipe to her mouth, and began the air again—they were the same notes;—yet were ten times sweeter: It is the evening service to the Virgin, said the young man—but who has taught her to play it, or how she came by her pipe, no one knows; we think that Heaven has assisted her in both, for ever since she has been unsettled in her mind it seems her only consolation—she has never once had the pipe out of her hand, but plays that service upon it almost night and day.

'The postillion delivered this with so much discretion and natural eloquence that I could not help deciphering something in his face above his condition, and should have sifted out his history had not poor *Maria* taken such full possession of me.

'We had got up by this time almost to the bank where *Maria* was sitting: she was in a thin white jacket, with her hair, all but two tresses, drawn up into a silk net, with a few olive leaves twisted a little fantastically on one side—she was beautiful; and if ever I felt the full force of an honest heart-ache it was the moment I saw her—

'—God help her! poor damsel! above a hundred masses, said the postillion, have been said in the several parish churches and convents around, for her—but without effect. We have still hopes, as she is sensible for short intervals, that the Virgin at last will restore her to herself; but her parents, who know her best, are hopeless upon that score, and think her senses are lost for ever.

'As the postillion spoke this, *Maria* made a cadence so melancholy, so tender and querulous, that I sprang out of the chaise to help her, and found myself sitting betwixt her and her goat before I relapsed from my enthusiasm.

'*Maria* look'd wistfully for some time at me, and then at her goat—and then at me—and then at her goat again, and so on, alternately—

'—Well, *Maria*, said I, softly—What resemblance do you find?'

Here, of course, the goat saves the situation. We come back to Coleridge's definition of humour: 'The little is made great, and the great little, in order to destroy both; because all is equal in contrast with the infinite.'

If the injustice done to Sterne by our modern degradation of the word 'sentimentality' were generally admitted, then we could more safely use the cognate word 'sensibility' to describe the general background of his work. It has usually been assumed that it had no background. Critics have taken too literally Sterne's joke, that having written one word he trusted to Providence for the next. They have been deceived by their inability to appreciate the method of *Tristram Shandy* into thinking not merely that it had no method (there is some excuse for that fault, for it is a subtle matter), but also into imagining that where there was no method there was no mind. That was because they were incapable of taking this humorist seriously. It may be urged that no one should take a humorist seriously, but apart from the fact that this shows a misconception of humour, why should Sterne be treated any less seriously than his compeers? Rabelais and Cervantes have been treated with perfect seriousness, and learned works have been written, not on their humour, but on their thought. In the case of Rabelais and Cervantes an intellectual quality is obvious enough. To keep to Locke's differentiation, their ideas were derived from reflection; whereas, in Sterne's case, the ideas were derived mainly from sensation. The background in his case was *sensibility*; and sensibility is intimately related to *conscience*; and conscience to *morality*. Between these states of mind—they are but different aspects of the same state of mind—there is involved the element of humour. One of the most significant things about Sterne is that he makes this interrelation of elements so clear.

His favourite sermon was the one he included in *Tristram Shandy*: that on the Abuses of Conscience. His theme was, that in conscience there is no inherent goodness; it is not a law unto itself, infallible or invariable. Conscience is rather a principle, seated within the mind, which enables us to interpret our conduct in the light of laws that are already given us in Religion and Morality. Conscience, in fact, is moral sensibility, but it is a sensibility operating within a fixed world. This is anything but a romantic doctrine; it is, indeed, the essential classical doctrine. And that is why, in spite of his popularity among some of the romantics, Sterne's genius is really to be reckoned on the side of the classical forces in literature.

His humour is evidence of that. All real humorists are classicists, because it is in the nature of a classicist to see things finite, and see things infinite, but not to confuse these two categories. The classicist, like the humorist, acknowledges the 'hollowness and farce of the world, and its disproportion to the godlike within us'—and this is Coleridge's definition of humour. It might just as well be a definition of classicism. The romanticist, on the other hand, merges all things into the infinite, sees all men as gods, or, at the other extreme, sees nothing but the unrelated trivialities of existence—the jumble, the glitter, the breathless jollity of it all.

We have, then, this inner principle which we may call conscience and which is the sense of religion and of morality; or we may call the same principle sensibility, and then it is the sense of humour. And it is a curious fact, which Coleridge has pointed out, that we find no real humour among the ancients:

'Humour took its rise in the Middle Ages; and the Devil, the Vice of the Mysteries, incorporates the modern humour in its elements. It is a spirit measured by disproportionate finites. The Devil is not, indeed, perfectly humorous; but that is only because he is the extreme of all humour.'

That is a very profound observation, and suggests as a possible truth that the greatest degree of humour is the complement of the greatest degree of religion. Old Nick, as he was good-humouredly called, only lost his reality because he was divested of his humour, gradually becoming a figure of horror as his significance and power passed from the realm of the finite and physical to that of the infinite and metaphysical.

There remain two very important aspects of Sterne's genius, which must be briefly touched upon in any general estimate of his place in literature—namely, his mastery of English prose style and his mastery of the art of narrative. His style is one of deceptive ease, but we know that it cost him great pains. The first draft of the first two volumes of *Tristram Shandy* was written rapidly—in less than six months; but an interval of another six months elapsed before the volumes were published, and during this time the manuscript was circulated and met with a good deal of criticism. As a result of these criticisms and of his own reflection, Sterne is said to have reduced the bulk of the volume by half. 'I have burnt more wit than I have published' was his own confession. And we know from the evidence of his Letter Book that even in matters of ordinary correspondence he exercised extraordinary care, drafting and emending and copying out even the most intimately trivial notes.

We have in the passage quoted from Suard's memoir the secret of his style—perhaps not the 'secret', because that is an impalpable energy which defies analysis—but at least its more formal origins. These are to be found in his confessed devotion to the literature of the Bible and to the writings of Locke. Of the Bible he has spoken elsewhere, in that sermon which Newman praised in his *Idea of a University*. The distinction which Sterne makes between true and false eloquence shows his real understanding of the art of writing, and his definition of true eloquence as 'a surprising mixture of simplicity and majesty' is one of quite excellent exactness. His indebtedness to Locke in this matter might not have been suspected but for the solemn declaration of his devotion to this philosopher which he made to Suard; but on comparing the styles of Locke and Sterne we find a decided similarity. It is not easy to eliminate the humour of the one and the abstract reasoning of the other and pierce to the radical elements of their composition and rhetoric. But if we admit the unity of style between Sterne's Sermons and his humorous works—and any one who has read both will not be disposed to deny this unity—and then compare the two authors on a cognate or identical subject,[1] the resemblance is found to be very remarkable. But the source of his style does not matter so much as its significance. There can be no doubt that it has had a decisive effect on the development of English prose style in deflecting it from the path of latinization into which it had entered during the second half of the seventeenth and first half of the eighteenth centuries. Sterne, more than any other writer of his age, re-established the native tradition, returning to the original genius of the language and making the basis of his style an English idiom that had been lost almost since Milton's day.

As examples of his expressive power there is almost every paragraph of *Tristram Shandy* and *A Sentimental Journey*. No books in English literature are so consistently brilliant and vivid in their style. An ease of rhythm and limpidity of phrase continue page after page and never dissipate into the fog of the impersonal, the pedantic, the dull, or the undistinguished. Consider how that power lives in a single famous phrase: 'God tempers the wind to the shorn lamb.' Even the considerable body of deliberate plagiarisms[2] do nothing but increase our wonder that such a little juggling should mean so great a

[1] Such as Sterne, Sermon xi, vol. vi, 'On Enthusiasm', and Locke, *Human Understanding,* Book IV, chap. xix, 'Of Enthusiasm'.

[2] See Dr. John Ferriar's *Illustrations of Sterne* (2nd edition, 1812), *passim.*

transmogrification. Here is a sentence from Bacon's essay on Death:[1]

'Groans and convulsions, and discoloured faces, and friends weeping, and blacks, and obsequies, and the like, show Death terrible.'

Sterne takes it, shakes it out a little, alters its rhythm and adds the vivid particularization in which he most reveals his genius, and gives us this wonderful sentence:

'There is no terror, brother Toby, in its looks, but what it borrows from groans and convulsions—and the blowing of noses, and the wiping away of tears with the bottoms of curtains in a dying man's room.'

Sterne's constructive genius is a more difficult question; it is so much less obvious. We have all been deceived by those squiggly lines which he drew in the sixth book of *Tristram Shandy* to represent the course of his narrative. But any dissatisfaction with the digressive spirit of Sterne's works arises from a misunderstanding of the methods proper to humoristic writing. The conception of plot, which we have continually in mind owing to our preoccupation with drama and fiction, has nothing to do with the question. It is possible that here again Sterne is indebted to Locke, and a contemporary German critic, Rudolf Kassner, has suggested that from the moment when Mr. Shandy was so unfeelingly interrupted in the first chapter of *Tristram* by his wife's stupid question about the clock, there is an elaborate play upon Locke's theory of duration. Sterne certainly seems to have taken hints from this part of the *Essay concerning Human Understanding* (Book II, ch. 14), but the real basis of his method is profounder. To quote Coleridge again, for the last time:

'You must bear in mind, in order to do justice to Rabelais and Sterne, that by right of humoristic universality each part is essentially a whole in itself. Hence the digressive spirit is not mere wantonness, but in fact the very form and vehicle of our

[1] Compare also Jeremy Taylor, *Holy Dying*, chap. iii, sec. 7, 4, for a very similar expression of the same thought.

genius. The connection, such as was needed, is given by the continuity of the characters.'

The characters persist, but the incidents are intermittent. They are finite flashes against an infinite background. This method, which is essential to humour, has a deeper significance for fiction in general. Continuity can be achieved in various ways, but in fiction we have in the past thought too exclusively of the continuity of action, of dramatic interest—in short, we have thought of a *mechanical* continuity. To that kind of continuity we nowadays oppose *psychological* continuity, and this is achieved either, as notably in the case of Henry James, by conceiving everything in the terms of a single consciousness; or else, as in the case of Marcel Proust, by attempting to get beyond the system of association and habit which constitutes our normal life and so down to the memory of that intermittent life of feeling which is the only subjective reality. Sterne is very modern in this sense. He is the precursor of all psychological fiction, which is as though we were to say: of all that is most significant in modern literature. But his influence animates more than a literary form. He was the freest spirit of his century, said Goethe; and Nietzsche called him the freest writer of all time. Neither Goethe nor Nietzsche stopped to define the nature of this freedom, but it seems to have some analogy to the care-free, ghost-free self-reliance of the epic hero. In this Sterne's heroes differ from the typical heroes of the Renaissance. Hamlet, Don Quixote, Faust—these are great mythical figures embodying the consciousness of a race or of an epoch, and in effect thereby transcending their actuality or humanity. But Uncle Toby and Corporal Trim, and above all Mr. Shandy, are, like Odysseus, at once mythical and human, and therefore held by us in a peculiar relation of both grandeur and intimacy.

PARTICULAR STUDIES

8

HAWTHORNE

Mr. Lloyd Morris's biography of Hawthorne[1] is a work of genuine merit and deserves the attention which a serious study of Hawthorne's genius should attract. As a biography it belongs to the modern school of 'biography made easy'—it 'runs as lightly as a novel', never halting to make a footnote or support a fact. When it is well done, there is no valid objection to this method; we take the biographer on trust and he presents us, after much labour and deliberation, with a work of art which is, in effect, the outcome of a sound judgement, a skilful control of material, and a scientific probity. It is true that Mr. Julian Hawthorne, the son of the novelist, has accused Mr. Morris[2] of distorting his father's character in essential particulars; he was robust and 'common-sensical', whereas Mr. Morris has made him a very Gentle Fanny, anaemic, morbid, and mysterious. But though we must give due weight to a son's impression of his father's personality, we must also remember that nowhere is a man so hidden as in his own family circle, and that the character he wears habitually in other men's eyes is often very different from the personality he creates within himself. Mr. Morris sees, not a body that moves and speaks in the daily round of life, but a mind whose real dwelling was in the remoter world of fancy and whose

[1] *The Rebellious Puritan. Portrait of Mr. Hawthorne.* By Lloyd Morris. (London and New York, 1928.)
[2] *Saturday Review of Literature*, 16th April 1927.

speech was certain works of art; and in his attempt to portray that more essential Hawthorne he has our sympathy and a good deal of our admiration.

That Hawthorne was not quite the breezy man of the world of his son's idealization is proved, if need be, by the curious fascination which he exercised on minds so perceptive and so worthy of him as Emerson and Melville. Emerson was impressed by 'the painful solitude of the man', yearned for his intimate friendship, but felt a barrier of 'unwillingness and caprice'. Hawthorne, we know, had a deep scorn for all metaphysical reasoning; he 'admired Emerson as a poet of deep beauty and austere tenderness, but sought nothing from him as a philosopher'. 'For myself', he wrote in *The Old Manse*, 'there had been epochs of my life when I, too, might have asked of this prophet the master word that should solve me the riddle of the universe; but now, being happy, I felt as if there were no question to be put.' Hawthorne, we feel, was a greater man than Emerson; he held to some truth that gave him the mastery and the inevitable scorn. Herman Melville's cry was deeper: 'Whence come you, Hawthorne? By what right do you drink from my flagon of life? And when I put it to my lips—lo, they are yours and not mine. I feel that the Godhead is broken up like the Bread at the Supper, and that we are the pieces. Hence this infinite fraternity of feeling.' Hawthorne recoiled from the intensity of Melville's conception of friendship; perhaps, Mr. Morris suggests, he did not understand it. 'He was incapable of sharing the ecstasies and pangs which their relations yielded to Melville. No doubt he desired neither ecstasies nor pangs. No doubt he desired only peace.' Hawthorne had no more liking for mysticism than for metaphysics, but in his rejection of Melville we cannot be equally sure of the rightness of his attitude. It does not go without saying that Hawthorne was the greater man. The greater artist, yes; but Melville's 'divine magnanimities' encompassed far more than Hawthorne's equanimity. In Hawthorne, simple happiness; in Melville, the 'profoundest sense of being'. 'Ineffable socialities are in me. . . . It is a strange feeling—no hopefulness is in it, no despair. Content—that is it; and irresponsibility; but without licentious inclination.'

Hawthorne's happiness was perhaps due to nothing more than the simplicity of his life. It is not fair (to this extent I agree with Mr. Julian Hawthorne) to call him a Puritan, even a rebellious one. In no sense is his art what the psychologists call a compensation—in no sense a reaction to environment or education, a working-off of repressions, a rationalization of fixed ideas. Hawthorne was born with a lively sensibility and that freedom of mind which best conduces to a temperate art; and there seems to have been no attempt to interfere with his natural development. The only necessities that ever seriously galled him were economic. He led a strangely secluded life in his adolescent years, but not stranger than that of any youth of his temperament born into the dreary waste of provincial life. His defects (which have often the appearance of being inhibitions) are really defects of education—as is most obviously shown in his aversion, later in life, to the nude statues he found everywhere about him in Rome. His remark that 'man is no longer a naked animal; his clothes are as natural to him as his skin, and sculptors have no more right to undress him than to flay him', strikes us with the force of its crudity rather than its prudery. It was not so much a 'strange, vague, long-dormant heritage of his strait-laced Puritan ancestry' as a simple lack of experience. There is surely plenty of evidence in his writings (in the descriptions of Zenobia in *The Blithedale Romance*, for example) to show that the sensuous elements in nature appealed to him in a normal way. Except that the Puritan was an integral part of the historical consciousness which he set himself out to portray, it is difficult to see how the label ever came to be applied so freely to Hawthorne. Actually he was the very antithesis of a Puritan.

It has already been observed that he was no mystic, and was, if anything, repelled by mysticism. But he was absorbed in something which is often confused with mysticism—in mystery or mysteriousness. And this fact is really the key to his character, if we can arrive at an understanding of it. There is in *Our Old Home* a passage which gives us a clue. In itself the passage is a remarkable anticipation of more recent interpretations of Gothic art. Hawthorne is describing Lichfield Cathedral:

'To my uninstructed vision, it seemed the object best worth gazing at in the whole world; and now, after beholding a great many more, I remember it with less prodigal admiration only because others are as magnificent as itself. The traces remaining in my memory represent it as airy rather than massive. A multitude of beautiful shapes appeared to be comprehended within its single outline; it was a kind of kaleidoscopic mystery, so rich a variety of aspects did it assume from each altered point of view, through the presentation of a different face, and the rearrangement of its peaks and pinnacles and the three battlemented towers, with the spires that shot heavenward from all three, but one loftier than its fellows. Thus it impressed you at every change, as a newly created structure of the passing moment, in which yet you lovingly recognized the half-vanished structure of the instant before, and felt, moreover, a joyful faith in the indestructible existence of all this cloudlike vicissitude. A Gothic cathedral is surely the most wonderful work which mortal man has yet achieved, so vast, so intricate, and so profoundly simple, with such strange, delightful recesses in its grand figure, so difficult to comprehend within one idea, and yet all so consonant that it ultimately draws the beholder and his universe into its harmony. It is the only thing in the world that is vast enough and rich enough.

'Not that I felt, or was worthy to feel, an unmingled enjoyment in gazing at this wonder. I could not elevate myself to its spiritual height, any more than I could have climbed from the ground to the summit of one of its pinnacles. Ascending but a little way, I continually fell back and lay in a kind of despair, conscious that a flood of uncomprehended beauty was pouring down upon me, of which I could appropriate only the minutest portion. After a hundred years, incalculably as my higher sympathies might be invigorated by so divine an employment, I should still be a gazer from below and at an awful distance, as yet remotely excluded from the interior mystery. But it was something gained, even to have that painful sense of my own limitations, and that half-smothered yearning to soar beyond them.'

This sense of an almost giddy vertiginous gulf between human finiteness and the infinity of the Absolute, whether in art or in religion, is the peculiar Northern or Gothic sensibility; and Hawthorne is a very pure representative of it. Nevertheless, he might well feel the painful sense of his own limitations at the sight of a Gothic cathedral, because this sense of the finite and the infinite, and of the infinite in the finite, can only be expressed through the access of an emotional force such as comes from an organized and universal religion. Hawthorne, of course, lacked this support, and fell back on that substitute which has proved a weariness to so many of his readers—symbolism. It is quite extraordinary how large a part this method of expression plays in his work. The greater number of his short stories and the four longer romances are either built round a symbol or liberally strewn with symbolic illustrations. The frequent introduction of mesmerism and spiritualism as factors in the plot merely shows the contagion of contemporary enthusiasms, and is a warning of how psycho-analysis in modern fiction may strike a reader fifty years hence. But the symbolism of which *The Scarlet Letter* is the most familiar example cannot so easily be dismissed. Or, at least, to dismiss it is to dismiss the essential quality of Hawthorne's art.

This quality was well described by Henry James in that biography of Hawthorne which is such a significant document in modern criticism, as an 'element of cold and ingenious phantasy', and was further characterized as 'passionless'. Henry James did not really appreciate this quality; one can hardly imagine Henry James appreciating Spenser and Bunyan, who are its great exemplifiers. He remarks, with reference to *The Scarlet Letter*, that 'the absence of a certain something warm and straightforward, a trifle more grossly human and vulgarly natural, which one finds in *Adam Blair*, will always make Hawthorne's tale less touching to a large number of even very intelligent readers, than a love story told with the robust, synthetic pathos which served Lockhart so well'. This was written in 1879, early in James's own career; and by the irony of events this is just the sort of criticism which is now being levelled against James's own later work. In fact, though he hardly realized it, James moved in his later years very near to the 'cold and ingenious phantasy', the 'passionless' quality of Hawthorne's tales; for what but allegories, revolving round symbols, are such novels as *The Golden Bowl*, *The Wings of the Dove*, and *The Ivory Tower*? The difference is merely one of the degree of intelligence involved. Is it possible that the cause determining the form was the same in both cases?

Let us further characterize this form as two-dimensional. It lacks the third dimension of depth, or passion. Hawthorne, who was well aware of the limits of his talent (and this has a great deal to do with his strength) observed of his *Twice-Told Tales* that:

'They have the pale tint of flowers that blossomed in too retired a shade—the coolness of a meditative habit, which diffuses itself through the feeling and observation of every sketch. Instead of passion, there is sentiment; and even in what purport to be pictures of actual life, we have allegory, not always so warmly dressed in its habiliments of flesh and blood, as to be taken into the reader's mind without a shiver. Whether from lack of power, or an unconquerable reserve, the Author's touches have often an effect of tameness; the merriest man can hardly contrive to laugh at his broadest humour; the tenderest woman, one would suppose, will hardly shed warm tears at his deepest pathos. The book, if you would see anything in it, requires to be read in the clear, brown, twilight atmosphere in which it was written; if opened in the sunshine, it is apt to look exceedingly like a volume of blank pages.'

And in another place Hawthorne confesses that his native propensities were towards Fairy Land.

All these self-descriptions are meant modestly enough, but they should not be taken as disparagements. Hawthorne's art belongs to that order of fancy which was defined by Coleridge as 'a mode of memory emancipated from the order of time and space', and as having 'no other counters to play with but fixities and definites'. Rather than disparage such works of phantasy, we should respect them as giving free play to the intelligence. Here alone in the world of fiction can the mind range unobstructed by emotion; and here, surely, is the possibility of an art as universal and as indestructible as the 'cloudlike vicissitudes' of Gothic architecture. Its very passionless quality, moreover, assures it of that objectivity which is the aim and distinction of all classical art; and objectivity was a characteristic which Henry James, without these considerations in mind, noted in Hawthorne's writing. It is precisely this objectivity which saves his treatment of Puritanism from any suggestion of inner compulsion.

But we must press this matter further, to ask how it came about that Hawthorne developed this particular type of art—whether, in other words, there was any compulsion determining the actual quality of his art. This involves us in a very delicate, a very significant, and a very complex problem. It can be briefly stated in words which Henry James used in this connection, and which may stand as a text for the whole debate—'that the flower of art blooms only where the soil is deep, that it takes a great deal of history to produce a little literature, that it needs a complex social machinery to set a writer in motion'. Henry James himself took this text very much to heart; it was the problem he himself had to solve, and Hawthorne was the terrible warning he always kept before his eyes. For his definite conclusion was that Hawthorne's art had suffered, and suffered disastrously, irremediably, from the thinness and insipidity of the atmosphere he had been compelled to live in. There is no doubt that in the panic induced by his own situation Henry James tended to depreciate too much the quality of Hawthorne's work. Above all, he failed to appreciate at its true value what we might call Hawthorne's provincialism. Whatever America of to-day may be, New England of a hundred years ago, in spite of its political independence, was spiritually an outer province of the British Isles. Now a province, though it lacks many of the positive virtues of a metropolis, has some rather negative virtues of its own. It is more confined in its outlook, but tends to send its roots deeper into the soil with which it is, moreover, in directer contact. Much of the best of our literature is essentially provincial—Sterne and the Brontës, and even Wordsworth. But, Henry James would have objected, provincial or not, these authors had a background, whereas in America there is 'no State, in the European sense of the word, and indeed barely a specific national name. No sovereign, no court, no personal loyalty, no aristocracy, no church, no clergy, no army, no diplomatic service, no country gentlemen, no palaces, no castles, nor manors, nor old country-houses, nor parsonages, nor thatched cottages, nor ivied ruins; no cathedrals, nor abbeys, nor little Norman churches; no great Universities nor public schools—no Oxford, nor Eton, nor Harrow; no literature, no novels, no museums, no pictures, no political society, no sporting class—no Epsom nor Ascot!'

'What was left?' cried Henry James. 'Why, simply the whole of life,' retorted Howells in a review of *Hawthorne*. James's own answer was that 'the American knows that a good deal remains; what it is that remains—that is his secret, his joke, as one may say. It would be cruel, in this terrible denudation, to deny him the consolation of his national gift, that "American humour" of which of late years we have heard so much.'

This is altogether too scornful. It is true that this same

'humour' is still the most trying feature of American writing. Facetiousness is the greatest blemish on Hawthorne's style; it is almost everywhere, and but for its presence Hawthorne would rank with a select company of four or five of our purest writers. An essay like *The Old Manse*, descriptive writing such as is found in *Our Old Home* (surely the best book on England ever written by an American), and, occasionally, intense nervous narrative such as he gives us in *The Scarlet Letter* and *The Blithedale Romance*—these cannot be matched by anything visibly dependent on Eton or Ascot. I will quote two examples:

'He spoke languidly, and only those few words, like a watch with an inelastic spring, that just ticks a moment or two, and stops again. He seemed a very forlorn old man. In the wantonness of youth, strength, and comfortable condition—making my prey of people's individualities, as my custom was—I tried to identify my mind with the old fellow's, and take his view of the world, as if looking through a smoke-blackened glass at the sun. It robbed the landscape of all its life. Those pleasantly swelling slopes of our farm, descending towards the wide meadows, through which sluggishly circled the brimful tide of the Charles, bathing the long sedges on its hither and further shores; the broad sunny gleam over the winding water; that peculiar picturesqueness of the scene where capes and headlands put themselves boldly forth upon the perfect level of the meadow, as into a green lake, with inlets between the promontories; the shadowy woodland, with twinkling showers of light falling into its depths; the sultry heat-vapour, which rose everywhere like incense, and in which my soul delighted, as indicating so rich a fervour in the passionate day, and in the earth that was burning with its love;—I beheld all these things as through old Moodie's eyes. When my eyes are dimmer than they have yet come to be, I will go thither again, and see if I did not catch the tone of his mind aright, and if the cold and lifeless tint of his perceptions be not then repeated in my own.'

S

This shows very exact observation, and a careful, conscious use of words, a subtle sense of rhythm. In the second passage, also from *The Blithedale Romance*, we have the same objectivity applied to a narrative of action:

'We floated past the stump. Silas Foster plied his rake manfully, poking it as far as he could into the water, and immersing the whole length of his arm besides. Hollingsworth at first sat motionless, with the hooked pole elevated in the air. But, by and by, with a nervous and jerky movement, he began to plunge it into the blackness that upbore us, setting his teeth, and making precisely such thrusts, methought, as if he were stabbing at a deadly enemy. I bent over the side of the boat. So obscure, however, so awfully mysterious, was that dark stream, that—and the thought made me shiver like a leaf—I might as well have tried to look into the enigma of the eternal world, to discover what had become of Zenobia's soul, as into the river's depths, to find her body. And there, perhaps, she lay, with her face upward, while the shadow of the boat, and my own pale face peering downward, passed slowly betwixt her and the sky!

'Once, twice, thrice, I paddled the boat up stream, and again suffered it to glide, with the river's slow, funereal motion, downward. Silas Foster had raked up a large mass of stuff, which, as it came towards the surface, looked somewhat like a flowing garment, but proved to be a monstrous tuft of water-weeds. Hollingsworth, with a gigantic effort, upheaved a sunken log. When once free of the bottom, it rose partly out of the water—all weedy and slimy, a devilish-looking object, which the moon had not shone upon for half a hundred years —then plunged again, and sullenly returned to its old resting-place, for the remnant of the century.'

But it would be impossible to quote a line further, because facetiousness, in the shape of Silas Foster, stalks all through this otherwise magnificent chapter. Perhaps it would have been juster to quote that other midnight scene, from *The Scarlet Letter*, where Dimmesdale mounts the scaffold on which Hester had suffered ignominy; for in that scene Hawthorne's descriptive powers reach an intensity he never equalled elsewhere. But then this scene dissolves into supernatural manifestations of symbolic import which, in their context, have an effect of triviality or irrelevance. It is but another aspect, the serious aspect, of the phenomenon of oblique reference. Whether as humour or as allegory, this phenomenon is the same in all American writers: they walk all round the circumference of a subject and imagine they have been at the centre. Was this not the very quality which Henry James brought with him to Europe and instead of surrendering, merely transmuted into intellectual forms? That, at any rate, is the superficial aspect of his genius.

This phenomenon, however, is merely a question of style. On the question of substance I must hark back to Hawthorne's provincialism, and insist that here was a positive colour, a depth, a density—something of an integrity worth cultivating. It was a tender growth, but how vivid! We might with pleasure turn oftener to the literary charm, the historical interest, the delicate phantasy with which Hawthorne evokes the New England scene, the New England past, the New England character. It is all so authentic; and if in his devotion to it Hawthorne sacrificed the finer graces of ancient culture and the surer power of established tradition, who shall say what the alternative would have cost in moral questionings— the alternative being, as Henry James was to demonstrate, expatriation? It is perhaps not a general question at all—not a question about which the critic has a right to generalize. We can only observe the dilemma, observe that Hawthorne and Henry James avoided it in different ways, and wonder whether a gain in aesthetic values is full compensation for a loss in moral virtue. That there was a third, and a desperate, solution is proved by the case of Poe, who impaled himself on the horns of the dilemma. He could neither accept for good or ill the provincialism he lived among, nor make the necessary effort to escape from it.

This quality in Hawthorne which I have described as provincialism—his particular atmosphere or essence—and the beautiful prose in which it finds expression—these would not in themselves have sufficed to give Hawthorne the high position he occupies in English literature. The heart also was involved. In his Preface to *The House of the Seven Gables* (Hawthorne's prefaces are as important as Henry James's) he once again shows us that he knew all the time what he was about:

'When a writer calls his work a Romance, it need hardly be observed that he wishes to claim a certain latitude, both as to its fashion and material, which he would not have felt himself entitled to assume, had he professed to be writing a Novel. The latter form of composition is presumed to aim at a very minute fidelity, not merely to the possible, but to the probable and ordinary course of man's experience. The former—while, as a work of art, it must rigidly subject itself to laws, and while it sins unpardonably so far as it may swerve aside from the truth of the human heart—has fairly a right to present that truth under circumstances, to a great extent, of the writer's own choosing or creation.'

'The truth of the human heart' is perhaps what Howells meant by the whole of human life. It is a sentimental phrase, of course, and Henry James might have argued that the heart can be as impoverished as the body or the mind by a waste environment. Perhaps it can, in an abstract and very evolutionary sense. But it would be obvious nonsense to deny to the New Englander of the nineteenth century, above all to one of such refined sensibilities as Hawthorne, the fullest range of human emotions. And where there are emotions there can be tragedy, and all the forms of literature leading up to tragedy. No one has seriously contended that the inhabitants of America are without original sin—if we may assume the validity of that very necessary dogma; and where there is original sin there also is an original sense of values; and art, especially the art of the novelist, is the working out of such a sense of values. From this point of view two clauses of Henry James's text prove false; neither a deep soil nor a long history is a condition essential for art; and the remaining clause, that it needs a complex social machinery to set a writer in motion, is merely a relative condition. Hawthorne was obviously set in motion, so presumably the simple machinery of New England society was adequate in that sense; and though lack of encouragement and lack of appreciation may finally defeat the strongest creative impulse, this impulse in itself is a subjective phenomenon. In so far as art is original (and that is the last essential test of art), it is innate, and independent of social categories. It is only the socialization of art—the process by means of which the art is made available for the community through structures like the epic, the drama and the novel—it is only this process which suffers from the absence of a tradition. The poet is then apt to write for himself, or for some ideal futurity, and to be so much the less universal.

Hawthorne, however, wrote for the New England society of his time, and his art is admirably proportioned to the nature of this community. It was, above all, a very self-conscious community. It took itself very seriously—not only in the sense that it deliberately cultivated its newly founded nationality and was already on the look-out for national heroes and national poets, but also in the sense that it tried very hard to behave itself in the eyes of the world. It was preoccupied especially with moral problems; and in making these the concern of his writing, Hawthorne was consciously or unconsciously taking advantage of whatever virtue of depth there was in the immature society around him. The Puritan conscience might at first glance seem an unpromising subject for the delicate visionary that Hawthorne in his early tales had shown himself to be; but his gift of objectivity enabled him to play lightly with the heaviest of materials. 'He continued,' as Henry James expressed it, 'by an exquisite process best known to himself, to transmute this heavy moral burden into the very substance of the imagination, to make it evaporate in the light and charming fumes of artistic production.'[1] Henry James then goes on to define very exactly the nature of this transmutation:

'Nothing is more curious and interesting than this almost exclusively *imported* character of the sense of sin in Hawthorne's mind; it seems to exist there merely for an artistic or literary purpose. He had ample cognizance of the Puritan conscience; it was his natural heritage; it was reproduced in him; looking into his soul, he found it there. But his relation to it was only, as one may say, intellectual; it was not moral and theological. He played with it and used it as a pigment; he treated it, as the metaphysicians say, objectively. He was not discomposed, disturbed, haunted by it, in the manner of its usual and regular victims, who had not the little postern door of fancy to slip through, to the other side of the wall. It was, indeed, to his imaginative vision, the great fact of man's nature; the light element that had been mingled with his own

---

[1] In this connection it is interesting to compare a short story in *Twice-Told Tales* called 'The Minister's Black Veil' with *The Scarlet Letter*. The theme is the same in both cases. But in 'The Minister's Black Veil' the hidden remorse of the Rev. Mr. Hooper is merely symbolized in the black veil which he wears over his face, and the nature of his remorse is never known; the story remains strictly allegorical. In *The Scarlet Letter*, however, we are very soon made aware of the nature of the Rev. Mr. Dimmesdale's remorse, and though we never revel in the modern manner in the details out of which the tragic situation arises, the tragedy itself is worked out on the plane of reality. The phantasy which is the predominant quality of the short tales is in the longer romances reduced to a very subordinate place, and is even then to be regretted. So great is the difference between these two phases of Hawthorne's work that we begin to wonder whether he was subject to some decisive influence at the time he wrote *The Scarlet Letter* (1850). That particular kind of intensity was then rare enough, but manifest in two novels published from a Yorkshire parsonage in 1847. The great similarity between the characters of Chillingworth and Heathcliff would support a suggestion that Hawthorne was inspired in some degree by *Wuthering Heights*; and later we find a confession scene in *The Marble Faun* (1860) closely duplicating a similar scene in *Villette* (1852). Such influences are inevitable, and in writers of independent genius such as Hawthorne they are all to the good, opening out veins which would otherwise remain buried. In any case, such influences are not fruitful unless there is a prior aptitude in the author influenced.

composition always clung to this rugged prominence of moral responsibility, like the mist that hovers about the mountain. It was a necessary condition for a man of Hawthorne's stock that if his imagination should take licence to amuse itself, it should at least select this grim precinct of the Puritan morality for its play-ground.'

This is so truly expressed that it leaves little more to be said. But Hawthorne's example is one of very wide significance, and one that can benefit a generation which is singularly confused on the subject of the relationship of morality to art. Hawthorne was a 'pure' artist in the modern sense—as 'pure' as Poe or Landor, Flaubert or Mallarmé. And yet he was preoccupied with moral problems—as, to a great extent, was Flaubert also. The distinction is, of course, that he did not desire a solution of them—not a solution, at any rate, on the moral plane. His scorn of the self-concentrated philanthropist, and of the meddler in other people's affairs generally, is evident everywhere—but especially in *The Blithedale Romance*, which might have been written for the express purpose of making this attitude clear. The only agent he employed in his moral dramas was the conscience; and all his romances might be described as studies in remorse, which is conscience accusing itself. The extraordinary thing, above all in *The Scarlet Letter*, is the degree of intensity with which the theme is invested. Indeed, that is the extraordinary thing about Hawthorne altogether, and the one factor which more than any other inclines us to rank him as a major artist—the capacity, that is, which he has for putting an emotional emphasis into subjects so dispassionately conceived. The resulting art is 'classical', but it is reached by the reverse of the normal classical procedure of putting a rational curb on to subjects emotionally conceived. The subjects are indeed 'grim', but the imagination has thrown over them its own peculiar radiance and glory.

PARTICULAR STUDIES

9
CHARLOTTE AND EMILY BRONTË

Heredity is a factor which we cannot neglect in considering the course of any human life, but in ascribing any importance to it, we should be careful to distinguish rather sharply between intelligence or mental development, which is the product of natural selection in the race and of education in the individual, and what for want of another word we must call genius, which, when it is of any value, is intelligence directed into personal and wayward channels. It is merely the instrument of genius—the brain considered as a muscle—that is susceptible to hereditary influences. The rest is the product of environment and chance—particularly of the psychological events introduced into life by human relationships.

When we have to reckon with any degree of historical remoteness, heredity becomes a very obscure influence, and the observed facts, in a case like that of the Brontë family, are far too unreliable and unsystematic to be of much use. We see two human strains, themselves the products of incalculable forces, which unite and give issue to genius. The process, one can persist in believing, is as natural as a chemical combination, but it is impossible to reduce it to an equation. We can at the best only point to tendencies and characteristics in the parent stock and hazard that these are some of the elements responsible—and these are but vague, obvious features which it would be difficult to use with any scientific precision.

In the case of the Brontës we have, on the one side, a stock

of somewhat barbarous origin, culminating in a man of deter-
mination and capability, a man who 'early gave tokens of
extraordinary quickness and intelligence'. Patrick Brontë had
opened a public school at the age of sixteen, and at the age of
twenty-five was still ambitious enough to proceed to Cambridge, where he took his degree after four years' study. Mrs.
Gaskell's rather picturesque description of his passionate nature
has been discredited in some of its details, but enough authentic evidence remains to evoke for us a grim puritanical mask,
expressing, even while it repressed, the fires beneath. Mrs.
Brontë brought characteristics which were of a more ordinary
nature, though perhaps no less essential to the result. She was
intelligent, placid, and ailing. Her delicate constitution passed
to her children, and perhaps this factor, more than any other,
determined their neurotic tendency. A neurosis, however,
generally needs more than ill health for its inducement: it
needs a psychic shock of some kind, and perhaps the mother
provided this also by her early death in 1821, when Charlotte
was but five and Emily three years old. The strong instinctive
link between mother and child is never thus abruptly broken
without unseen compensations and reverberations. The enormous body of childish writings still existing in Charlotte's
case, but until recently withheld for its lack of literary qualities, may conceivably be of great significance from this point
of view. I will merely suggest that we have in Charlotte's
seemingly endless fictive evocations of the Duke of Wellington a phantasy of a kind made familiar to us by the researches
of psycho-analysts. 'Charlotte's little stories', writes Mr.
Shorter, 'commence in her thirteenth year, and go on until
she is twenty-three. From thirteen to eighteen she would seem
to have had one absorbing hero—the Duke of Wellington.
Whether the stories be fairy tales or dramas of modern life,
they all alike introduce the Marquis of Douro.'[1] Interpretations
of such a phantasy as this might differ: Adler would see in it
an unconscious attempt on the part of the neurotic weakling

[1] Clement Shorter: *The Brontës, Life and Letters* (1908), p. 72.

to free herself from a feeling of inferiority[1] by the creation of a compensating ideal of superiority; Jung would find the unconscious origin of such a hero phantasy quite simply in a longing for the lost mother, whereas Freud would probably treat it as the sublimation of a repressed love for the father. But whatever interpretation is adopted, a sense of inferiority, of incompleteness, is seen as the essential character of the neurosis underlying the phantasy.

In the case of Emily the same causes produced a 'masculine protest' of a more complex kind, showing, indeed, the typical features of what I think we must, with the psycho-analyst, regard as some kind of psychical hermaphroditism. The outward expression of this state was evident enough. In her childhood the villagers thought her more like a boy than a girl. 'She should have been a man: a great navigator!' cried M. Heger, despite his horror of her intractability. Charlotte refers to 'a certain harshness in her powerful and peculiar character'. 'Stronger than a man, simpler than a child, her nature stood alone.' Yet Emily was not given to expressing herself by outward speech or action; she was sombre and reserved—was, in fact, of a shy, introspective cast; from which clue the psychologist will realize how much deeper and more powerful must have been the masculine assumptions of her mind. These found their fit expression, in due course, in *Wuthering Heights*, whose very peculiar merits show that mingling of the strong and the sweet which some critics make the criterion of all great works of the imagination, and which, in her case, was but the direct expression of her nature.

We might pass further, in illustration of our point, to the cases of Anne and Branwell. The former as an example of

[1] There are many direct betrayals in Charlotte's correspondence of this deeply-felt sense of inferiority. The following passage from the reminiscences of her school friend, Mary Taylor, is significant: 'She always showed physical feebleness in everything. She ate no animal food at school. It was about this time I told her she was very ugly. Some years afterwards I told her I thought I had been very impertinent. She replied: "You did me a great deal of good, Polly, so don't repent of it." '

religious melancholy, and the latter as an example of disinte-
grated personality, offer familiar characteristics: they are true
to type. But consideration of them is much less important,
because it does not bear on a creative artist of much significance. It is sufficient to observe that though all four cases
present very diverse symptoms, they are all traceable to the
one cause: the early rupture of the maternal bond of affection
and protection, the intolerance of a stern, impassive father, the
formation of inferiority complexes in the children, and the
consequent compensations by phantasy.

What it is now necessary to emphasize strongly, in concluding this psychological excursus, is that art is a triumph
over neurosis; that though it originates in a neurotic tendency,
it is a coming-out-against this tendency; and that in the case
of the three sisters the sublimation was achieved. Their art is
not neurotic in kind; no art is. It is only when we search for
causes and origins (as we have a perfect right to do) that we
discover the neurosis; in the final effect, according to the
measure of its success, all is health and harmony.

In dealing with these psychological questions we have, I
think, emphasized the kind of environment that leaves the
deepest mark on the formation of character and genius. But
we are left with the environment of place, of locality. This
influence is most in question in the case of Emily, that 'nursling
of the moors', and indeed her poems show, I think, the most
intense rendering of the embodied presence of nature that
anywhere exists in English literature.

> *The earth that wakes* one *human heart to feeling*
> *Can centre both the worlds of Heaven and Hell.*

In these two lines she reaches a climax in her philosophy of
nature, and shows a depth of emotional perception which was
not exceeded even by Wordsworth.

But the immediate influence of natural scenes differs from
this general evocation of the spirit of nature. There is about
the moors of Yorkshire, where they yet remain, a quality that

works strongly on the senses. Their sparseness and loneliness drive you to an intimacy with whatever life does exist there; a small thing like the scent of bog-myrtle can kindle a keen emotion. There is a severity in the unrelieved reach of gradual hill country; the eye drifts into distant prospects, seeks the sky-line that is not a line, but a subtle merging of tones; the human mind *is* perhaps heard more distinctly in this inorganic stillness—only when, however, it has learned to think, and to express its thoughts. The moors, like any other local endowment, are merely material for observation and perception, and if into their confines there happens to enter a mind of exceptional dimensions, this mind will use its environment to some purpose. Such was the case with Emily Brontë. Charlotte, writing that eloquent and penetrating Preface to the second edition of *Wuthering Heights*, expresses this fact with all her rhetorical force:

'*Wuthering Heights* was hewn in a wild workshop, with simple tools, out of homely materials. The statuary found a granite block on a solitary moor; gazing thereon, he saw how from the crag might be elicited a head, savage, swart, sinister; a form moulded with at least one element of grandeur—power. He wrought with a rude chisel, and from no model but the vision of his meditations.'

We should note how objective the attitude of the artist is made. A more facile conception would have imbued the statuary with the moor's savage elements, and made the image but the reflection of an entranced imagination. But the vision of her meditations was the product of an applied mind; and that this fixed itself mainly on a rustic scene was but the result of chance limitations—limitations, however, which we do not regret, since they drove that vision so deeply into the heart of the subject.

A far more effective factor, both in the case of Emily and of Charlotte, was what we might call quite simply education, but which resolves, upon deeper analysis, into the personal influence of Constantin Heger. In Charlotte's case it seems that this aggressive intellect—masculine, fiery, compact—came opportunely to occupy the stronghold of the unconscious evacuated by the Duke of Wellington, whose lustre had no doubt waned with the growth of experience and intelligence. From the psychological point of view, that is all that need be said of a personal relationship which has been the subject of much speculation; though the intense nature that the hero worship was to assume, before the end of Charlotte's stay in Brussels, was, as I shall make out later, a determining experience in her life.

The immediate importance of this contact was its purely literary consequences. Charlotte and Emily learned the meaning of style—and style not in the English sense of picturesqueness, but in the French sense of clarity and brevity. Spirits that were romantic, or at any rate Celtic, submitted to the discipline of a strictly Latin mind—Latin in its scepticism, its dryness, and its dignity. Mrs. Gaskell printed a *devoir* of Charlotte's corrected by M. Heger, where the process may be seen in action. In the simple and halting French then at Charlotte's command we already experience the peculiar force and vividness of her impressions; but the corrections and marginal comments of M. Heger are the precepts, not of a schoolmaster, but of a master of the art of writing. 'He told me', relates Mrs. Gaskell, 'that one day this summer [when the Brontës had been for about four months receiving instruction from him] he read to them Victor Hugo's celebrated portrait of Mirabeau, "mais, dans ma leçon je me bornais à ce qui concerne *Mirabeau Orateur*. C'est après l'analyse de ce morçeau, considéré surtout de point de vue du fond, de la disposition, de ce qu'on pourrait appeler *la charpente* qu'ont été faits les deux portraits que je vous donne." He went on to say that he had pointed out to them the fault in Victor Hugo's style as being exaggeration in conception, and, at the same time, he had made them notice the extreme beauty of his "nuances" of expression. They were then dismissed to choose the subject of a similar kind of portrait. This selection M. Heger always left to them; for "it is necessary", he observed, "before sitting down to write on a subject, to have thoughts and feelings about it, I cannot tell on what subject your heart and mind have been excited. I must leave that to you." '

When Charlotte finally left the Heger institute at Brussels, some eighteen months after the composition of the *devoir* referred to, the intense desire to write, which had been hers since childhood, assumed a more definite urgency. It was not merely that she had perfected, under the Professor's care, the methods of self-expression; she had also endured a nervous crisis of an indefinite nature but of a deep effect. She herself (in a letter to Miss Wooler in 1846) described her state as *hypochondria*: 'I endured it but a year and assuredly I can never forget the concentrated anguish of certain insufferable moments, and the heavy gloom of many long hours, besides the preternatural horrors which seemed to clothe existence and nature, and which made life a continual walking nightmare. Under such circumstances the morbid nerves can know neither peace nor enjoyment; whatever touches pierces them: sensation for them is suffering.' Mrs. Gaskell pictures some of the circumstances of this period. Charlotte had been left during the *grandes vacances* in the great deserted pensionnat, with only one teacher for a companion. 'This teacher, a Frenchwoman, had always been uncongenial to her; but, left to each other's sole companionship, Charlotte soon discovered that her associate was more profligate, more steeped in a kind of cold, systematic sensuality, than she had before imagined it possible for a human being to be; and her whole nature revolted from this woman's society. A low nervous fever was gaining upon Miss Brontë. She had never been a good sleeper, but now she could not sleep at all. Whatever had been disagreeable, or obnoxious, to her during the day, was presented when it was over with exaggerated vividness to her disordered fancy. . . . In the daytime, driven abroad by loathing of her companion and by the weak restlessness of fever, she tried to walk herself into such a state of bodily fatigue as would induce sleep.... The shades of evening made her retrace her footsteps —sick for want of food, but not hungry; fatigued with long continued exercise—yet restless still, and doomed to another weary, haunted night of sleeplessness.' During one such anguished progress, she found herself before a confessional in Ste. Gudule's, and, her strong Protestant prejudices succumbing to what she calls 'an odd whim', she abandoned herself to that psychopathic consolation. 'I was determined to confess,' she writes to Emily. 'I actually did confess—a real confession.' The vivid use she made of the incident, in *Villette*, is only the most obvious record of this spiritual climax; the complete pathological phase (where sensation, as she says, was suffering) constituted, I think, the fundamental experience upon which she built her whole conception of imaginative reality.[1]

I have here used an epithet, 'imaginative', which it is necessary to use at all times with care and generally to avoid. It is one of those epithets that normally cloak a lack of thought or a failure of analysis. Nevertheless, I think it will be found, when reduced to its definite limits, to connote a certain process in the mind of the creative writer for which no other more suitable term can be used. The merely descriptive distinction between the fancy and the imagination, which has so long served in the sphere of literary criticism, is no longer adequate. It is not based on any corresponding psychological distinction; and even when the elements of fancy are excluded, we are left with no clear boundaries within which we can

[1] In considering this period of her life, though I ignore, I do not deny what the four letters from Charlotte to Constantin Heger, published by *The Times* in 1913, are a sufficient proof of: the importance of her feelings for Professor Heger in the causation of this pathological state. There can be no question of the existence, in her mind, of an appalling conflict between the strength of her emotion and the considerations—social, moral, and religious—which caused her to hide, even from herself, the nature of this emotion. The result was a decided 'complex', and I should be disposed to agree with a psychologist who identified her whole neurotic condition at this period with such a specific repression. I do not consider the *cause* of her state too closely because all I am concerned with is its effect upon her creative mind.

confine the activities of the imagination. It is merely a distinction, as Pater pointed out, between degrees of intensity. It
would not, however, serve any useful purpose to import into
literary criticism the purely technical conception of the imagination current in the old psychology, however precise such a
use might be. We merely want a more definite understanding
of the way in which ideas and images are associated in that
abnormal manner we term imaginative. It was in the capture
of such states of excitement that Wordsworth quite rightly
saw the function of the poet. And although in the case of
fiction the plane of conception is different, being more relative, less absolute—a detailed construction of dramatic events
rather than a generalized expression of states of consciousness
or thought—nevertheless, the psychological mechanism is the
same. True imagination is a kind of logic; it is the capacity to
deduce from the nature of an experienced reality, the nature
of other unexperienced realities. Upon the depth and totality
of the original experience will depend the reach and validity
of the imaginative process. If the process is kept to a quasi-
logical rigidity, it may be observed that merely one kind of
experience, sufficiently realized, will suffice for an almost
unlimited progression of imaginative analogies: the one experience will be ballast enough to carry the author through
any fictive evocation of feelings and actions. The case of
Dostoevsky is very illustrative of this truth; and the life of
Charlotte Brontë is well worth consideration precisely because
the process, the logic, is there seen so uncontaminated by subsidiary influences.

Experience alone does not, of course, make the poet or
novelist; it merely qualifies him. It must be united with a
previous disposition to create an imaginary world, the origin
of which, as I have suggested, is to be found in psychological
factors at work during infancy and adolescence. Charlotte
early had 'the desire (almost amounting to illness) of expressing herself in some way,—writing or drawing'.[1] At school she

[1] Mrs. Gaskell's account of conversations with Charlotte. See *Life*, chap.
xxvii.

developed a talent, under the guise of play, of 'making things out'. 'This habit', one of her school friends relates, 'of "making out" interests for themselves that most children get who have none in actual life, was very strong in her. The whole family used to "make out" histories, and invent characters and events. I told her sometimes they were like growing potatoes in a cellar. She said, sadly, "Yes! I know we are!".' The greater bulk of the unpublished Brontë manuscripts seems to consist of an elaborate 'cycle' of stories and poems, written over a long period of years and concerned with the politics and chivalry of a kingdom imagined in every detail. To revert to the old antithesis, these were works of idle fancy; but when bleak disillusionment was added to the already sufficiently bleak existence of these children, when expression became a more serious necessity as an escape from emotional agitations too strong to be repressed with impunity, then the mere mechanism of literary expression was ready at their command.

This is to put the matter on its deterministic level; it is perhaps of more profit to note the conscious reactions of Charlotte to these emotional and mental transitions. There are two points to notice: her theory of the relation of experience to imagination; and the evolution, at her hands, of the analytic method in fiction. The best expression of the first point was elicited during Charlotte's brief correspondence with G. H. Lewes—a literary encounter very characteristic of the period and about which an effect of exquisite comedy lurks. On 6th November 1847 she wrote in reply to a friendly letter of Lewes's, dictated by his enthusiasm for *Jane Eyre*: 'You advise me, too, not to stray far from the ground of experience, as I become weak when I enter the region of fiction, and you say, "real experience is perennially interesting, and to all men". I feel that this is also true; but, dear sir, is not the real experience of each individual very limited? And if a writer dwells upon that solely or principally, is he not in danger of repeating himself, and also of becoming an egotist? Then, too, imagination is a strong, restless faculty, which claims to be heard and exercised: are we to be quite deaf to her cry, and insensate to her struggles? When she shows us bright pictures, are we never to look at them, and try to reproduce them? And when she is eloquent, and speaks rapidly and urgently in our ear, are we not to write to her dictation?'

In reading this passage we must remember that Charlotte writes conscious of what she could but regard as a salutary lesson in the strategy of authorship: this was the complete failure of her first novel, *The Professor*, in which, as Mrs. Gaskell says, 'she went to the extreme of reality, depicting characters as they had shown themselves to her in actual life'. And in the letter to Lewes already quoted, Charlotte herself confessed: 'When I first began to write, so impressed was I with the truth of the principles you advocate, that I determined to take Nature and Truth as my sole guides, and to follow their very footprints; I restrained imagination, eschewed romance, repressed excitement; over-bright colouring, too, I avoided, and sought to produce something which should be soft, grave, and true.' But the publishers would have none of it, and the convenient theory of art for art's sake not being yet a part of the literary consciousness, she had decided to modify her virtuous course. She abandoned the mere transcript of experience and adopted the imaginative process I have tried to define.[1] It is here that we must realize the essential strength of her character and genius; a weaker writer would have had recourse to the less intense forms of imaginative activity; but Charlotte, driven, perhaps, by sub-

[1] It is interesting to note her own subsequent and detached opinion of the qualities which, nevertheless, did result from her first method. In a letter to W. S. Williams dated 14th December 1847, she writes: 'A few days since I looked over *The Professor*. I found the beginning very feeble, the whole narrative deficient in incident and in general attractiveness. Yet the middle and latter portion of the work, all that relates to Brussels, the Belgian school, etc., is as good as I can write; it contains more pith, more substance, more reality, in my judgement, than much of *Jane Eyre*. It gives, I think, a new view of a grade, an occupation, and a class of characters—all very commonplace, very insignificant in themselves, but not more so than the materials composing that portion of *Jane Eyre* which seems to please most generally.'

conscious forces, determined, in her own phrase, to be 'her own woman'. She determined to see justly rather than to feel kindly; and when she was almost agonized by the suggestion, emanating from the *Quarterly*, but eagerly repeated even by the kind of people she herself thought nice, that *Jane Eyre* was a 'wicked book', even then she had the courage of her magnificent retort: 'I am resolved not to write otherwise. *I shall bend as my powers tend.*'

Her powers resided in her intuitive logic, though she rather tended to mask the incidence of her faculty. 'We only suffer reality to *suggest*, never to *dictate*,' she writes to her old school friend; and some years later, with *Villette* fresh from her pen, she even went so far as to enunciate this slightly insincere maxim: 'I hold that a work of fiction ought to be a work of creation: that the *real* should be sparingly introduced in pages dedicated to the *ideal*.' This hardly tallies with her own criticism of *Villette*: 'I greatly apprehend that the weakest character in the book is the one I aimed at making the most beautiful; and, if this be the case, the fault lies in its wanting the germ of the *real*—in its being purely imaginary.' We have in this latter statement, self-analysed and self-confessed, the whole secret of her strength. Her practice of fiction resolves always into a nucleus of experience and the growth, from this nucleus, of an imaginative organism 'given off', as in nature, cell by cell, with inexorable continuity.

Combined with this process, a part of its mechanism, was the gift of analysis. Some years before she began to write, even before her education at Brussels, she was aware of her capabilities in this direction. She warned a rejected suitor, who wished to become her 'friend', that 'it has always been my habit to study the character of those amongst whom I chance to be thrown. . . . As for me, you do not know me: I am not the serious, grave, cool-headed individual you would suppose: you would think me romantic and eccentric; you would say I was satirical and severe.' The two faculties of her writing are clearly foreshadowed here: imagination and analysis.

There is no need to enlarge upon this second quality; it is so obviously her distinction. The consistency of its exercise—as, for example, in the character of Madame Beck—is perhaps for her date a matter for wonder. She herself remarks of Balzac: 'By-and-by I seemed to enter into the mystery of his craft, and to discover, with delight, where his force lay: is it not in the analysis of motive, and in a subtle perception of the most obscure and secret workings of the mind?' But at the time of her first introduction to Balzac's work, her own gift was already fully formed. I find no evidence anywhere that she knew the work of Stendhal, or the solitary masterpiece of Benjamin Constant; but she introduced into English literature the very qualities of psychological observation and analysis by which these writers had instituted a new epoch in the literature of France.

The influence she exercised on the development of the English novel was more profound than is often acknowledged: it is *Villette*, more than any work of Thackeray or George Eliot, that we must recognize as the pioneer of an extension of the province and function of the novelist's art only completely worked into the tradition of the English novel by Meredith and Henry James. To her contemporaries this revolutionary element in her work was quite evident, and though they did not stop to consider its real nature, they disliked it strongly because it was strange. Open-minded critics of the stamp of Lewes and Thackeray were willing to acknowledge the power and originality of her art, but the more average minds of the time experienced a sense of shock, deepening to outrage when it gradually became evident that the mysterious Currer Bell belonged to the gentler sex. The particular charge, first raised against *Jane Eyre*, but repeated in the case of *Shirley*, was one of 'coarseness'. What her accusers meant by their term cannot be very vivid to our modern consciousness: all they meant would, I think, easily be included in our concept 'realism'. But even Mrs. Gaskell, who by no means shared all the prudery of her age, thought it necessary to apologize for this lapse on the part of her heroine; and did so in these curious sentences:

'I do not deny for myself the existence of coarseness here and there in her works, otherwise so entirely noble. I only ask those who read them to consider her life,—which has been openly laid bare before them,—and to say how it could be otherwise. She saw few men; and among these few were one or two with whom she had been acquainted since early childhood,—who had shown her much friendliness and kindness, —through whose family she had received many pleasures,— for whose intellect she had a great respect,—but who talked before her, if not to her, with as little reticence as Rochester talked to Jane Eyre. Take this in connection with her poor brother's sad life, and the outspoken people among whom she lived,—remember her strong feeling of the duty of representing life as it really is, not as it ought to be,—and then do her justice for all that she was, and all that she would have been (had God spared her), rather than censure her because circumstances forced her to touch pitch, as it were, and by it her hand was for a moment defiled.' (*Life*, ch. xxvi.)

Charlotte herself could not comprehend the charge; and her unconsciousness of the very existence of what her critics so plainly realized, brings before us in all its uniqueness the amazing quality of *innocence* which distinguishes, not only her own work, but that of her sisters also. It is because the art was so innocent that it is so real. One can only account for the phenomenon by the unparalleled isolation of their lives. Though from an early age they devoured every scrap of literature that came within their reach, it is doubtful if anything of a directly inspiring kind ever came their way before Charlotte's and Emily's departure for Brussels. At Haworth they seem to have been confined to a diet of newspapers, sermons, and the Bible; and at Brussels, though in the matter of style and composition their reading there had incalculable influence, yet it seems certain that, with the possible exception of Hoffmann and Rousseau, it did not include anything that could form a model for their own efforts. At any rate, whatever the explanation, it is certain that when the three sisters solemnly and in unison sat down to compose their first serious novels, they did so without any prepossessions. They are the least influenced and most original geniuses in the whole history of the English novel. What Charlotte in her Introduction to *Wuthering Heights* wrote of the others, was equally true of herself: 'Neither Ellis nor Acton was learned: they had no thoughts of filling their pitchers at the well-spring of other minds; they always wrote from the impulse of nature, the dictates of intuition, and from such stores of observation as their limited experience had enabled them to amass.'

It is this quality of innocence that gives to *Wuthering Heights* its terrible and unique intensity. If I have written of Charlotte to the neglect of Emily, it is not that for one moment I make the mistake of attaching more importance to her. It is merely that in the case of Charlotte the evidence is so much more ample. The psychology of Emily is at once less complex and more profoundly hidden. She is one of the strangest geniuses in our literature, and her kinship is with Baudelaire and Poe. It is not merely that her imagination traverses the same sombre shadows, but also like these two anguished minds, she is for ever perplexed by the problem of evil—'conquered good and conquering ill'. Her absorption in metaphysical problems has no parallel in the poetry of her age, and in her 'Last Lines' rises to an intensity of emotional thought not surpassed in the whole range of English literature. Yet this same mind was capable of the purest lyrical utterance—in which, however, the sense of mortality seems to linger:

> Fall, leaves, fall; die, flowers, away;
> Lengthen night, and shorten day!
> Every leaf speaks bliss to me,
> Fluttering from the autumn tree.
>
> I shall smile when wreaths of snow
> Blossom where the rose should grow;

CHARLOTTE AND EMILY BRONTË

I shall sing when night's decay
Ushers in a drearier day.

Emily Brontë's poetry, which is at once explicit and profound, with sense finely annealed to cadence, is the most essential poetry ever written by a woman in the English tongue. Her mind, far more daring than Charlotte's, soared above particular creeds and attained in a few momentary manifestations those universal forms of thought common only to minds of the first order. Her best poems suffer, at present, by being bound up with much that is juvenile and occasional in kind. *Wuthering Heights* remains, the towering rock of Charlotte's metaphor, extremely definite, completely achieved, and of an amazing unity of tone.

We are left with one other element, common to Emily and Charlotte, which needs a word of notice. A certain lack of reticence had shocked the ruck of their Victorian critics; a smaller and a rarer band were disturbed by the evident rapture. It fell to Harriet Martineau, economist, moralist, agnostic, and a very typical representative of her age, to bring this criticism to a head. Despite a friendship she had formed for Charlotte, she had felt bound to air her misgivings in *The Daily News*, and in a review of *Villette* had insisted that Charlotte made love too general and too absorbing a factor in women's lives, protesting against the assumption that 'events and characters are to be regarded through the medium of one passion only'. Charlotte demurred, but Miss Martineau, indomitable and pitiless, wrote to her: 'I do not like the love, either the kind or the degree of it; and its prevalence in the book and effect on the action of it, help to explain the passages in the reviews which you consulted me about, and seem to afford *some* foundation for the criticisms they offered.' Charlotte retired abashed; she had but followed 'the impulses of nature and the dictates of intuition'. And about this very book she had written to her publisher: 'Unless I am mistaken, the emotion of the book will be found to be kept throughout in tolerable subjection.' Emotion in subjection—that is the very definition of art! And because Miss Martineau did not realize this, she has become a curious paleolithic dummy, an Aunt Sally ready for our modern ironists, whilst Charlotte still lives in her books with all the directness of a real personality.

But it is not Miss Martineau who was destined to stand as antitype to the Brontës: a subtler and finer antagonist had been in the field for some time. It speaks a good deal for Charlotte's critical perception that she realized the implications of Miss Austen's talent as soon as she became aware of it, rather late in her life, and, though only in the privacy of her correspondence with her publisher, she then defined the limitations of that talent in terms which still remain unanswerable. In a letter written in 1850 she says: 'She does her business of delineating the surface of the lives of genteel English people curiously well. There is a Chinese fidelity, a miniature delicacy in the painting. She ruffles her reader by nothing vehement, disturbs him by nothing profound. The passions are perfectly unknown to her; she rejects even a speaking acquaintance with that stormy sisterhood. Even to the feelings she vouchsafes no more than an occasional graceful but distant recognition—too frequent converse with them would ruffle the smooth elegance of her progress. Her business is not half so much with the human heart as with the human eyes, mouth, hands, and feet. What sees keenly, speaks aptly, moves flexibly, it suits her to study; but what throbs fast and full, though hidden, what the blood rushes through, what is the unseen seat of life and the sentient target of death—this Miss Austen ignores.' The justice of that analysis remains, to confront the present sophisticated rage for Jane Austen. But it also remains the statement of an extreme position, the weakness of which would have been exceedingly patent to the precise sensibility of the author of *Pride and Prejudice*. If she had lived long enough she might have criticized *Jane Eyre* in terms of almost exact contradiction. The psychologist does not venture to take sides in such a pitched battle, but resorts to his theory of types, and sees here the dry bones of his structure take on perfect flesh. It would be difficult to discover a more exact illustration of the main distinction he draws between faculties directed inwards, to the observation of feeling, and faculties directed outwards, to the observation of external things. The psychologist must halt at this distinction, unless he suggests, as a scientific ideal, some harmony or balance of these tendencies. But the critic must pursue the matter to a judgement. It will not, for that purpose, suffice to identify the ordered conception of objective facts with the classical spirit, or the research of passion with the romantic spirit—though it is tempting in this case to think of Jane Austen, as a typical (though rare, because feminine) embodiment of classicism, and Pater seized on *Wuthering Heights*, in preference to any work of Scott's, as the 'really characteristic fruit' of the spirit of romanticism. That only proves once more the inadequacy of these outworn shibboleths, since from another point of view *Wuthering Heights*, with its unerring unity of conception and its full catharsis of the emotions of pity and terror, is one of the very few occasions on which the novel has reached the dignity of classical tragedy. And, in the other case, it would be hard to concede the full meaning of classicism to Jane Austen's universe of undertones.

We return to Charlotte's phrase—emotion in subjection—and contend that this is the only normal sense in which the classical spirit should be endured. The rest is pedantry, academic closures, and the 'literature of our grandfathers'. To apply the distinction to Jane Austen is hardly fair: she belongs to the spirit of comedy, which has never been easily classified, always existing as a free and detached criticism of life and literature. Jane Austen, in essentials, takes her place with Congreve, if with anybody in English letters; and maybe, after all, in making her the antitype to the Brontës we are but displaying the old discordant masks side by side. Is it an equal opposition? Well, not quite. Charlotte Brontë is again the critic—'Miss Austen being, as you say, without "sentiment", without *poetry*, maybe *is* sensible, real (more *real* than *true*), but she cannot be great.' And that might be said equally well of Congreve, or of any representative of the comic spirit. It is a question of attitude. It is, finally, a question of courage—of throwing into the attempt for truth not only intelligence, spirit, faith, but also feeling, emotion, self.

PARTICULAR STUDIES

BAGEHOT

The greatest difficulty in any attempt at a critical appreciation of a Mid-Victorian figure lies in a certain deceptive normality which they one and all seem to possess. We think of the age in general as a very stolid one, and we are apt to imagine that its representatives were wholly immobile beneath their frock-coats and florid whiskers. Their works present a certain orderly appearance—are solid, serious, and painstaking; and if they do venture upon vain questionings, they do so always with an air of maturity and decorum. Bagehot is, perhaps, a prime representative of this order in the public mind; but in this case, as perhaps in others, the popular conception is singularly false. In another age, and with a different environment, he might have given us cause to rank him as a typical genius and to seek for him all the psychological attributes of genius. That, in any case, he differed from our usual conception of a picturesque genius, such as Blake or Shelley, is not to be denied; to range him with Coleridge and Arnold might cause surprise—but, nevertheless, it is to comparisons of such a nature that we shall be driven. And it is not merely a question of social habit; the name of Coleridge is there to guard against that assumption. It is rather a question of mental faculties, and a more useful line of separation may be drawn between the active or practical genius and the passive or speculative genius. It is a distinction to which Bagehot himself contributed some incisive strokes:

'Certain minds, the moment we think of them, suggest to us the ideas of symmetry and proportion. Plato's name, for example, calls up at once the impression of something ordered, measured, and settled; it is the exact contrary of everything eccentric, immature, or undeveloped. The opinions of such a mind are often erroneous, and some of them may, from change of time, of intellectual *data*, or from chance, seem not to be quite worthy of it; but the mode in which those opinions are expressed, and (as far as we can make it out) the mode in which they are framed, affect us, as we have said, with a sensation of symmetricalness. . . . We may lay it down as the condition of a regular or symmetrical genius, that it should have the exact combination of powers suited to graceful and easy success in an exercise of mind great enough to task the whole intellectual nature.

'On the other hand, men of irregular or unsymmetrical genius are eminent for some one or some few peculiarities of mind, have possibly special defects on other sides of their intellectual nature, at any rate want what the scientific men of the present day would call the *definite proportion* of faculties and qualities suited to the exact work they have in hand.'

It may seem at first sight that Bagehot is here making a distinction of externals; that we of to-day, with our psychological methods at hand, can make a finer and profounder analysis. But in further explanation of his meaning Bagehot has a passage which shows the presence of a psychological insight far ahead of the experimental researches of his time. To this characteristic of his we must return, but first let us proceed with the distinction:

'Possibly it may be laid down that one of two elements is essential to a symmetrical mind. It is evident that such a mind must either apply itself to that which is theoretical or that which is practical, to the world of abstraction or to the world of objects and realities. In the former case the deductive understanding, which masters first principles, and makes deductions from them, the thin ether of the intellect—the "mind itself by

300

itself"—must evidently assume a great prominence. To attempt to comprehend principles without it is to try to swim without arms, or to fly without wings. Accordingly, in the mind of Plato, and in others like him, the abstract and deducing understanding fills a great place; the imagination seems a kind of eye to descry its *data*; the artistic instinct an arranging impulse, which sets in order its inferences and conclusions. On the other hand, if a symmetrical mind busy itself with the active side of human life, with the world of concrete men and real things, its principal quality will be a practical sagacity, which forms with ease a distinct view and just appreciation of all the mingled objects that the world presents—which allots to each its own place, and its intrinsic and appropriate rank.'

Bagehot then gives Chaucer as an example of this second type of regular genius, and then concludes:

'Eminence in one or other of these marking faculties—either in the deductive abstract intellect or the practical seeing sagacity—seems essential to the mental constitution of a symmetrical genius, at least in man. There are, after all, but two principal all-important spheres in human life—thought and action; and we can hardly conceive of a masculine mind symmetrically developed which did not evince its symmetry by an evident perfection in one or other of those pursuits, which did not leave the trace of its distinct reflection upon the one, or its large insight upon the other of them.'

These are distinctions which in modern psychology have come to assume a normative character; and a work like Jung's *Psychological Types* is largely an expansion of the same kind of fundamental division here made explicit by Bagehot.

These distinctions are, of course, abstractions; and though Plato and Chaucer may serve as more or less precise types, our definitions tend to break down before a test case like Shakespeare. We can, indeed, call his genius irregular, though it be an irregularity due to the excess of certain faculties; or we can boldly say that he is of the type of 'practical seeing sagacity' rather than of 'deductive abstract intellect'. But the truth is rather that the character of all men, of whatever degree of genius, is determined not by the exclusive existence of one or the other of these traits, but rather by its merely relative predominance; and certain peculiarly elusive types, possessed of both tendencies in equal power, seem to hover between their alternating predominance.

Bagehot himself was of the regular type, though certain circumstances of his life seem to have predisposed him to a sensitive awareness of opposing qualities. He was born rather more than a century ago at Langport, in Somerset, and came of an old and landed family more recently established as local bankers. Perhaps the only abnormal fact of his early life was the difference of religion between his parents. His father was by birth and tradition a Unitarian; his mother, despite her marriage, retained her strong faith in the Established Church. We have to read a little between the lines of Mrs. Russell Barrington's *Life of Bagehot*, but it is fairly obvious that a strong attachment, none the less strong for being partially unconscious, existed between mother and son; and there was perhaps a compensating lack of sympathy between son and father. The first important outcome of this disposition of religious forces was that Bagehot was debarred from Oxford by his father's rigid objection to doctrinal tests; he went to University College, London, instead, and the results of this step were far-reaching. Bagehot never seems to have regretted Oxford; nor need we, for the freshness and fairness which strike us as distinguishing him among his contemporaries could not have escaped the retrograde influences then and there at work. It so happened that, instead of these influences working on his mind and imagination through the direct example of Newman, they came to him as the melancholy wreckage of the mind that was Arthur Clough. But that is to anticipate a little.

While still at Bristol College, where he went to school, Bagehot had come under the influence of Dr. Pritchard, a famous ethnologist, and the learned circle of which he was the centre. Bagehot's mind was then given a scientific bias which it never lost; and when he went eventually to University College his main interests became mathematical and philosophical. He took his degree in 1847, and then went into lodgings with the purpose of pursuing his studies in philosophy for the M.A. degree. It is at this period that we get the fullest insight into his essential character. His mother suffered from fits of insanity: and this tragic circumstance, more than anything else, determined his character and career. An unbroken persistence of comfortable affection might have resulted in a pedestrian and unquestioning intellect; but at the critical stage of his mental development, Bagehot's whole emotional existence was shaken by this dreadful fact. He thus became endowed with a sensitiveness which, combined with his natural intellectuality, determined his particular quality. At the age of twenty-one he went through a phase of morbidity and melancholy for which he found the exact description in a passage from Keats's Preface to *Endymion*: 'The imagination of a boy is healthy, and the mature imagination of a man is healthy; but there is a space of life between, in which the soul is in a ferment, the character undecided, the way of life uncertain, the ambition thick-sighted.' He quoted this passage in his essay on Hartley Coleridge, and there is little doubt that his own experience had confirmed its truth. It was at this period that the potential influences of his time thickly beset him. He seems to have retreated from Newman for curious and characteristically subtle reasons. He thought that Newman was deficient in self-consciousness, and therefore comparatively deficient in aspiration, in the sense of being but little occupied with the future state of his own mind. He accused him of a want of precise moral convictions: the overactivity and restlessness of his mind resulted, to Bagehot's view, in a great facility of analysing to a certain extent, but also in a 'great disinclination (almost an inability) to analyse further'. And Bagehot adds, in the letter from which we are quoting:

'To finish about Newman, I do not think his want of self-consciousness can be the reason for his wanting precise moral convictions. Arnold, who was not self-conscious at all scarcely, had very precise notions of duty. I think in Newman's case the reason is that his intellect is more subtle than his sense in discriminating: he can conceive finer shades of feeling and motive than his conscience will confidently estimate.'

And then came the influence of Clough. Bagehot took the gold medal in Intellectual and Moral Philosophy with his Master's degree in 1848, but he emerged with broken health. In the same year Clough was made Principal of University Hall, which had been established as a hall of residence in connection with University College largely through Bagehot's efforts. During the following two years Bagehot and Clough saw a good deal of each other; and Richard Holt Hutton, who was Bagehot's greatest friend at this time, has recorded his opinion that Clough was 'the man who had, I think, a greater intellectual fascination for Walter Bagehot than any of his contemporaries'. Clough possessed, and was completely possessed by, that subtle scepticism which was only one component of Bagehot's constitution. Bagehot had, besides, a 'secret vigour' which carried him beyond scepticism: he accepted, in a robust and ready fashion, an irrational fund of faith. This is, of course, the crucial fact about Bagehot's intelligence; according to our own beliefs and temperaments we accept it as the quality that gives to his work all its sanity and symmetry, or we regret that a mind so well endowed with talent should have voluntarily resigned all enquiry into the fundamental questions of philosophy. Our standards are involved: With what scale shall we measure this man? The man himself remains the same.

Bagehot realized all this, and in his essay on his friend's poems, published after Clough's death in 1861, he reviews not only the fate to which Clough succumbed but also the fate which he, Bagehot, had escaped. He traced the animating cause to the teaching of Dr. Arnold. Clough 'had by nature, probably, an exceedingly real mind, in the good sense of that expression and the bad sense. The actual visible world as it was, and he saw it, exercised over him a compulsory influence.' But 'he could not dissolve the world into credible ideas and then believe those ideas, as many poets have done. He could not catch up a creed, as ordinary men do. He had a *straining*, inquisitive, critical mind; he scrutinized every idea before he took it in: he did not allow the moral forces of life to act as they should; he was not content to gain a belief "by going on living".'

And Bagehot proceeds to show that for such a mind Arnold's teaching was of the worst possible sort:

'He was one of Arnold's favourite pupils because he gave heed so much to Arnold's teaching; and exactly because he gave heed to it was it bad for him. He required quite another sort of teaching: to be told to take things easily; not to try to be wise overmuch; to be "something beside critical"; to go on living quietly and obviously and see what truth would come to him. Mr. Clough had to his latest years what may be noticed in others of Arnold's disciples—a fatigued way of looking at great subjects. It seemed as if he had been put into them before his time, had seen through them, heard all which could be said about them, had been bored by them, and had come to want something else.'

A mind thus 'demoralized' was, as Bagehot saw it, exposed to a still worse danger: the Oxford of Newman:

'The doctrinal teaching which Arnold impressed on the youth about him was one personal to Arnold himself, which arose out of the peculiarities of his own character, which can only be explained by them. As soon as an inquisitive mind was thrown into a new intellectual atmosphere, and was obliged to naturalize itself in it, to consider the creed it had learned with reference to the facts which it encountered and met, much of that creed must fade away.'

Arnold flattered himself, said Bagehot, that he was a principal opponent of Newman; but he was rather a principal fellow labourer, and by removing 'the happy apathy' of the common English boy, Arnold was but anxiously preparing the very soil for Newman's unsettling fervour. The way was open for all those subtle questionings which, as Bagehot held in that letter of fifteen years earlier from which we have quoted, never end in certainty or security of mind.

This digression on Clough's fate would not be justified if it did not illustrate so admirably the emotional aspects of Bagehot's own character. He has been accused of hardness, of mere intellectuality, but in truth, as his friend Hutton said, he had 'the visionary nature to which the commonest things often seemed the most marvellous, and the marvellous things the most intrinsically probable'. For this reason he avoided the obvious outlet for his energies. He wrote of the Whig critics (Jeffrey and the early Edinburgh reviewers):

'Their tendency inclining to the quiet footsteps of custom, they like to trace the exact fulfilment of admitted rules, a just accordance with the familiar features of ancient merit. But they are most averse to mysticism. A clear, precise, discriminating intellect shrinks at once from the symbolic, the unbounded, the indefinite. The misfortune is that mysticism is true. There certainly are kinds of truth, borne in as it were instinctively on the human intellect, most influential on the character and the heart, yet hardly capable of stringent statement, difficult to limit by an elaborate definition. Their course is shadowy; the mind seems rather to have seen than to see them, more to feel after than to definitely apprehend them. They commonly involve an infinite element, which cannot, of course, be stated precisely, or else a first principle—an original tendency—of our intellectual constitution, which it is impossible not to feel, and yet which it is hard to extricate in terms and words.'

This passage, more than any other in Bagehot's writings, is to be kept in mind in estimating his character. By the kind of interests he affected, and the nature of his upbringing and training, we might have expected a closer sympathy with the

Whig point of view. But Bagehot was a Tory of a very definite type—of a type more intellectual than was usual in the nineteenth century. By virtue of his particular kind of scientific conservatism—the conservatism which sees that the only way to preserve a tradition is to prolong it—he belongs to the school of Bolingbroke and Burke. In another aspect he belongs to the school of Sir Walter Scott, and was an appreciator, and even an exemplifier, of the 'Cavalier' character. 'The essence of Toryism', he wrote, 'is enjoyment.' 'Over the "Cavalier" mind this world passes with a thrill of delight; there is an exultation in a daily event, zest in the "regular thing", joy at an old feast.' 'A Cavalier is always young. The buoyant life rises before us rich in hope, strong in vigour, irregular in action; men young and ardent, framed in the prodigality of nature'; open to every enjoyment, alive to every passion; eager, impulsive; brave without discipline, noble without principle, prizing luxury, despising danger, capable of high sentiment . . .'—this was the ideal he opposed to Macaulay's chill defect of sympathy, to Clarendon, decorous and grim, and to Hume, 'a saving, calculating north-countryman—fat, impassive—who lived on eightpence a day'.

Undoubtedly in this matter Bagehot reverted to something fundamental in the English temperament—to something which was Chaucer's and Shakespeare's and Ben Jonson's, but which later became crushed by the multiplication of a severer cast of mind. It is just at this point that we must be careful to distinguish between the subtle and the 'plain' aspects of Bagehot's intelligence. His conservatism was not an outcome of his subtlety but a foil to it; it was, like his religion, an accepted tradition which he might use as a resting-place and a fund of strength but never submit to the refining anxiety of his mind. Some things are too great and simple for that process; hence that sense of poise and equanimity which was his achieved possession. And so his conservatism was the conservatism of simple acceptance, not of fear. The latter type, so prevalent again to-day, he has analysed in a masterly passage on the polity of Lord Eldon. He does not fail to define another type of conservatism to which he had naturally been inclined, but the limitations of which he did not hesitate to expose. The type is still with us, so that the reader can readily test the acuteness of his description of it:

'There was another cause beside fear which then inclined, and which in similar times of miscellaneous revolution will ever incline, subtle rather than creative intellects to a narrow conservatism. Such intellects require an exact creed; they want to be able clearly to distinguish themselves from those around them, to tell to each man where they differ and why they differ; they cannot make assumptions; they cannot, like the merely practical man, be content with rough and obvious axioms; they require a *theory*. Such a want it is difficult to satisfy in an age of confusion and tumult, when old habits are shaken, old views overthrown, ancient assumptions rudely questioned, ancient inferences utterly denied, when each man has a different view from his neighbour, when an intellectual change has set father and son at variance, when a man's own household are the special foes of his favourite and self-adopted creed. A bold and original mind breaks through these vexations, and forms for itself a theory satisfactory to its notions, and sufficient for its wants. A weak mind yields a passive obedience to those among whom it is thrown. But a mind which is searching without being creative, which is accurate and logical enough to see defects, without being combinative or inventive enough to provide remedies—which, in the old language, is discriminative rather than discursive—is wholly unable, out of the medley of new suggestions, to provide itself with an adequate belief; and it naturally falls back on the *status quo*.'

A discernment so original as this is evidence in Bagehot himself of a creative intelligence. To share to the extent of understanding 'the subtlest quintessence of the most restless and refining abstraction' of Hume or Montaigne, and yet to avoid the easy reaction into which they fell—'the stupidest, crudest acquiescence in the concrete and present world'—such was Bagehot's achievement. His promise was greater. It almost seems as if he came near to defining the specific problem of modern thought, and even possibly had the equipment for the necessary structure of a modern theology. Or was it merely another case of watertight compartments? We do not know, and his most direct statement on such questions, an essay on 'The Ignorance of Man', does not go beyond the affirmation of revelation.

There are still one or two facts to record which bear on the development of Bagehot's character. After taking his final degree, it was decided that he should study law; and this he set himself to do. In due course he was called to the Bar, but he immediately gave up the profession and returned home to Langport, on the solicitations of his mother. He then entered the family business, and from that time his life is settled. It should only be noted that the previous year (1851) he had fled to Paris to rid himself of mental depression, and there had the luck to fall in with a revolution. The immediate outcome was a series of letters on the *Coup d'État*, in which he first revealed to the world that he could write 'quick sentences [as Woodrow Wilson has called them] of political analysis which were fit to serve both as history and as prophecy'. These letters are remarkable for a cynicism to which he was not so much addicted at a later period, but from a literary point of view we can afford to neglect them in favour of the series of critical essays which he began to write as soon as he was settled in his father's counting-house. He was then twenty-six and he had six clear years before him; in that period he wrote nearly all, and certainly most of his best, literary criticism. In 1858 he was married. His father-in-law was James Wilson, Financial Secretary to the Treasury and proprietor of the *Economist*. Bagehot was thrown upon influences which tended to develop his scientific rather than his literary interests, and in an ensuing period of six years he wrote only five literary essays. Then they stop altogether, and on all such topics he remains mute to the time of his death, in 1877.

But meanwhile these other interests had matured; and in 1867 he published *The English Constitution*. This was followed in 1870 by *Physics and Politics*, and in 1873 by *Lombard Street*. These three books perhaps with most people constitute Bagehot's chief claim to fame. And indeed they are almost unparalleled classics, belonging to a small group of which Sir Henry Maine's *Ancient Law* is the prototype, in which scientific subjects are endowed with literary qualities by sheer perspicuity of style and sustained animation of interest. These works are secure in their own particular sphere; our only complaint is that they have in some measure detracted from the singular interest of Bagehot's literary criticism. This is almost the best of its time, and only the speculative figure of Matthew Arnold prevents us from pronouncing it quite the best. Arnold's criticism was more deliberate; in a sense it was more cultured. It was scarcely more decisive. What Arnold has gained in the suffrage of time, he lost in immediate effect. In Bagehot's words, what he gained in subtlety he lost in boldness. Perhaps Bagehot would have discerned in the Doctor's son all the worst elements that he had found implanted in Clough; but he does not seem to have expressed himself on the subject, though he was a great admirer of Arnold's poems. Arnold, however, was well aware of Bagehot, and already in 1856 had 'traced the same hand' in a series of articles in the *National Review*, which articles seemed to him 'to be of the very first quality, showing not talent only, but a concern for the *simple truth* which is rare in English literature as it is in English politics and English religion'. Perhaps this is evidence of Arnold's defection from his father's teaching ('a fatigued way of looking at great subjects'); at any rate, it shows a just estimate of the essential quality of Bagehot's criticism, and there is really little else to say about it, except to show the manner of it. This is nowhere so admirably evident as in the estimates he gives of some of his contemporaries. This is always the severest test of a critic, and if we can still read this part of his criticism with interest, we need have no fear for the rest. There is no nineteenth-century critic, Coleridge and Arnold not excepted, who comes out of such a test so admirably as Bagehot. His essays on two such diverse subjects as Dickens and Clough are not only the first but also the last words on these themes. This is a large claim for such a subject as Dickens, who has been the recipient of so much criticism—but how much of it is really criticism? How much of it is not rather the acceptance of a popular estimate and a rationalization of this estimate? If Bagehot made a mistake, it was to imagine that the popularity was impermanent; but his mistake saved him from the inhibitions that have affected later critics, and he had no hesitation in exposing 'the natural fate of an unequal mind employing itself on a vast and various subject'.

At the base of all Bagehot's criticism was a certain theory of imagination. He held that 'the materials for the creative faculty must be provided by the receptive faculty. Before a man can imagine what will seem to be realities, he must be familiar with what are the realities'. But, as he wrote in his essay on Shakespeare, 'To a great experience one thing is essential, an experiencing nature'. In these two observations Bagehot came nearer to an understanding of the process of literary inspiration than any other critic, with the possible exception of Coleridge. He realized that an imagination which does not build on experience is a baseless fabric; and though this is not an original view, it is one that is often forgotten. His further corollary, that there is no real experience without an experiencing nature, embodies a profounder truth; but this he illustrates rather than explains. Goethe, for example, is contrasted with Shakespeare, and Macaulay with Scott. He does not accuse Goethe and Scott of a lack of imagination—who would?—but he points in the former case 'to the tone of his character and the habits of his mind. He moved hither and thither through life, but he was always a man apart. He mixed with unnumbered kinds of men, with Courts and academies, students and women, camps and artists, but everywhere he was with them yet not of them. In every scene he was there, and he made it clear that he was there with reserve and as a stranger. He went there *to experience.*'

This unexperiencing nature perhaps amounts to no more than a lack of sympathy, but if it were always recognized that sympathy is a necessary component of experience, criticism would be a briefer and more illuminating science.

It is well to remember Bagehot's insistence on sympathy because, in advancing a further and very distinctive characteristic of his criticism, we are in danger of reverting to that false impression of mere hard intellectuality. 'What is not possible', he once wrote, 'is to combine the pursuit of pleasure and the enjoyment of comfort with the characteristic pleasures of a strong mind'; and this was his indictment of the eighteenth century—through which, however, he recognized there ran 'a tonic of business', of political business. His description of the period as 'that in which men ceased to write for students and had not yet begun to write for women' has hardly been bettered. It defines three centuries in a sentence. But what he did admire in the eighteenth century, and in Gibbon in particular, was 'a masculine tone; a firm strong perspicuous narrative of matter of fact, a plain argument, a contempt for everything which distinct definite people cannot entirely and thoroughly comprehend'. And this is the manner of his own writing and the basis of his conception of style: 'The most perfect books have been written not by those who thought much of books but by those who thought little, by those who were under the restraint of a sensitive talking world, to which books had contributed something and a various eager life the rest.' Bagehot himself came near to this ideal; he was not merely a critic and economist but also a banker and politician; not merely the author of a most penetrative essay on Bishop Butler but also a good horseman and the owner of a pack of beagles. If anything was lacking it was the 'sensitive talking world'.

These varied interests gave to his mind a universality which is rare in literature but of incomparable value. It may seem,

BAGEHOT

on a superficial view, that Bagehot dissipated his energies over too wide a field; that if he had concentrated on criticism, on politics, or on economics, he might have attained the highest possible reputation in one of these narrower spheres. That would be to mistake the quality of the man and to misjudge the proper value of criticism. The opinion of such a man on one literary topic is worth the life-work of a solitary pedant. This universality, combined with that regularity which we noted earlier in this appreciation, gives him that *centrality* of mind which, on a different scale, he had admired in Béranger: 'He puts things together; he refers things to a principle; rather, they group themselves in his intelligence insensibly round a principle. There is nothing *distrait* in his genius; the man has attained to be himself; a cool oneness, a poised personality, pervades him.'

Such was the character of Bagehot himself; it omits only his wit and his humour, and these may be left to take care of themselves. Had he lived longer his achievement would have been different: he was still developing. But his niche is enviable as it is: *The English Constitution* has a unique place in our literature, and it is doubtful if any book since Hobbes's *Leviathan* has had so much influence on minds which exercise real power. 'Had he lived to apply his method', wrote Lord Bryce, 'he might have exercised almost the same kind of influence that Montesquieu exerted in the middle of the eighteenth, and Tocqueville in the earlier part of the nine-teenth century; and we feel in him the power of an intellect altogether worthy to be compared even with that of the earlier and greater of those two illustrious men.' But it is doubtful if that intellect would ever have returned to pure literature; some psychological inhibition seems to have inter-vened and reformed his interests. We are reminded of a passage in his essay on Bishop Butler:

'Those who know a place or a person best are not those most likely to describe it best; their knowledge is so familiar that they cannot bring it out in words. A deep, steady, under-

313

current of strong feeling is precisely what affects men's highest opinions most, and exactly what prevents men from being able adequately to describe them. In the absence of the delineative faculty, without the power to state their true reasons, minds of this deep and steadfast class are apt to put up with reasons which lie on the surface. They are caught by an appearance of fairness, affect a dry and intellectual tone, endeavour to establish their conclusions without the premises which are necessary—without mention of the grounds on which, in their own minds, they really rest.'

Did Bagehot himself come to this pass? Did the final insanity and death of his mother release a psychic source too keen for analysis and analogical probing? Did that mind then affect a dry and intellectual tone without mention—perhaps without awareness—of the motive that animated it? The literary critic can only ask these questions: another science must answer them.

PARTICULAR STUDIES

II

COVENTRY PATMORE

Coventry Patmore has been described as 'the most neglected of our notable poets';[1] even his grave, we were told, was untended, and fit to illustrate one of his best lines:

> The darnell'd garden of unheedful death.

And this would seem to be all the comment which time has made on the proud words which Patmore placed in front of the collected edition of his poems:

'I have respected posterity; and, should there be a posterity which cares for letters, I dare to hope it will respect me.'

Perhaps we have not lived long enough to earn the name of posterity; perhaps we do not care sufficiently for letters to honour the grave of a poet who made no compromise with the public of his own day, and can therefore expect none from the public of ours. But that is not the real truth. Whenever a critic of faithful conscience recalls the poets of this period—Tennyson, Arnold, Clough, Patmore, Browning, Rossetti—it is on the name of Patmore that he lingers with a still lively sense of wonder. The rest have been fully estimated, and their influence, if not exhausted, is predictable. Patmore is still potential; but to what extent, and whether purely as a poet or more likely as a mystic, are questions which must be answered in this essay.

[1] By Mr. Clifford Bax in a letter to *The Times Literary Supplement*, 12th May 1932.

That arrogance which dominates all contemporary accounts of Patmore's personality is the first quality we must dwell on, because it is a reflex of the man's relation to his age. No poet, indeed, no personality of the whole period stands in such direct opposition to all its beliefs and ideals—perhaps we should say, finally stood in such opposition, for Patmore's settled attitude did not develop until middle age. He began his career with family circumstances which explain a good deal—a harsh unsympathetic mother, and a father, who though sympathetic to the extent of spoiling him in every direction—particularly in the direction of a literary career—was regarded by the world at large as a cad and imposter, till he finally fled the country to escape his financial entanglements. Such circumstances are bound to produce in a sensitive nature 'defence' compensations which take on the appearance of self-assertion and intellectual arrogance. And these are perhaps the very factors which, whilst they explain the 'drive' of a personality like Patmore's, also give us a clue to its creative limitations.

Patmore once declared that he was the only poet of his generation, except Barnes, who steadily maintained a literary conscience. This is perfectly true. He was a 'clerk' who never betrayed that tradition of intellectual integrity of which every poet should be the trustee. Everything he wrote was written with a great sense of responsibility, not only to the public, but to his own inner light or inspiration. Though his first considerable work, *The Angel in the House,* won an immense popularity, he deliberately turned his back on his success, to pursue a path implicit in his faith which led him to intellectual heights where no considerable public could then follow, and which will always be reserved for the select. In politics he was bitterly opposed to all parties. Gladstone he abhorred so thoroughly that he could write of him:

His leprosy's so perfect that men call him clean;

and his scorn of Disraeli and 'the false English Nobles' was equally vitriolic. In contrast to the prevailing economic and political optimism, he adopted views of unrelieved pessimism. He saw himself (alone with Barnes!) as the last classical author of a civilization on the verge of extinction:

'Unpalatable and unacceptable as the suggestion may be, it cannot be denied by persons who are able and willing to look facts in the face that there are already strong indications of a relapse into a long-protracted period of social and political disorganization, so complete that there shall be no means of leisure or even living for a learned class, nor any audience for what it has to impart. Such recrudescences of civilization have occurred, and they may occur again, though the prospect may be as incredible to most Europeans at the present moment as it must have been to the lieges of the Eternal City at the height and sudden turning-point of its popular glory and seemingly consolidated order.'

In religion he became, again in opposition to the intellectual trend of his period, a Catholic of the most intransigeant type; and even in his religion he was so little in sympathy with its temporal vessels that he continually murmured against the priesthood and even against the Pope.

This attitude was maintained with a courage and absence of reserve which we cannot but admire. 'Plain-speaking,' he says in one of his essays, 'does not vitiate. Even coarseness is health compared with those suppressed forms of the disease of impurity which come of our modern undivine silences.' And it was one of his first principles that there existed an absolute incompatibility between genius and any kind of insincerity. This belief is stated with great force in an essay in *Religio Poetae*, the purpose of which is to distinguish the intellect from the understanding (or discursive reason) and the memory as the peculiar faculty of genius:

'The intellect is the faculty of the "seer". It discerns truth as a living thing; and, according as it is in less or greater power, it discerns with a more or less far-seeing glance the relationships of principles to each other, and of facts, circumstances, and the realities of nature to principles, without anything that can be properly called ratiocination. It cannot be cultivated, as the understanding and memory can be and need to be; and it cannot in the ordinary course of things be injured, except by one means—namely, dishonesty, that is, habitual denial by the will, for the sake of interested or vicious motives, of its own perceptions. Genius and high moral—not necessarily physical —courage are therefore found to be constant companions. Indeed, it is difficult to say how far an absolute moral courage in acknowledging intuitions may not be of the very nature of genius: and whether it might not be described as a sort of interior sanctity which dares to see and confess to itself that it sees, though its vision should place it in a minority of one.'

This courage Patmore himself possessed in the highest degree, and certainly he did not shrink from finding himself in a minority of one. Admitting this, it only remains for us to consider critically the quality of his vision and his ability to body it forth.

Perhaps we might consider the more technical question first. By this I mean Patmore's whole conception of poetry as an art, and then his own particular style. Both aspects of the question give rise to the most searching doubts. The problem is simplified for us by the compactness and cohesion of Patmore's verse. It can without loss be reduced to two parts— to two sequences of poems distinct in style if not in matter. *The Angel in the House* was one of the most characteristic and certainly one of the most successful poems of the whole Victorian age: it had sold over a quarter of a million copies before the author's death. The first part was originally published in 1854; the final part in 1863. It belongs to that bastard type of literature—the novel in verse—and has much of the atmosphere and, for those who like it, the charm of the domestic fiction of the period. It was fairly characterized by Edmund Gosse as 'humdrum stories of girls that smell of bread and butter', but it cannot be dismissed at that. Of its philosophy I shall have something to say presently; meanwhile its subject-matter raises a question of importance which has never been squarely faced by Patmore's apologists. If necessary we might go back to Aristotle for reasons, but surely it may be laid down as self-evident that poetry and life are anything but identical. The sphere of poetry is at once rarer and more remote than the sphere of life, a truth which will only imply a separation of art and life to those who confuse life with existence. Art involves aesthetic distance. Contemporary subjects can only be treated if invested with dignity or obscurity—and Patmore's 'girls' have neither. The theme which Patmore proposed to himself was right enough. 'The Siren woman', he claimed, 'had been often sung by the Pagan Poets of all time, and the Fairy woman by the Troubadours of the Middle Ages. But that Love in which all Loves centre, and that Woman who is the rightful sustainer of them all, the Inspiration of Youth, and the Consolation of Age, that Love and that Woman had seldom been sung sincerely and effectually.' That is true enough, but such love need not necessarily be pictured in the decorous and depressing atmosphere of a Victorian Deanery. It is significant that the original of the Dean was in real life a Nonconformist minister, but even Patmore saw that he could not make poetry out of nonconformity: it was his mistake to imagine that the snobbish atmosphere of a Cathedral Close would make all the difference. When it was too late Patmore realized his mistake, and he spent the last phase of his life dreaming of, and preparing for, a great poem on the Marriage of the Virgin, in which the same love was to be celebrated, but with distance and circumstance worthy of the theme.

This defect of presentation explains why *The Angel* is not read to-day; and I can imagine no posterity which will reverse our present inclination in this matter. It has become and will remain a literary curiosity, not justified by any remarkable beauties even of texture or expression. For it has to be admitted, next, that Patmore at this stage of his inspiration was no inevitable poet. He chose a simple metre for his simple subject—iambic octosyllabic—and laboured hard to make it smooth. But as Tennyson said, some of his lines seemed 'hammered up out of old nails', and though such lines were pointed out to him, he was often incapable of seeing anything wrong with them, and there are plenty left in the final version. That would not matter so much if there were corresponding jewels of highest light, to outshine these defects, but actually the texture is sustained at an even level of apt but uninspired expression. It is wit-writing of an extremely competent and felicitous kind, but is not, and perhaps never pretended to be, lyrical poetry of any emotional intensity.

This is the more remarkable because no poet since Wordsworth and Coleridge, not even Matthew Arnold, had such a clear conception of the poet's function. In that essay, extremely compressed with sense, which gives the title to the volume *Religio Poetae*, we find the best expression of Patmore's views. The Poet is compared with the Saint: he is above all the *perceiver*, 'nothing having any interest for him unless he can, as it were, see it and touch it with the spiritual senses, with which he is pre-eminently endowed'.

'The Poet, again, is not more singular for the delicacy of his spiritual insight, which enables him to see celestial beauty and substantial reality where all is blank to most others, than for the surprising range and alertness of vision, whereby he detects, in external nature, those likenesses and echoes by which spiritual realities can alone be rendered credible and more or less apparent, or subject to "real apprehension", in persons of inferior perceptive powers. Such likenesses, when chosen by the imagination, not the fancy, of the true Poet, are *real* words —the only real words; for "that which is unseen is known by that which is seen", and natural similitudes often contain and are truly the visible *ultimates* of the unseen. . . .

'He gives the world to eat only of the Tree of Life, reality; and will not so much as touch the Tree of Knowledge, as the writer of Genesis ironically calls the Tree of Learning that leads to denial of knowledge. He is the very reverse of a "scientist".'

This emphasis on the realism of words is in advance of anything suggested by Coleridge. It is to be found in Vico, whom Patmore could hardly have read, but only receives its full development in the present-day theories of Croce and Vivante. It was his firm faith in this theory which reconciled Patmore to the intermittency of his inspiration. When a poet *knows* what poetry is, he cannot be false to his genius. It would be a spiritual betrayal which could only end in spiritual death. Patmore had genius enough to perceive this, and I think that it was this very concentration on the nature of poetry which led him towards the wider mysticism of the Catholic faith. In another essay in *Religio Poetae* he says:

'The most peculiar and characteristic mark of genius is insight into subjects which are dark to ordinary vision and for which ordinary language has no adequate expression. Imagination is rather the language of genius: the power which traverses at a single glance the whole external universe, and seizes on the likenesses and images, and their combinations, which are best able to embody ideas and feelings otherwise inexpressible; so that the "things which are unseen are known by the things which are seen".'

And elsewhere he says: 'Sensible things alone can be expressed fully and directly by sensible terms. Symbols and parable, and metaphors—which are parables on a small scale —are the only means of adequately conveying, or rather hinting, supersensual knowledge.' Patmore's own poetry, in its final and most important phase, was to become just such a hinting at supersensual knowledge. But this change of spirit was dependent on a change of form.

Patmore's poetic technique received an immense impetus from his invention of what was virtually a new verse-form— the 'ode' which he began to use about 1865. A certain degree of originality in formal structure has perhaps been a condition of all exceptional poetry—novelty of means acting as a spur to any kind of individual attainment. Edmund Gosse was of the opinion that Patmore found the analogy for his 'ode' in the *Canzoniere* of Petrarch. Patmore himself tried to find sanction for his form in the historical development of the ode in English poetry, but these pedantic notions of his are not very convincing. The form, in fact, developed under the stress of a particular mode of feeling. To quote a comparatively simple example:

A FAREWELL

With all my will, but much against my heart,
We two now part.
My Very Dear,
Our solace is, the sad road lies so clear.
It needs no art,
With faint, averted feet
And many a tear,
In our opposed paths to persevere.
Go thou to East, I West.
We will not say
There's any hope, it is so far away.
But, O, my Best,
When the one darling of our widowhead,
The nursling Grief,
Is dead,
And no dews blur our eyes
To see the peach-bloom come in evening skies,
Perchance we may,
Where now this night is day,
And even through faith of still averted feet,
Making full circle of our banishment,
Amazed meet;
The bitter journey to the bourne so sweet
Seasoning the termless feast of our content
With tears of recognition never dry.

It will be seen that the Patmorean ode is, in short, an iambic measure (like that of *The Angel in the House*), which, however, breaks away from the regularity of the octosyllabic couplet or quatrain to indulge in what Patmore himself called 'the fine irregular rock of the free tetrameter.' The verse in these Odes moves 'in long undulating strains' which are modulated by pauses and irregularly occurring rhymes, the rhymed words determining the length of the lines which vary arbitrarily from two to ten or even twelve syllables. It is therefore a metre of extraordinary freedom and impetuous force—which only needed the internal freedom introduced by Patmore's friend Hopkins to give us all the constituents of modern free verse. 'The beauty and incomparable variety of the metre', wrote Patmore in a letter published in Mr. Champneys' *Memoirs*, 'opens up quite a new prospect to me of the possibilities of poetry'; and again: 'I have hit upon *the* finest metre that ever was invented, and on *the* finest mine of wholly unworked material that ever fell to the lot of an English poet.' It is interesting to note that some years after he had invented this measure, Patmore entered into a long correspondence with the poet mentioned above, whose technical innovations were to become the greatest source of inspiration to our own generation. Gerard Manley Hopkins's letters to Patmore are said to be 'numerous, long and of great interest', and 'so excellent, so full of the writer's individuality, of acute if sometimes whimsical judgements, that they are all worthy of preservation'; but Mr. Champneys refrains from publishing them as being too technical for the general reader. They have since appeared and show that Hopkins was, in some degree, influenced by Patmore; and that Hopkins induced Patmore to make many revisions in his poems.

The Odes, begun about 1865, represent Patmore's output for the rest of his life—about thirty years; and yet they only occupy a hundred pages in the collected edition of his works. This comparative paucity may be explained by the high standard of literary morality which Patmore set himself. 'Every one of my books', he wrote, 'has been written after many years of reflection on its subject—reflection for my own benefit, not primarily with a view to the book, and has been merely the easy and rapid overflowing into words of the fullness of thought at last attained. And as a corollary to this we find him saying: 'My best things were written most quickly. "Amelia" took four days; "Deliciæ Sapientiæ de Amore" two hours; several of the best Odes even less.' Perhaps it was a mistake thus to wait for thought voluntarily to move harmonious numbers—perhaps it is always a mistake to conceive poetry as a species of divine visitation—Hopkins was of that opinion. But Patmore made this attendance on inspiration almost an article of religious faith, and though he worked in preparation for a poem with solemn deliberation, he never once forced his muse to unwilling expression.

Possibly an explanation of the intermittency of his inspiration is to be found in the nature of Patmore's personality. He himself was fond of making a distinction between the masculine and the feminine mind in literature. For instance, in his essay on 'Mrs. Meynell', he says: 'A strong and predominatingly masculine mind has often much to say, but a very imperfect ability to say it; the predominatingly feminine mind can say anything, but has nothing to say; but with the double-sexed insight of genius, realities and expressions are wedded from their first conceptions, and, even in their least imposing development are living powers, and of more practical importance than the results of the highest efforts of mind when either of its factors greatly predominates over the other.' He found Mrs. Meynell too deficient in this 'ultimate womanhood, the expressional body', to give her a right to be counted among the classical poets. The same charge might, I think, be made against Patmore himself. Edmund Gosse[1] records that 'during the debatable period between his first wife's death and his second marriage, Patmore's ideas with regard to poetry underwent a very remarkable change. In later life he was accustomed to insist on the essential oneness of his work, and to point to its uniform features. But setting his eloquent casuistry aside, the reader cannot fail to see a very broad chasm

1 *Coventry Patmore*, by Edmund Gosse (1905), pp. 124-5.

lying between what he wrote up to 1862, and what he wrote after that date. In the first place the appeal to a popular judgement, to a wide circle of amiable readers, entirely disappears. Patmore, with the removal of so many earthly ties, and with the growth of what was mystical and transcendental in his temperament, became haughty in his attitude to the world. His conscientiousness as an artist was quickened, and at the same time he gave way to a species of intellectual arrogance which had always been dormant in his nature, but which now took the upper hand.'

This intellectual arrogance represents a certain settling of his fluent feminine personality, the psychological condition of his poetic force, along firm lines of masculine character inhibitive to this force, and there can be little doubt that this tendency was immensely accelerated by the decision he had to make about this time—he had not only to compromise in some degree with his doctrine of the inviolability of nuptial love, but concurrently was impelled by his conscience to make the final act of submission and become a member of the Catholic Church. The complex strands of this psychological development cannot be unravelled here, and I am far from suggesting that this individual case reveals any general rule; but in plain fact Patmore did emerge from this mental turmoil with his masculine arrogance intensified, and with the frequency of his poetic impulse in consequence impaired.

It is time now to consider the substance of Patmore's poetry. Arthur Symons once described Patmore as 'a poet of one idea and of one metre', and it is indeed amazing to see the alacrity with which he first adopted his central idea, and the tenacity with which he developed it and intensified it. Already in the more philosophical parts of *The Angel in the House*—in those Preludes and Devices which interrupt the narrative and in 'the Wedding Sermon' with which it concludes—Patmore had outlined his conception of love. Incidentally, these Preludes often display a complex fusion of phantasy and wit which gives them a place in the English school of metaphysical

325

poetry: I quote 'The Amaranth' as an example of this type:

> *Feasts satiate; stars distress with height;*
> *Friendship means well, but misses reach,*
> *And wearies in its best delight*
> *Vex'd with the vanities of speech;*
> *Too long regarded, roses even*
> *Afflict the mind with fond unrest;*
> *And to converse direct with Heaven*
> *Is oft a labour in the breast;*
> *What'er the up-looking soul admires,*
> *Whate'er the senses' banquet be,*
> *Fatigues at last with vain desires,*
> *Or sickens by satiety;*
> *But truly my delight was more*
> *In her to whom I'm bound for aye*
> *Yesterday than the day before,*
> *And more to-day than yesterday.*

As for the philosophy which underlies the whole structure of *The Angel*, and which was to be developed into rarer mystical concepts in the Odes, it has never been better summarized than by Patmore himself in an essay on 'Love and Poetry' which appears in *Religio Poetae.*

'The whole of after-life depends very much upon how life's transient transfiguration in youth by love is subsequently regarded; and the greatest of all the functions of the poet is to aid in his readers the fulfilment of the cry, which is that of nature as well as religion: "Let not my heart forget the things mine eyes have seen." The greatest perversion of the poet's function is to falsify the memory of that transfiguration of the senses and to make light of its sacramental character. This character is instantly recognized by the unvitiated heart and apprehension of every youth and maiden; but it is very easily forgotten and profaned by most, unless its sanctity is upheld by priests and poets. Poets are naturally its prophets—all the more powerful because, like the prophets of old, they are wholly independent of the priests, and are often the first to discover and rebuke the lifelessness into which that order is always tending to fall. If society is to survive its apparently impending dangers, it must be mainly by guarding and increasing the purity of the sources in which society begins. The world is finding out, as it has often done before, that it cannot do without religion. Love is the first thing to wither under its loss. What love does in transfiguring life, that religion does in transfiguring love: as any one may see who compares one state or time with another. Love is sure to be something less than human if it is not something more; and the so-called extravagances of the youthful heart, which always claim a character for divinity in its emotions, fall necessarily into sordid, if not shameful, reaction, if those claims are not justified to the understanding by the faith which declares man and woman to be priest and priestess to each other of relations inherent in Divinity itself, and proclaimed in the words "Let us make man in our own image" and "male and female created he them".'

The mystical developments of this philosophy received a perfect prose expression in that lost masterpiece, the *Sponsa Dei*, which Patmore destroyed when Hopkins warned him that it was 'telling secrets', and that he ought to submit it to his spiritual director. Edmund Gosse, who had read the manuscript, says that 'no existing specimen of Patmore's prose seems to me so delicate, or penetrated by quite so high a charm of style'. And the subject, he says, 'was certainly audacious. It was not more or less than an interpretation of the love between the soul and God by an analogy of the love between a woman and a man; it was, indeed, a transcendental treatise on divine desire seen through the veil of human desire. The purity and crystalline passion of the writer carried him safely over the most astounding difficulties.'

One cannot help regretting the destruction of this work (as we regret the poems which Hopkins, for similar scruples, himself destroyed), but actually I doubt if much of the substance of Patmore's doctrine has been lost. It is all implicit in the Odes, and in that book of maxims which is one of the greatest of Patmore's achievements: *The Rod, the Root, and the Flower* (an English work which it is not wholly ridiculous to compare with Pascal's *Pensées*). The following Ode 'To the Body' may be given as an example of the daring, and the impetuosity (there are only three sentences in it), and the final intensity of Patmore's poetry:

> *Creation's and Creator's crowning good;*
> *Wall of infinitude;*
> *Foundation of the sky,*
> *In Heaven forecast*
> *And long'd for from eternity,*
> *Though laid the last;*
> *Reverberating dome,*
> *Of music cunningly built home*
> *Against the void and indolent disgrace*
> *Of unresponsive space;*
> *Little sequester'd pleasure-house*
> *For God and for His Spouse;*
> *Elaborately, yea, past conceiving, fair,*
> *Since, from the graced decorum of the hair,*
> *Ev'n to the tingling, sweet*
> *Soles of the simple, earth-confiding feet,*
> *And from the inmost heart*
> *Outwards unto the thin*
> *Silk curtains of the skin,*
> *Every least part*
> *Astonish'd hears*
> *And sweet replies to some like region of the spheres;*
> *Form'd for a dignity prophets but darkly name,*
> *Less shameless men cry 'Shame!'*
> *So rich with wealth conceal'd*
> *That Heaven and Hell fight chiefly for this field;*

328

Clinging to everything that pleases thee
With indefectible fidelity;
Alas, so true
To all thy friendships that no grace
Thee from thy sin can wholly disembrace;
Which thus 'bides with thee as the Jebusite,
That, maugre all God's promises could do,
The chosen People never conquer'd quite;
Who therefore lived with them,
And that by formal truce and as of right,
In metropolitan Jerusalem.
For which false fealty
Thou needs must, for a season, lie
In the grave's arms, foul and unshriven,
Albeit, in Heaven,
Thy crimson-throbbing Glow
Into its old abode aye pants to go,
And does with envy see
Enoch, Elijah, and the Lady, she
Who left the roses in her body's lieu.
O, if the pleasures I have known in thee
But my poor faith's poor first fruits be,
What quintessential, keen, ethereal bliss
Then shall be his
Who has thy birth-time's consecrating dew
For death's sweet chrism retain'd,
Quick, tender, virginal, and unprofaned!

Even at its best Patmore's poetry is spoilt by ugly inversions and elisions, inexcusable considering the freedom of the form. But in these last Odes, we are hardly aware of such faults: the thought is irredeemably fused in the expression, and the result is true poetry of the rarest and perhaps the highest kind—metaphysical poetry, such as Lucretius, Dante, Donne, Crashaw and Wordsworth wrote. Those who limit poetry by a narrow lyrical conception of the art will find little to charm

their indolence in Patmore. But those who are braced to the
highest levels of the art, where the flowers are few and fugi-
tive, where Nature and Humanity, to adapt a saying of Patmore's, are beautified and developed instead of being withered
up by religious thought, will find in the best of the Odes a
fund of inspired poetry for which they would willingly sacrifice the whole baggage of the Victorian legacy in general.
And they will find this poetry amply supported by Patmore's
prose, to which justice is not often done—prose which has 'the
virile qualities of simplicity, continuity and positiveness'.

Of the fundamental faith to which all Patmore's writings
are finally related, it would be presumptuous to do more than
point out quite dispassionately its vigour, its broad-minded-
ness, and its essential freedom. It was a faith opposed to the
whole trend, literary and scientific, of Patmore's period. Patmore was not afraid to scale his isolated peak, but in this he
had the good sense to abate some of his usual arrogance. His
last word is given in the Preface to *The Rod, the Root, and the
Flower,* written in 1895, the year before his death:

'Far be it from me to pose as other than a mere reporter,
using the poetic intellect and imagination so as in part to conceive those happy realities of life which in many have been
and are an actual and abiding possession; and to express them
in such a manner that thousands who lead beautiful and substantially Catholic lives, whether outside or within the visible
Church, may be assisted in the only true learning, which is
to know better that which they already know.'

PARTICULAR STUDIES

12

GERARD MANLEY HOPKINS

(i)

The life of Gerard Manley Hopkins, like the lives of most poets, was outwardly monotonous; how can the life of the true poet, who is the direct opposite of the man of action, be otherwise? He was born on the 11th June 1844, his father and mother being of cultured middle-class stock. He died at the age of forty-five in 1889. Between these two necessary events, there are only two others which have any vital significance—his conversion to the Catholic Church in 1866, and his ordination to the priesthood in 1877. Nevertheless, a life was never more intensely lived: for he lived acutely with all his senses. He became a poet, but he might have been a musician—all his life, we are told, he was composing songs and melodies; and he might have been a painter—he had great aptitude in drawing and was advised to adopt painting as a profession. Finally, he had another kind of sensibility which is so often overlooked —I mean that sensibility for the quality and contour of ideas, on which the true metaphysician depends. He dreamed his way through childhood—bookish, pallid, desperately strong-willed and courageous; precocious, perhaps not a little pretentious. He wrote long elaborate prize-poems at school, poems too full of learning to have any suggestion of original genius. At Oxford he came under the influence of Jowett, and was, one of his friends[1] tells us, 'at first a little tinged with the

---

[1] William Addis: quoted in *Gerard Manley Hopkins*, by G. F. Lahey. S.J. (Oxford, 1930), a memoir to which I owe these details of Hopkins's life.

liberalism prevalent among reading men'. But only at first. The same friend describes a walking tour he took with Hopkins in 1865, during which they visited the Benedictine monastery at Belmont, near Hereford. There they had a long conversation with Canon Raynal, afterwards Abbot. Hopkins was impressed. His mood gave birth to a poem in which his first genuine note is struck:

> *I have desired to go*
> *Where springs not fail,*
> *To fields where flies no sharp and sided hail*
> *And a few lilies blow.*

> *And I have asked to be*
> *Where no storms come,*
> *Where the green swell is in the havens dumb*
> *And out of the swing of the sea.*

That 'Heaven-haven', so complete in its spiritual complacency, was never to be Hopkins's own lot. His faith was to be tense, but not firm; it was to be all the stronger because held in opposition to his obstinate reasonings.

Oxford in the 'sixties was still reckoning with the Tractarian Movement. A youth of the innate religious tendencies of Hopkins was inevitably drawn into the discipleship of Dr. Pusey. But beyond Dr. Pusey was the greater mind, the clearer intelligence, the poetic sensibility of Newman. He rose like a great golden eagle above all the contemporaries of Hopkins, and under his wings Hopkins inevitably sheltered. In 1866 we find him addressing Newman 'with great hesitation', but coming straight to the point:

'I am anxious to become a Catholic . . . I do not want to be helped to any conclusions of belief, for I am thankful to say my mind is made up, but the necessity of becoming a Catholic (although I have long foreseen where the only consistent position would lie) coming on me suddenly has put me into painful confusion of mind about my immediate duty in my circumstances. I wished also to know what it would be morally my duty to hold on certain formally open points, because the same reasoning which makes the Tractarian ground contradictory would almost lead one also to shrink from what Mr. Oakley calls a minimizing Catholicism.'

His mind was already made up. So much so that some extremely eloquent and appealing letters written to him by H. P. Liddon, Pusey's closest supporter, had no effect. We learn from one of these letters that Hopkins had put forward what Liddon called 'the precarious hypothesis of a personal illumination'. But we cannot analyse all the factors which led to this conversion. Though I believe most converts claim to reach supernatural faith by way of reason, Hopkins himself seems to have felt that the gulf between nature and super-nature, between the finite and the infinite, could not be bridged by a process of logic.

The great interests which they shared, Catholicism and poetry, eventually brought Gerard Hopkins and Coventry Patmore into contact, and Patmore paid a tribute to Hopkins at the time of his death which throws a very valuable light on the quality of the faith he held. In a letter to Robert Bridges, Patmore wrote:

'Gerard Hopkins was the only orthodox, and as far as I could see, saintly man in whom religion had absolutely no narrowing effect upon his general opinions and sympathies. A Catholic of the most scrupulous strictness, he could never-theless see the Holy Spirit in all goodness, truth and beauty; and there was something in all his words and manners which were at once a rebuke and an attraction to all who could only aspire to be like him.'

It is important to realize the character of this 'freedom in faith' because a consideration of Hopkins's poetry brings us close to a problem which has agitated modern criticism a good deal—I mean the relation of poetry to the poet's beliefs. The problem has been discussed in relation to Dante by Mr. Eliot, and more generally by Mr. Richards in his book on *Practical*

Criticism. These critics are mainly occupied in discussing whether it is necessary to share a poet's beliefs in order fully to enjoy his poetry. The aspect of the problem that arises in the case of Hopkins is even more vital—the precise effect of a poet's religious beliefs on the nature of his poetry.

(ii)

In Hopkins's poetry, as perhaps in the work of other poets, we can distinguish (1) poetry which is the direct expression of religious beliefs, (2) poetry which has no direct or causal relation to any such beliefs at all, and (3) poetry which is not so much the expression of belief in any strict sense but more precisely of doubt. All Hopkins's poems of any importance can be grouped under these three categories. When this has been done, I think that there would be general agreement that in poetic value the second and third categories are immensely superior to the first. Indeed, so inferior are such strictly religious poems as 'Barnfloor and Winepress', 'Nondum', 'Easter', 'Ad Mariam', 'Rosa Mystica', and one or two others, that Robert Bridges rightly excluded them from the first edition of the *Poems*. Of the *Poems* published by Dr. Bridges, one or two might conceivably be classified as poems of positive belief, like the exquisite 'Heaven-Haven' and 'The Habit of Perfection'. 'The Wreck of the Deutschland', the long poem which Hopkins himself held in such high regard, is a poem of contrition, of fear and submission rather than of the love of God:

> Be adored among men,
>   God, three-numberèd form;
> Wring thy rebel, dogged in den,
>   Man's malice, with wrecking and storm.
> Beyond saying sweet, past telling of tongue,
>   Thou art lightning and love, I found it, a winter and warm;
>   Father and fondler of heart thou hast wrung,
>   Hast thy dark descending and most art merciful then.

334

2

34# GERARD MANLEY HOPKINS

This is the beauty of terror, the 'terrible pathos' of the phrase in which Canon Dixon so perfectly defined Hopkins's quality.

Of the poetry which has no direct or causal relation to beliefs of any kind, poems such as 'Penmaen Pool', 'The Starlight Night', 'Spring', 'The Sea and the Skylark', 'The Windhover', 'Pied Beauty', 'Hurrahing in Harvest', 'The Caged Skylark', 'Inversnaid', 'Harry Ploughman', and the two 'Echoes', the poetic force comes from a vital awareness of the objective beauty of the world. That awareness— 'sensualism' as Dr. Bridges calls it—is best and sufficiently revealed in original metaphors such as 'mealed-with-yellow sallows', 'piece-bright paling', 'daylight's dauphin', 'a stallion stalwart, very violet-sweet', and many others of their kind, in which the poet reforges words to match the shape and sharpness of his feelings. Dr. Bridges, in the context I have already quoted from,[1] speaks of 'the naked encounter of sensualism and asceticism which hurts the "Golden Echo" '— a phrase I cannot in any sense apply to the poem in question; for while I appreciate the magnificent sensualism of this poem, I fail to detect any asceticism in the ordinary secular meaning of the word. But that in general there was a conflict of this sort in Hopkins is revealed, not only by the fact that he destroyed many of his poems which he found inconsistent with his religious discipline, but most clearly in his curious criticism of Keats:

'. . . Since I last wrote, I have re-read Keats a little, and the force of your criticism on him has struck me more than it did. It is impossible not to feel with weariness how his verse is at every turn abandoning itself to an unmanly and enervating luxury. It appears too that he said something like "O, for a life of impressions instead of thoughts". It was, I suppose, the life he tried to lead. The impressions are not likely to have been all innocent, and they soon ceased in death. His contemporaries, as Wordsworth, Byron, Shelley, and even Leigh

1 Notes to the *Poems* (2nd edition, Oxford, 1930), pp. 94-99.

335

Hunt, right or wrong, still concerned themselves with great causes, as liberty and religion; but he lived in mythology and fairyland, the life of a dreamer: nevertheless, I feel and see in him the beginnings of something opposite to this, of an interest in higher things, and of powerful and active thought. . . . His mind had, as it seems to me, the distinctly masculine powers in abundance, his character the manly virtues; but, while he gave himself up to dreaming and self-indulgence, of course they were in abeyance. Nor do I mean that he would have turned to a life of virtue—only God can know that—but that his genius would have taken to an austerer utterance in art. Reason, thought, what he did not want to live by, would have asserted itself presently, and perhaps have been as much more powerful than that of his contemporaries as his sensibility or impressionableness, by which he did want to live, was keener and richer than theirs.'

The implication of this criticism is that the poet, by nature a dreamer and a sensualist, only raises himself to greatness by concerning himself with 'great causes, as liberty and religion'. In what sense did Hopkins so sublimate his poetic powers? In a poem like 'Pied Beauty' we see the process openly enacted. After a catalogue of dappled things, things which owe their beauty to contrast, inconsistency and change, Hopkins concludes by a neat inversion—an invocation to God who, fathering forth such things, is Himself changeless. In 'Hurrahing in Harvest' again we have an extended metaphor: the senses glean the Saviour in all the beauty of Summer's end. 'The Windhover' is completely objective in its senseful catalogues: but Hopkins gets over his scruples by dedicating the poem 'To Christ our Lord'. But this is a patent deception. It does not alter the naked sensualism of the poem; and there is no asceticism in this poem; nor essentially in any of the other poems of this group. They are tributes to God's glory, as all poetry must be; but they are tributes of the senses; and a right conception of God and of religion is not hurt by such tributes.

In the third section, poems expressive not so much of belief as of doubt, I would place those final sonnets, Nos. 40, 41, 44, 45, 46, 47 and 50 in the published *Poems*. These all date from the last years of Hopkins's life—the first six from 1885, the other from 1889, the actual year of his death. But even earlier poems express at least despair: 'Spring and Fall'—the blight man was born for; the 'Sybil's Leaves'—the self-wrung rack where thoughts against thoughts grind. But the sonnets themselves are complete in their gloom, awful in their anguish. I need only quote that last terrible sonnet:

> *Thou art indeed just, Lord, if I contend*
> *With thee; but, sir, so what I plead is just.*
> *Why do sinners' ways prosper? and why must*
> *Disappointment all I endeavour end?*
>
> *Wert though my enemy, O thou my friend,*
> *How wouldst thou worse, I wonder, than thou dost*
> *Defeat, thwart me? Oh, the sots and thralls of lust*
> *Do in spare hours more thrive than I that spend,*
> *Sir, life upon thy cause. See, banks and brakes*
> *Now, leavèd how thick! lacèd they are again*
> *With fretty chervil, look, and fresh wind shakes*
> *Them; birds build—but not I build; no, but strain*
> *Time's eunuch, and not breed one work that wakes.*
> *Mine, O thou lord of life, send my roots rain.*

Is there any evidence in the known facts of Hopkins's life which throws light on this state of mind? Father Lahey, in his memoir of Hopkins, speaks of the three sorrows of his last years. The first two were due to external causes and do not concern us here; but Father Lahey then writes:

'Of Hopkins's third sorrow it is more difficult to speak. It sprang from causes which have their origin in true mysticism. Hopkins, smiling and joyful with his friends, was at the same time on the bleak heights of spiritual night with his God. All writers on mysticism—St. Teresa, St. John of the Cross, Poulain, Maumigny, etc.—have told us that this severe trial is the greatest and most cherished *gift* from One Who has accepted literally His servants' oblation. Hopkins was always remembered by all who met him as essentially a priest, a deep and prayerful religious. With the fine uncompromising courage of his initial conversion, he pursued his never-ending quest after spiritual perfection. The celebrated "terrible" sonnets are only terrible in the same way that the beauty of Jesus Christ is terrible. Only the strong pinions of an eagle can realize the cherished happiness of such suffering. It is a place where Golgotha and Thabor meet. Read in this light his poems cease to be tragic.'

The relation of doubt to belief is another and a profounder question than the one which concerns us now. No one who has thought about such matters fails to realize the paradoxical significance of the cry of the dumb child's father: 'Lord, I believe; help Thou mine unbelief.' As Father Lahey points out, this absence of spiritual complacency is of the very essence of Christian mysticism. An absence of spiritual complacency may also well be of the very nature of poetic sensibility.

Of that psychological aspect of creativity in the poet I have dealt at length in my essay on *The Nature of Poetry*.[1] I will only give here, for present application, a brief summary of the argument. We are born with sensibility and come into a world of ready-formulated ideas. As we develop, we may either adapt our sensibility to receive these ideas; or we may painfully create ideas of our own (disciplinary dogmas) which the freely expanding personality can hold in tension. In the latter case the space between self and dogma is *bridged*—there is a bridge, not an abysm of despair—by doubt. My contention is, that a creative gift or poetic sensibility is only consistent with such a state of spiritual tension and acuity. True originality is due to a conflict between sensibility and belief; both exist in the personality, but in counter-action. The evidence is clear to read in all genuine mysticism and poetry; and nowhere

[1] See pages 21–40.

more clearly than in the poetry and mysticism of Gerard Hopkins.[1]

(iii)

The terrible sincerity of the process of Hopkins's thought inevitably led him to an originality of expression which rejected the ready-made counters of contemporary poetics. His originality in this respect is both verbal and metrical, and perhaps the innovations he introduced into metre prevent more than anything else the appreciation of his poetry. Except for a few early poems, which need not be taken into account, practically every poem written by Hopkins presents rhythmical irregularities. The poet himself attempted a theoretical justification of these, and it is an extremely ingenious piece of work. But there can be no possible doubt— and it is important to emphasize this—that the rhythm of Hopkins's poems, considered individually, was intuitive in origin——

> *'Since all the make of man*
> *Is law's indifference.'*

The theory was invented later to justify his actual powers. It makes its first appearance in his correspondence in 1877, and in his letters to Bridges and Dixon, Hopkins shows that he understood the technique of English poetry as no poet since Dryden had understood it—Dryden whom he describes so well in one of these letters as 'the most masculine of our poets; his style and his rhythms lay the strongest stress of all our literature on the naked thew and sinew of the English language'. Such a description looks innocent enough, but it implies the great realization that poetry must start from the nature of a language—must flow with a language's inflexions

[1] Cf. André Gide: 'La force poétique aurait-elle décru en moi avec mes sentiments chrétiens. . . . Je ne crois pas; mais plutot avec ma perplexité. Chacun de mes livres a été, jusqu'à présent, la mise en valeur d'une incertitude.' *Pages de Journal*, p. 665. *La Nouvelle Revue française*, May 1935.

and quantities, must, in a word, be *natural*. Such was the secret of Greek poetry, and of Anglo-Saxon poetry; and it is the virtue of most of our poets that they instinctively reject Italianate rhythms, and other foreign impositions, and fall into this natural rhythm, which Hopkins called sprung rhythm. There are many statements and restatements of what he meant by this rhythm in the course of these letters; the best is perhaps that contained in a letter to Canon Dixon (Letter XII).[1]

'Its principle is that all rhythm and all verse consists of feet and each foot must contain one stress of verse-accent: so far is common to it and Common Rhythm; to this it adds that the stress alone is essential to a foot and that therefore even one stressed syllable may make a foot and consequently two or more stresses may come running, which in common rhythm can, regularly speaking, never happen. But there may and mostly there does belong to a foot an unaccented portion or "slack": now in common rhythm, in which less is made of stress, in which less stress is laid, the slack must be always one or else two syllables, never less than one and never more than two, and in most measures fixedly one or fixedly two; but in sprung rhythm, the stress being more *of* a stress, being more important, allows of greater variation in the slack and this latter may range from three syllables to none at all—*regularly*, so that paeons (three short syllables and one long or three slacks and one stressy) are regular in sprung rhythm, but in common rhythm can occur only by licence; moreover may in the same measure have this range.'

The effect of this distinction on the normal conception of poetic measure is revolutionary. Bridges was horrified; Dixon intrigued. 'Presumptious jugglery', Bridges called it, misspelling in his indignation. Hopkins replied that he used

---

[1] *The Letters of Gerard Manley Hopkins to Robert Bridges. The Correspondence of Gerard Manley Hopkins and Richard Watson Dixon.* Edited with notes and an Introduction by Claude Colleer Abbott. (Oxford University Press). Two volumes, 1935.

sprung rhythm 'because it is the nearest to the rhythm of prose, that is the native and natural rhythm of speech, the least forced, the most rhetorical and emphatic of all possible rhythms, combining, as it seems to me, opposite and, one would have thought, incompatible excellences, markedness of rhythm—that is rhythm's self—and naturalness of expression.' But Bridges was never convinced; I doubt if he ever really saw the point of the discovery—his own later experiments in the measure were feeble; he certainly never realized the importance of it, and the possibility that through Hopkins a renaissance of English poetry would come about would have seemed fantastic to him.

The preface in which he formulates his theories more precisely was written about 1883—in the midst, that is to say, of his main creative period. He begins by saying that his poems are written some in Running Rhythm, by which he means the common rhythm in English use, and some in Sprung Rhythm, and some in a mixture of the two. Common English rhythm, the standard rhythm in use from the sixteenth to the nineteenth centuries, is measured by feet of either two or three syllables and never more or less. Every foot has one principal stress or accent, and for purposes of scanning Hopkins held that it is a great convenience to follow the example of music and take the stress always first, as the accent or chief accent always comes first in a musical bar. If this is done there will be in common English verse only two possible feet—the so-called Trochaic and Dactylic, though these two may sometimes be mixed.

'But because', Hopkins goes on to explain, 'verse written strictly in these feet and by these principles will become same and tame, the poets have brought in licences and departures from rule to give variety. . . . These irregularities are chiefly Reversed Feet and Reversed or Counterpoint Rhythm, which two things are two steps or degrees of licence in the same kind.'

By a reversed foot, he adds, perhaps unnecessarily: 'I mean

putting the stress where, to judge from the rest of the measure, the slack should be, and the slack where the stress; and this is done freely at the beginning of the line, and, in the course of a line, after the pause; only scarcely ever in the second foot and never in the last, for these places are characteristic and sensitive and cannot well be touched.'

The following two verses from 'The Habit of Perfection', one of Hopkins's early poems, shows an isolated instance of a reversed foot in the third line; otherwise it is in standard iambic metre:

> Elected Silence, sing to me
> And beat upon my whorlèd ear,
> Pipe me to pastures still and be
> The music that I care to hear.
>
> Shape nothing, lips; be lovely-dumb:
> It is the shut, the curfew sent
> From there where all surrenders come
> Which only makes you eloquent.

This is, of course, all very simple and unremarkable, and has been the practice of every good poet from Chaucer down: as Hopkins says, it is nothing but the irregularity which all natural growth and motion shows.

'If however the reversal is repeated in two feet running, especially so as to include the sensitive second foot, it must be due either to great want of ear or else it is a calculated effect, the super-inducing or *mounting* of a new rhythm upon the old; and since the new or mounted rhythm is actually heard, and at the same time the mind naturally supplies' the standard rhythm which by rights we should be hearing, 'two rhythms are in some manner running at once and we have something answerable to counterpoint in music, which is two or more strains of tune going on together, and this is Counterpoint Rhythm. Of this kind of verse Milton is the great master and the choruses of *Samson Agonistes* are written throughout in it.'

Let us take a simple example from Hopkins's 'God's Grandeur':

> The world is charged with the grandeur of God.
>   It will flame out, like shining from shook foil;
>   It gathers to a greatness, like the ooze of oil
> Crushed. Why do men then now not reck his rod?
> Generations have trod, have trod, have trod;
>   And all is seared with trade; bleared, smeared with toil;
>   And wears man's smudge and shares man's smell: the soil
> Is bare now, nor can foot feel, being shod.
>
> And for all this, nature is never spent;
>   There lives the dearest freshness deep down things;
> And though the last lights off the black West went
>   Oh, morning, at the brown brink eastward, springs—
> Because the Holy Ghost over the bent
>   World broods with warm breast and with ah! bright wings.

Here again the underlying measure is standard iambic; but in nearly every line of the sonnet, a foot is reversed and we hear against the running rhythm, this rhythm pointed counter to the proper flow.

If you counterpoint throughout a poem, the original rhythm will be destroyed or lost, and that is actually what happens to the choruses of *Samson Agonistes*. Then the result is what Hopkins calls Sprung Rhythm. It is a rhythm of incomparable freedom: any two stresses may either follow one another running, or may be divided by one, two or three slack syllables. The feet are assumed to be equally long or strong, and their seeming inequality is made up by pause or stressing. Such rhythm cannot be counterpointed. Note also that it is natural for the lines to be *rove over* as Hopkins expressed it, that is, for the scanning of each line immediately to take up that of the one before, so that if the first has one or more syllables at its end, the second must have so many less at its beginning; and in fact the scanning runs on without break from the beginning of a stanza to the end, and all the stanza is one long strain, though written in lines asunder.

Further, Hopkins claims that two licences are natural to Sprung Rhythm. The one is rests, as in music, the other is *hangers* or *outrides*, that is one, two or three slack syllables added to a foot and not counted in the normal scanning. They are so called because they seem to hang below the line or ride forward or backward from it in another dimension than the line itself. 'Felix Randal' is a typical example of such sprung rhythm:

> *Felix Randal the farrier, O he is dead then? my duty all ended,*
> *Who have watched his mould of man, big-boned and hardy-*
> *   handsome*
> *Pining, pining, till when reason rambled in it and some*
> *Fatal four disorders, fleshed there, all contended?*
>
> *Sickness broke him. Impatient he cursed at first, but mended*
> *Being anointed and all; though a heavenlier heart began some*
> *Months earlier, since I had our sweet reprieve and ransom*
> *Tendered to him. Ah well, God rest him all road ever he*
> *   offended!*
>
> *This seeing the sick endears them to us, us too it endears.*
> *My tongue had taught thee comfort, touch had quenched thy tears,*
> *Thy tears had touched my heart, child, Felix, poor Felix Randal;*
>
> *How far from then forethought of, all thy more boisterous years,*
> *When thou at the random grim forge, powerful amidst peers,*
> *Didst fettle for the great grey drayhorse his bright and battering*
> *   sandal!*

Hopkins himself observed that such rhythm, as we have noted, is the rhythm of common speech and of written prose, when rhythm is perceived in them; 'the least forced, the most rhetorical and emphatic of all possible rhythms, combining, as it seems to me, opposite and, one would have thought, incompatible excellences, markedness of rhythm—that is rhythm's self—and naturalness of expression'. It is the rhythm of all but the most monotonously regular music, so that it arises in the words of choruses and refrains and in songs written closely to music. It is found in nursery rhymes, weather saws, and so on; and it arises in common verse when reversed or counterpointed. And I would add, it is the rhythm of all the genuine *vers libre* or free verse which has arisen since Hopkins's time.

This being so, the question arises: how came such a natural and universal rhythm to be neglected in English poetry? Perhaps we should rather ask: how did the standard running rhythm come into existence? and having once come into existence, why did it become such a fixed norm? Not only Greek and Latin lyric verse, which are in sprung rhythm, but the whole tradition of Teutonic and Norse poetry favours the principle of sprung rhythm. So that we may say, that the tradition of sprung rhythm to which Hopkins returned has a tradition within our own linguistic world at least twice as long as the tradition of running rhythm. For running rhythm was only established in England in the sixteenth century, whereas sprung rhythm had existed for at least eight centuries before that time. Our early metre is usually known as alliterative, and is entirely without rhyme. In this metre each line is divided by a pause, and each half-line contains two or more stresses, and an irregular number of slacks: the stresses in each whole line have the same initial sounds, and on account of this the metre is called alliterative. The only difference between this metre and Hopkins's is that Hopkins adds rhyme, and used alliteration on no fixed principle. But it will already have been noticed that he nevertheless makes considerable use of alliteration. In a few of his poems the total effect of alliteration is not much less than in a purely alliterative poem like *Piers Plowman*. 'The Windhover' is a supreme example:

I caught this morning morning's minion, king-
  dom of daylight's dauphin, dapple-dawn-drawn Falcon, in his
    riding
Of the rolling level underneath him steady air, and striding
High there, how he rung upon the rein of a wimpling wing
In his ecstasy! then off, off forth on swing,
    As a skate's heel sweeps smooth on a bow-bend: the hurl and
      gliding
  Rebuffed the big wind. My heart in hiding
Stirred for a bird,—the achieve of, the mastery of the thing!

Brute beauty and valour and act, oh, air, pride, plume, here
  Buckle! AND the fire that breaks from thee then, a billion
Times told lovelier, more dangerous, O my chevalier!

    No wonder of it: shéer plód makes plough down sillion
Shine, and blue-bleak embers, ah my dear,
    Fall, gall themselves, and gash gold-vermilion.

In short, we might say that Hopkins is eager to use every device the language can hold to increase the force of his rhythm and the richness of his phrasing. Point, counterpoint, rests, running-over rhythms, hangers or outrides, slurs; end-rhymes, internal rhymes, assonance and alliteration—all are used to make the verse sparkle like rich irregular crystals in the gleaming flow of the poet's limpid thought.

The other aspect of his technique is one which, to my way of thinking, is still more central to the poetic reality: I mean his fresh and individual vocabulary. No true poet hesitates to invent words when his sensibility finds no satisfaction in current phrases. Words like 'shivelight' and 'firedint' are probably such inventions. But most of Hopkins's innovations are in the nature of new combinations of existing words, sometimes contracted similes, or metaphors, and in this respect his vocabulary has a surface similarity to that of James Joyce. Examples of such phrases are to be found in almost every poem: 'the beadbonny ash', 'fallowbootfellow', 'windlaced', 'churlsgrace', 'footfretted', 'clammyish lashtender combs', 'wildworth', and so on. Commoner phrases like 'beetle-browed', or 'star-eyed' are of the same kind, made in the same way, and freely used by him. Here again an explanation would take us far beyond the immediate subject; for it concerns the original nature of poetry—itself the emotional sound-complex uttered in primitive self-expression. Mr. Williams, whose graceful and appreciative introduction to the second edition of the *Poems* is a fair corrective to the pedantic undertones of Dr. Bridges in the first edition, has an excellent description of the phenomenon as it appeared in the composition of Hopkins's verse.

'It is as if the imagination, seeking for expression, has found both verb and substantive at one rush, had begun almost to say them at once, and had separated them only because the intellect had reduced the original unity into divided but related sounds.'

Poetry can only be renewed by discovering the original sense of word-formation; the words do not come pat in great poetry, but are torn out of the context of experience; they are not in the poet's mind, but in the nature of the things he describes. 'You must know', said Hopkins himself, 'that words like *charm* and *enchantment* will not do: the thought is of beauty as of something that can be physically kept and lost, and by physical things only, like keys; then the things must come from the *mundus muliebris*; and thirdly they must not be markedly old-fashioned. You will see that this limits the choice of words very much indeed.'

Of Hopkins's imagery, there is not much in general to be said, but that 'not much' is all. He had that acute and sharp sensuous awareness essential to all great poets. He was physically aware of textures, surfaces, colours, patterns of every kind; aware acutely of earth's diurnal course, of growth and decay, of animality in man and of vitality in all things. Everywhere there is passionate apprehension, passionate expression and equally that passion for form without which these other passions are spendthrift. But the form is inherent in the passion. 'For', as Emerson remarked with his occasional deep insight, 'it is not metres, but a metre-making argument, that makes a poem—a thought so passionate and alive, that, like the spirit of a plant or an animal, it has an architecture of its own, and adorns nature with a new thing.'

(iv)

Hopkins himself was aware of the quality of his genius, and therefore knew what to expect from his contemporaries. Even in his undergraduate days at Oxford, he could write:

'It is a happy thing that there is no royal road to poetry. The world should know by this time that one cannot reach Parnassus except by flying thither. Yet from time to time more men go up and either perish in its gullies fluttering excelsior flags or else come down again with full folios and blank countenances. Yet the old fallacy keeps its ground. Every age has its false alarms.'

The most obvious false alarm was Swinburne; but he was of the number who perish in the gullies of Parnassus. More false, because more seeming-fair, are those who come down again with full folios and blank countenances, and among these can be numbered some of Hopkins's closest friends. Probably the only one of his small circle who understood him fully was his fellow poet, Richard Watson Dixon. Canon Dixon, writing to Hopkins to urge him to write more poems, refers to their quality as 'something that I cannot describe, but know to myself by the inadequate word *terrible pathos*— something of what you call temper in poetry: a right temper which goes to the point of the terrible: the terrible crystal. Milton is the only one else who has anything like it, and he has it in a totally different way: he has it through indignation, through injured majesty, which is an inferior thing. . . .' There is a full understanding which we do not find in the published letters and writings of others who knew Hopkins—not in Coventry Patmore, who floundered in deep astonishment, and not, dare it be said, in his closest friend and final editor, the late Poet Laureate. To contend that Dr. Bridges did not understand the poetry of Hopkins would not be quite fair; he understood the craftsmanship of it, and was sensible to the beauty. But there seems to have been an essential lack of sympathy—not of personal sympathy, but of sympathy in poetic ideals. The preface to the notes which Dr. Bridges contributed to the first (1918) edition of the poems, reprinted in the new edition, is marked by a pedantic velleity which would only be excusable on the assumption that we are dealing with a poet of minor interest. That is, indeed, the attitude; please look at this odd fellow whom for friendship's sake I have rescued from oblivion. The emphasis on oddity and obscurity is quite extraordinary, and in the end all we are expected to have is a certain technical interest, leading to tolerance, and the discovery of 'rare masterly beauties'. Hopkins is convicted of affectation in metaphor, perversion of human feeling, exaggerated Marianism, the 'naked encounter of sensualism and asceticism which hurts the "Golden Echo",' purely artistic wantonness, definite faults of style, incredible childishness in rhyming—at times disagreeable and vulgar and even comic; and generally of deliberate and unnecessary obscurity. Everything, in such an indictment, must depend on the judge's set of laws, and in criticizing Dr. Bridges's treatment of Hopkins, I am wishing to say no more than that the Poet Laureate applied a code which was not that of the indicted. The lack of sympathy is shown precisely in this fact. Hopkins was a revolutionary; that is to say, his values were so fundamentally opposed to current practices, that only by an effort of the imagination could they be comprehended. Once they are comprehended, many apparent faults are justified, and there is no reason to dwell on any of them.

Hopkins was serene and modest in his self-confidence. He could admit the criticism of his friends, and yet quietly persist in his perverseness. To one of them he wrote, in 1879:

'No doubt my poetry errs on the side of oddness. I hope in time to have a more balanced and Miltonic style. But as air, melody is what strikes me most of all in music and design in painting, so design, pattern, or what I call *inscape* is what I, above all, aim at in poetry. Now it is the virtue of design, pattern, or inscape to be distinctive, and it is the vice of distinctiveness to become queer. This vice I cannot have escaped.'

And again, a little later:

'Moreover, the oddness may make them repulsive at first sight and yet Lang might have liked them on second reading. Indeed, when, on somebody returning me the *Eurydice*, I opened and read some lines, as one commonly reads whether prose or verse, with the eyes, so to say only, it struck me aghast with a kind of raw nakedness and unmitigated violence I was unprepared for; but take breath and read it with the ears, as I always wish to read, and my verse becomes all right.'

In his letters he is revealed as a man of quite exceptional nobility of mind, a man, too, of tender feeling and frank impulsive affection. His real quality was that chastity of mind which he describes in one of his best letters (Letter XCIX to Bridges):

'... if a gentleman feels that to be what we call a gentleman is a thing essentially higher than without being a gentleman to be ever so great an artist or thinker or if, to put it another way, an artist or thinker feels that were he to become in those ways ever so great he would still essentially be lower than a gentleman that was no artist and no thinker—and yet to be a gentleman is but on the brim of morals and rather a thing of manners than of morals properly—then how much more must art and philosophy and manners and breeding and everything else in the world be below the least degree of true virtue. This is that chastity of mind which seems to lie at the very heart and be the parent of all other good, the seeing at once what is best, the holding to that, and the not allowing anything else whatever to be even heard pleading to the contrary.'

But Hopkins realized that this was 'no snatching-matter'. 'The quality of a gentleman is so very fine a thing that it seems to me one should not be at all hasty in concluding that one possesses it.' His own humility was perfect, but he knew that there was an injunction on all poets and artists to let their light shine before men. 'I would have you and Canon Dixon and all true poets remember that fame, the being known, though in itself one of the most dangerous things to man, is nevertheless the true and appointed air, element, and setting of genius and its works.' For himself it was different; in joining the Society of Jesus he had deliberately renounced fame. In 1881 he told Dixon that he had destroyed all he had written before he entered the Society, and that at first he had meant to write no more. Then his superior suggested that he should write an ode on the wreck of the *Deutschland*, which he did with the results we know. He doubted the wisdom of writing any more poetry unless, so to speak, ordered to do so; but then he came to a compromise: 'However I shall, in my present mind, continue to compose, as occasion shall fairly allow, which I am afraid will be seldom and indeed for some years past has been scarcely ever, and let what I produce wait and take its chance; for a very spiritual man once told me that with things like composition the best sacrifice was not to destroy one's work but to leave it entirely to be disposed of by obedience.'

It is easy to regret that Hopkins's conscience would not allow him to spend time on poetry, but we must remember that the poet was the man—that his poetic make was complementary to his religious make, and that to ask for a different man is to ask for a different poet. If he had not been a priest, Hopkins would undoubtedly have written more verse—perhaps as much as Bridges or Browning or Swinburne. But he would not necessarily have been a better poet, and as it is, his small harvest is so rich and golden, that we would not exchange it for all the pallid stacks of verse piled up by his contemporaries. Dixon was distressed by the open conflict of religion and poetry, but respected the decision taken by Hopkins. What Bridges thought we do not know, but he had no sympathy for the religious life of his friend, even a definite antipathy. One wonders on what the friendship subsisted, so little were Hopkins's profoundest feelings appreciated by Bridges. But friendship is perhaps never solidly grounded on intellectual interests; Hopkins had known Bridges for ten years before he discovered (and then from a review!) that his friend wrote poetry. We can assume, therefore, that the attraction was instinctive, even physical. How otherwise could Hopkins have tolerated the conceit, the pedantry, the cruel lack of perception that were the return for all his frankness, humility, and grace? Bridges has cautiously destroyed his side of the correspondence, but that very caution is significant. A man has not such a care for his reputation but from what we call a good conceit of himself, which is a fault even Hopkins found in Bridges.

(v)

It would be natural to conclude with some estimate of Hopkins's influence on modern poetry. But let us first ask what we should look for under this heading. The influence of a poet can be either technical, affecting the practice of other poets; or it can be spiritual, affecting the point of view, the philosophy of life, of poets and readers alike. I do not pretend to estimate this second kind of influence in Hopkins's case; and in any event I think it is irrelevant to our strictly poetical enquiry. The acute sensibility of Hopkins has undoubtedly sharpened the perceptive faculties of all who are familiar with his verse; and there may be a few who have felt the profounder truths which he expresses with so much intensity. But such effects would be difficult to estimate. Nor can we come to any very definite conclusion about a technical influence. If by that we mean a mimetic affectation of Hopkins's mannerisms, then the less said about it the better. But the true influence of one poet on another does not show itself so baldly. It may be that in the return to sprung rhythm, in the extended use of alliteration, Hopkins has made a calculable impression on the poets who have been writing during the last ten or fifteen years. But we must remember that although Hopkins's poetry was written fifty years ago, it was not published until 1918. A few of his poems appeared in anthologies a few years earlier, but they were given no prominence, and received no particular attention. The *patent* influence of Hopkins has therefore hardly had time to work itself into the body of English poetry. But the *latent* influence—that is a different question. It is a question of an impregnating breath, breathed into the ear of every poet open to the rhythms of contemporary life, the music of our existence, and the tragedy of our fate. In this sense Hopkins is amongst the most vital poets of our time, and his influence will reach far into the future of English poetry.

PARTICULAR STUDIES

13

HENRY JAMES

There is scarcely a problem in the philosophy of criticism which the work of Henry James does not raise, and by raising it lead us to the possibilities of a solution. But these problems, posed by a master of the indirect method, are only slowly emerging into our positive awareness. In their larger aspects, we can distinguish three of them: they concern the novel itself, its form and features; the moral responsibility of the novelist; and the much wider question of the attitude which the artist ought to adopt towards the particular crisis which civilization has now reached. Only one of these problems is at all definitely elaborated in the critical writings of the author himself, and this is the purely technical one. To make ourselves familiar with the evolution of Henry James, from his early impersonal experiments in the 'sixties right through to the final magnificence of his later period, is to trace the historical development of the art of fiction at its intensest creative point. It is to be carried, as in some wonderful ship that somehow manages to keep pace with the sun, right from the world of *Adam Bede* to the world of *The Golden Bowl*. There are other craft in the water—we are in the wake of the rich and overladen argosy of Balzac; Meredith runs part of the course with us; and Turgenev is a rather remote sailing ship which we keep in sight all the way—but there is no doubt that the authentic craft, the only one to steer direct, is the very one we have boarded. The experience must be lived through to be appreciated in all its excitement and variety: the traveller's tale in this particular case can only have an air of specious generalization, the unsatisfying blandness of broad effects, a fatal want of vividness and actuality. But in this respect it suffers with all critical effort; for what is criticism but an abstraction from particulars, a surrogate for actuality, a theory to account for facts?

There is a strict sense in which the novels of Henry James are a fund of practical advice. The novice, by the study of them, could learn a hundred useful precepts, and save himself years of unnecessary labour. But the study must be severe, for the perfection is often so complete that we look in vain for any marks of the mould from which it was cast. The surface quality of the work has been a first and final consideration; for 'surface', as we shall see, bears a vital relation to the content and character of the author's wider mission—and we may as well note at once that 'mission' is not a word to be afraid of in this connection. But the 'surface' has its own objective qualities; and many of Henry James's precepts are universal enough in their application. Their particular significance must be found in the particular emphasis they get among all the other qualities of his style and method. They are most effectual when they have a disciplinary urgency. The avoided vices are fluidity and discursiveness—'the terrible fluidity of self-revelation' and the discursiveness into which the art of fiction so easily and inevitably falls in irresponsible hands. In a less personal reference Henry James could be vaguer in his requirements:

'The good health of an art which undertakes so immediately to reproduce life must demand that it be perfectly free. The only obligation to which in advance we may hold a novel, without incurring the accusation of being arbitrary, is that it be interesting. That general responsibility rests upon it, but it is the only one I can think of. The ways in which it is at liberty to accomplish this result (of interesting us) strike us as innumerable, and such as can only suffer from being marked out or fenced in by prescription. They are as various as the temperament of man, and they are successful in proportion as they reveal a particular mind, different from others. A novel is, in its broadest definition, a personal, a direct impression of life; that, to begin with, constitutes its value, which is greater or less according to the intensity of the impression.'

Here we seem to have no preciser value than interest or intensity. But in actual practice no one could be more relentless in his standard of achievement. For what, to him, did intensity imply but integrity? And once you have let slip this word, in the critical philosophy of Henry James, you have implied a whole organization of values not one of which is less valuable, less indispensable, than the rest. With one decree he has sacrificed all that merely detached descriptive writing which constitutes, one might guess, at least a quarter of the bulk of English fiction. But nothing is now more evident than the fact that this drastic pruning was essential to any further growth; and no critic would now reject the rules worked out by Henry James on this subject, which an American professor[1] has conveniently formulated as:

'Localization . . . must never detach itself, either on the one hand from the formative influences of environment on character, or on the other from the formative influences operating from character upon environment. . . . A third prescription, too stringent to impose itself as a law, but still a regulative principle in James's severe practice, subordinates all descriptions, whether of persons or of places, to the perceptions of the characters, and serves, when conscientiously applied, the salutary purpose of holding the lyrical expansiveness of the author in check.'

The last requirement is but an aspect of the general method of indirection for which, above all authors, Henry James is the sponsor—'that magnificent and masterly *indirectness* which means the only dramatic straightness and intensity'. But indirectness is after all only a name for a method, and it may be asked what purpose can justify a method admittedly so diffi-

[1] *Henry James, Man and Author*, by Pelham Edgar (London, 1926).

cult and involved. The answer brings us to the essential originality and modernity of our author.

Henry James perceived, in a real sense which is distinctive of classical art, and in a sense which gives us the real meaning of the Greek conception of dramatic unity, that the problem of 'presentation', of 'projection', of the translation of action into verbal expression, was a problem of time. It is a question of creating an *illusion* of duration which shall correspond with an actual *sense* of duration. The illusion can only be effective if the strands of interest which we pick up at the beginning of a story are so woven that they duplicate our consciousness of real events. But consciousness, whether real or induced, is not a simple fact: it is rather a process or state which is only realized upon the completion of some definite rhythm or pattern. In this it differs from awareness, which is an incomplete state of sensibility. We say loosely that we are 'conscious' of pain or pleasure, but it would be better to say that we are 'aware' of them. We become 'conscious' when pain or pleasure is organized into a recognizable unity—when it becomes a sentiment, such as pity or terror. For pity or terror, or love or hate, is a highly organized complex, depending for its duration on its inherent pattern or repetitive rhythm. Still more complex are those organizations of emotions and conscious states which we name personalities, and those too have their dependable rhythm or definite pattern. Now, in order to create personalities and set them in action (which is the object of fiction), it is necessary to repeat, on another plane, an analogous rhythm or pattern.

The discovery, or rediscovery and application to fiction, of this principle was the great technical advance made by Henry James. It is an advance of the very greatest importance: it is not too much to say that upon the making-good of this advance by future novelists the whole art of fiction depends. How Henry James came to make this discovery is a different question, which must be dismissed briefly here. There were two steps: In the first place, his intelligence grasped the nature of the problem to be solved, though perhaps other writers have gone thus far. But then Henry James had the further and abounding grace to perceive that the problem could not be solved formally, aesthetically, or in pure abstraction, but must be *applied* to the actual current of existence. The rhythms could not be invented, but must be caught up from the actual idioms of daily life; and equally the patterns must be outlined in the wider pattern of civilization. The first, or dynamic, aspect of duration is solved on the moral plane; the second, or static, aspect is the aggregation of acts committed on the moral plane, and constitutes the problem implied in our sense of tradition or civilization.

It is difficult to cope with the complexity of interrelations which gather thickly at this point. There is the writer's concern for perfection in his medium, and there is his concern for the truth and actuality of his material. These may be unrelated activities—and indeed are so in most writers, and even, in some, tend to conflict. But in others, and above all in Henry James, there is a further concern that the particular material in hand shall have its particular perfection of medium. The style and method are not only perfect, but also perfectly adapted to the subject-matter. And the complexity does not end there; for over the choice of theme, its development in the dramatic sense, there still hovers the possiblity of a further perfection in the formal arrangement or pattern of the action—so admirably illustrated for us in *The Awkward Age*. And further still, all these interrelated perfections can still offer the temptation of still another pattern, a pattern which is the whole glowing perfection of one's philosophy of life—a perfection which, if intelligently sustained, governs with one last implied necessity the formal organization of life—the interrelation, that is to say, of each and every activity.

Some of the implications of a doctrine of perfection are suggested by an illuminating comparison which Professor Edgar draws between Henry James and Racine:

'Perfection is of admittedly various kinds, but even in its

most consummate form it is not necessarily the mark of supreme greatness. Narrowly considered, there is more perfection of finish and design in half a dozen of the masterpieces of Racine than in any of Shakespeare's plays, yet we are satisfied to sacrifice something of the harmony of the one for the abundance and energy of the other. Now the perfection that James wrought for and not infrequently achieved is more Racinean than Shakespearean. Soft flowing contours and harmonies of line distinguish it—a disciplined energy, a temperate warmth, and a refinement of execution that suggests rather deliberation than spontaneity. In either writer, too, a like fastidiousness prevails, which in the interests of concentrated effect clears the stage of all superfluous figures and defines strictly the limits within which the action is permitted to develop. I do not wish to involve myself in a prolonged comparison of two writers whose methods exhibit such obvious affinities, for their dissimilarities would necessitate as copious a discussion. There is this remark, however, to make, that whereas Racine, who chooses his themes for their rich human implications, seems never to concern himself with manipulating them so as to produce the illusion of reality, James, on the other hand, selects subjects which do not appear, save to himself, to hold the promise of germination, but develops them in accordance with the strictest logic of life.'

'The logic of life' is a remote phrase, for nothing, in common experience, has so little logic about it. Life is not an armoured syllogism, but an elusive growth. Yet there is a logic concerned, and this is the logic of art or imagination. The very next sentence in Professor Edgar's book seems to contradict his phrase; for he says of Henry James that 'it was his theory that the artist is privileged to give the law to life, and to submit her haphazard processes, her waywardness, her profuse extravagance, or even her occasional meagreness, to a control more severe than the discipline she herself imposes'. And this, of course, is the truth of the matter: the imagination seizes upon one of the disjointed events of which life for the most part is made up, and develops that event into a fable which has not the casual and occasional aspect of existence but the harmonious autonomy of art. Art, in fiction, is not a true report, but a convincing fable. But the fable is always a deduction from experience; and the word 'develops', a few lines above, hides a process which may rightly be called logical. For when events do not 'happen', as in life, then they must be created in a region of speculation, an aery void where our only guide is an innate sense of their rightness. And 'right' not only in their probability and necessity but in all the other virtues of the Aristotelian canon—in unity, beauty, universality, and moral purpose.

The faith of the artist in these matters is that the logic of art will, if persisted in, somehow include the 'logic of life'. The presiding idea will, that is to say, somehow provide for every possible relation and complexity included in its scope. All possible aspects are realized in the round mass of the work; all possible values are compounded within its unity. To the degree of perfection attained by Flaubert (to take his most immediate predecessor in these matters) Henry James added another dimension; and this further dimension made all the difference between failure and success. In an essay on Flaubert Henry James once used a devastating image to evoke the general significance of *L'Éducation sentimentale*, describing it as 'a huge balloon, all of silk pieces strongly sewn together and patiently blown up, but that absolutely refuses to leave the ground'. It meant more than it can ever mean to us for a critic of the last generation to be able to discriminate in this fashion between a labour so extensive in scale and so perfect in finish and that labour's lack of any inner volume or enabling medium; because only one who had gone all the way with Flaubert until he had outstripped him and turned to survey him, only one whose mind could rise above the merely empirical elaboration of beauty to an intelligence controlling beauty, only Henry James could designate the falsity, the irony, the lack of any centre of sympathy, in the work of Flaubert:

'Thus it is that as the work of a "grand écrivain", large, laboured, immensely "written", with beautiful pages and a general emptiness, with a kind of leak in its stored sadness, moreover, by which its moral dignity escapes—thus it is that Flaubert's ill-starred novel is a curiosity for a literary museum.'

'Moral dignity' brings us nearer the burning heart of Henry James's world than any other phrase in the vocabulary of criticism; these two words summarize his significance, and all that is left to the critic is to ease out their concentrated meaning.

Henry James was born with a moral sense; and the first aspect of the significance of the moral problem in his work is nothing but the significance of the problem in his life. He first came to consciousness in a world of strict Puritanism, but only immediately to be plunged into the sensuous life and colour and tone of Mediterranean Europe. As a child and youth he flitted like a winged envoy between the opposed civilizations. A docile mind or a dogmatic might have come to an early decision and stayed irrevocably in one or other sphere. But James had a discriminating mind; he was sensitive to the values of both worlds, and also conscious of the fact that those values were irreconcilable. He did finally make a conscious choice, as we shall see, but the dualism of his appreciative sense gave a lasting tension to his mind. Professor Edgar has observed this same duality:

'In Henry James, and I would speak of both the novelist and the man, there is a curious blending of opposed elements. He would be the most sophisticated of men and writers if he were not so ingenuously naïve, and it may well be this unwonted union of *naïveté* and sophistication that establishes his identity, that gives his character its mould and his work its distinguishing quality.'

Puritanism is a private virtue, but a public vice. In the individual it implies a moral constraint whose outcome is probably a finer sense of intellectual and aesthetic discrimination. But in public life Puritanism withers and blasts every finer manifestation of the corporate life; it is fatal to joy and grace, and eventually to religion and art. Professor Edgar says that 'the defect of Puritanism is a lack of charity; its merit is that it has a standard of discrimination between right and wrong that resists the easy ebb and flow of occasion and arbitrates between our duties and our desires.' This is true, but not searching enough. The standard of discrimination, if it is not to be a meaningless tyranny, must be an individual creation: it must be relative to the individual alone; and Puritanism lacks charity because it presumes to apply the measure of a personal rectitude to other minds and other epochs; what is evolved from a particular set of circumstances is enforced as a universal code.

It is to the personal aspect of Puritanism that Henry James clings desperately; so desperately that his most moving creations, beautiful figures like Milly Theale or Maggie Verver, are embodiments of a fine moral integrity, of conscience in all its infinite reaches and delicate adjustments. Wherever Henry James takes this integrity of character as his theme, there he creates his most enduring impressions. And these impressions are enduring precisely because they have gained in delicate extension, in infinite spiritual ramifications and crystallizations, what they have lost—not lost, but expended —in mere brute force and physical capacity. In this sense it is a perfectly clear issue, fully realized and consciously carried to its conclusions by Henry James. How explicit it is, for example, in his criticism of the 'vulgarity' of d'Annunzio's love scenes, which he ascribes to the weakness of that author's sense of 'values':

'We begin to ask ourselves at an early stage what this queer passion may be in the representation of which the sense of beauty ostensibly finds its richest expression and which is yet attended by nothing else at all—neither duration, nor propagation, nor common kindness, nor common consistency with other relations, common congruity with the rest of life—to make its importance good. If beauty is the supreme need so let it be; nothing is more certain than that we can never get too much of it if only we get it of the right sort. It is therefore on this very ground—the ground of its own sufficiency—that Signor d'Annunzio's invocation of it collapses at our challenge. The vulgarity comes from the disorder really introduced into values, as I have called them; from the vitiation suffered—that we should have to record so mean an accident —by taste, impeccable taste, itself.'

Beauty is the supreme need, and vulgarity, or ugliness, comes from a disorder of values. But whose values? Physical passion itself, in the colours d'Annunzio lends it, is a value. Yes, but not of the right sort, is the answer we derive from the quoted criticism. And 'the right sort' is, for Henry James, the crux of the whole problem. It is, at any rate, the problem to which he devoted the whole of his life.

Just as previously we have seen him take the method of fiction into another depth or dimension of effect, giving it density and duration and wholeness, so now we see him taking the problem of conduct beyond individual implications and facing the wider, the vaster, and the more portentous problem of civilization. Implicit in his discovery that the values of Puritanism are individual, was his discovery that the values which Puritanism does not provide for—does, in effect, so far as it becomes a system or a creed, tend to destroy—were precisely the social values, the values of civilization. And it was with the birth of this consciousness that Henry James entered upon his peculiar destiny.

There has been an attempt to treat the definite decisions and preferences by which Henry James slowly but surely dissociated himself from the country of his origin as so many steps in a spiritual decline. It is felt that by renouncing the crude but incalculable potentialities of American life he displayed a fastidiousness which rejected the rough virtues of rude health for the iridescence of decay. An American critic, Mr. Van Wyck Brooks, has even gone so far as to attempt a correlation between this assumed moral decadence and the development of Henry James's style and method. This kind of criticism must, we feel, be condemned on its own evidence: it cannot for a moment be admitted that the later style and method of this author, complex and difficult as they may be, are, on any sound basis of knowledge or clear refinement of sensibility, inferior to the comparatively simpler, but in that measure less characteristic, style and method of the early works. We see rather a style beginning as a careful inference from particular models (there is Hawthorne, and George Eliot, and a temperate Ruskin in it), but slowly emerging into individuality and force until finally it becomes one of the most flexible and most adequate styles in English literature.

The truth is, rather, that a critic like Mr. Van Wyck Brooks quite misconceives the true significance of Henry James, and is incapable of appreciating his concept of values. You may, from the virgin soil of a new continent, look upon Europe as a land of dead values and decaying manners; you may think of our civilization as one that has run its course and must inevitably complete a fatal destiny. It is very possible to generalize in such a manner, and it is very fashionable. And there is no need, for the moment, to throw doubt on this facile fatalism, however unscientific and unreasonable it may appear to be. For without involving ourselves in any historical prophecies, we can freely admit the decay of manners and civilization in the modern world. But who realized this more keenly than Henry James himself? And precisely his mission, once he had found himself on solid ground, was the pitiful unmasking of this decay, and the reaffirmation of a few quiet, essential virtues within the fabric of society.

The virtues are quiet and infinitely individual and reticent; but they have a way, when considered, of reverberating to the confines of empires and civilization. The virtues of Lambert Strether in *The Ambassadors* (to take a simple case), the almost allegorical figures of Mrs. Newsome and Madame de Vionnet, and the other cardinal qualities built into the action of the book, all these make for a suspense such as no mere play of characters could secure, but which comes from the sense we have, as we read, of an invisible chorus of fates. More prosaically, we are aware of the conflict, within the exemplary consciousness of Strether, of two civilizations. It would be more exact to say: of civilization and its opposite, barbarism.

In *The Ambassadors* Henry James represented the tragedy of his own life: and a careful study of this book—which he himself regarded as his masterpiece—is a necessary preliminary to any understanding of the significance of his work. But it is doubtful whether this book, or any other of his writings, would countenance as the antithesis of civilization so brutal a term as barbarism. There is the gentler word provincialism, and it is a word he often used—so often that Howells protested against it in a review of Henry James's *Hawthorne*. It is a word rather typical of Henry James, and it indicates an attitude *within* a civilization. Types are seen as conforming, or as simply not conforming, to a single standard. A more dispassionate observer would see the extremes more violently: would see types tending in one direction, towards civilization, or in the opposite direction, towards barbarism. But this is too theoretical a position for Henry James; and the values of civilization are for him fully conditioned by the visual and tactile objects of which it is severally and sensibly constituted. *The Spoils of Poynton* gives us this relation most clearly. But in a letter to Howells—an answer to the protest just referred to—the doctrine is stated in all its naked force:

'I sympathize even less with your protest against the idea that it takes an old civilization to set a novelist in motion—a proposition that seems to me so true as to be a truism. It is on manners, customs, usages, habits, forms, upon all these things matured and established, that a novelist lives—they are the stuff his work is made of; and in saying that in the absence of those "dreary and worn-out paraphernalia" which I enumerate as being wanting in American society, "we have simply the whole of human life left", you beg (to my sense) the question. I should say we had just so much less of it as these same "paraphernalia" represent, and I think they represent an enormous quantity of it.'

Civilization for Henry James meant a perfectly definite historical phenomenon: it meant in general the continuous tradition of culture which Western Europe inherited from the ancient world; it meant more particularly the Renaissance tradition in which we still exist, in however attenuated and debased a fashion. But again it would be a mistake to imagine that Henry James's sense of civilization was historically apprehended; such aesthetic judgements as we find him making are often curiously lacking in all sense of historical perspective; he does not handle the actual spoils of civilization with any very genuine signs of appreciation, and his references to paintings and *objets d'art* are often clumsy enough. Nor do we ever discover that such things played any vital or individual part in his own life. It is all so much a feeling for the general glory, as so beautifully conveyed in that silvery flood of eloquence in which he recovers, in *A Small Boy and Others*, his first impression of the Galerie d'Apollon. His acutest realizations gathered round the spiritual significance of these symbols; and perhaps his preference for the reactions rather than the reagents is after all only his recognition that civilization is a matter of mental condition rather than of vulgar possession—a state of refinement which comes by instinct or inheritance, but never by conveyance.

Civilization was in his view a phenomenon of ever-increasing complexity, and to refuse the effort required to comprehend and develop this complexity was to deny the life of intelligence itself. Of two such denials he was conscious in a sure but intuitive manner. One is represented by the America he deserted, and the other, as well as by anything, by the Russia that confronted him in Tolstoi and Dostoievski. His attitude towards America was, as we have already seen, the animation and activation of his whole life and work: his attitude towards Russia was no less real, though it never occupied his attention to the same degree. It was a blind reaction which showed itself in an almost violent scorn of the two writers just mentioned—'fluid puddings, though not tasteless, because the amount of their own minds and souls in solution in the broth gives it savour and flavour, thanks to the strong, rank quality of their genius and experience'. And in another place he says: 'I think it is extremely provincial for a Russian to be very Russian . . . for the simple reason that certain national types are essentially and intrinsically provincial.' Perhaps he would have made that overworked label suffice as a connecting-link between his antipathies. Perhaps nowadays we can see stronger and more essential links: such links are being forged by events, and the process of 'americanization', which carries with it all the determinate forces of materialism and mechanism, nowhere seems so irresistible as among the comparatively traditionless peoples of Russia. The deepest significance of the Russian revolution is surely to be found in its renunciation of Europe. The force and effectiveness of that revolution can be explained only by a recognition of the historical fact that there has been no merging of the national ethos in any wider concept of humanism, but rather a renewal of it in all its integrity. Russia has retreated to her own fastnesses. The political doctrine with which the new régime is identified, although of European origin, is one which even its European adherents would admit to be totally disruptive of the cultural traditions of the West. To one who had solemnly declared his adherence to this tradition there could be no further vacillation: that declaration had been too deeply confirmed by anguish of mind and force of emotion. If to-day we wished to take from the world of literature two antithetical types representing the dominant but opposed forces of the modern world, we could not find two so completely significant as Dostoievski and Henry James. In the one is all energy, all nihilism, obscurity and confusion, the dreadful apocalypse of a conscience that has lost all civilized sanctions and has no foundations to its world; and in the other a calm, dominant,

reticent and fastidious intellect, ordering the gathered forces
of time to a manifestation of their most enduring glory.

INDEX

INDEX

INDEX

INDEX

INDEX

INDEX

Hopkins, Gerard Manley, 41, 45, 48,
323, 327, 331 seq., *alliteration*
345, 346, *character* 350, *conver-*
sion 331 seq., *criticism of Keats*
335, 336, *despair* 337, *form* 348,
humility 351, *influence on modern*
poetry 352, *life* 331, *mysticism*
339, *ordination* 331 seq., *self-*
confidence 349, *sensualism* 335,
336, *style* 339, *vocabulary* 346
House of the Seven Gables, The, 276
Howells, 272, 365
Hugo, Victor, 285
Hulme, T. E., 48, 162, 163
humanism, 162
Humanism and the Religious Attitude,
162
Human Understanding, 262
Hume, 77, 307, 308
humorist, 252
humoristic writing, 263
humour, 241, 245, 250, 260
American, 272
coprological, 246
English, 247
man of, 252
Humphrey Clinker, 237, 246
Hunt, Leigh, 335
'Hurrahing in Harvest', 335
Hutton, Richard Holt, 304, 306
Huygens, Constantyn, 186
Hyperion, 63, 65
hypochondria, 286

Iago, 118
Id, 26, 136, 137
Idea, 133
idea, 58
Idea of a University, 261
Idea of Great Poetry, The, 68
idealism, 115, 186, 205
idioms, 55
'Ignorance of Man, The', 309
Iliad, The, 59, 153, 248
illusion of duration, 357

Illustrations of Sterne, 262
imagery, 60, 68, 98, 104, 107, 109,
110
primordial, 145
imagination, 31, 194, 249, 255, 287,
288, 321
and logic, 203
incantation, 96
inhibition, 27
inscape, 350
inspiration, 37, 62, 127, 131 seq.,
134, 137 seq.
literary, 311
poetic, 87
instinct, gregarious, 28
intellect, 31, 249
'intellectual', 198
intelligence, 36, 121, 122
Intelligence in Expression, 43
Introduction à la Connaissance de
l'Esprit Humain, 176
introspection, 237
introversion, 129, 144, 241
intuition, 44, 189
invention, 46, 68
'Inversnaid', 335
Ion, 133
irony, 205
Isabella, or the Pot of Basil, 67
'I Saw a Chapel all of Gold', 126
Ivory Tower, The, 270

Jackson, William Walrond, 80
Jacopone, 49
Jacquerie revolt, 157
Jacques le Fataliste, 243
James, Henry, 37, 264, 269, 271, 272,
275 seq., 292, 354 seq., *and*
America 363, *and Dostoievski*
367, *and civilization* 363, *and*
Flaubert 360, 361, *indirectness*
356, *integrity* 356, *later style* 364,
moral sense 361, *perfection* 358,
and Racine 358, 359, *style* 358,
theme 358

374

INDEX

INDEX

INDEX

INDEX

Trim, Corporal, 250, 251, 264
Tristram Shandy, 243, 248 seq., 252, 259, 261 seq.
trochee, 341
Trois Réformateurs, Luther, Descartes, Rousseau, 186
Trunnion, Commodore, 242
Turgenev, 354
Twice-Told Tales, 270, 278
Tyler, Wat, 157 seq.

Unamuno, Miguel de, 170, 173, 176, 179
unconscious, 24, 38

Valenciennes, 156
Valéry, Paul, 96 seq.
values, aesthetic, 191
  ethical, 191
Vanessa, 210
Vauvenargues, 27, 174 seq., 192, 211, 220 seq., *and Voltaire*, 224
Vathek, 219
Venus de Medici, 238
verse, free, 48, 53, 55, 109, 323, 345
  Greek lyric, 345
  Latin lyric, 345
Vico, G., 42 seq., 92 seq., 98, 321
Villehardouin, 157
Villette, 278, 287, 291, 292, 295
Virgil, 89
Vivante, Leone, 43, 321
Voltaire, 204, 224, 238, *and Vauvenargues*, 224
Vossler, Karl, 99

Wallas, Mary, 224, 226, 231 seq.
war, 174
Warton, Thomas, 94
Waste Land, The, 53, 58
Wellington, Duke of, 281, 285

Western Europe, 366, 367
Whibley, Charles, 204
Whitehead, A. N., 187, 190 seq.
Whitman, 48
Wilkes, 238
Williams, Charles, 347
Williams, Harold, 290
Williams, W. S., 290
Wilson, James, 309
Wilson, Woodrow, 309
'Windhover, The', 335, 336, 345
Wings of the Dove, The, 270
wisdom, poetic, 93
wit, 240, 247, 250, 325
wit-writing, 45 seq., 320
Wood's halfpence, 200, 204
words, 95
  as analysis, 44
  in prose, 44
  their appearance, 45
  their association, 45
  their formation, 347
  their meaning, 45
  metaphorical use of, 42
  their music, 44, 60
Wordsworth, William, 14, 30, 39, 41, 45 seq., 57, 59, 80, 83, 107, 272, 283, 320, 329, 335
worship, 177, 180
'Wreck of the Deutschland, The', 92, 334, 351
Wuthering Heights, 278, 282, 284, 294, 295

Yeats, W. B., 48
Yogi, 110
Yorick's sermon, 253
York, 248
Yorkshire, moors of, 283

Zenobia, 267, 274